D1601176

"Strange Prophecies Anew"

"Strange Prophecies Anew"

Rereading Apocalypse in Blake, H. D., and Ginsberg

Tony Trigilio

Madison • Teaneck
Fairleigh Dickinson University Press
London: Associated University Presses

Associated University Presses
440 Forsgate Drive
Cranbury, NJ 08512

Associated University Presses
16 Barter Street
London WC1A 2AH, England

Associated University Presses
P.O. Box 338, Port Credit
Mississauga, Ontario
Canada L5G 4L8

The paper used in this publication meets the requirements
of the American National Standard for Permanence of Paper
for Printed Library Materials Z39.48–1984.

Library of Congress Cataloging-in-Publication Data

Trigilio, Tony, 1966–
    "Strange prophecies anew": rereading apocalypse in Blake, H. D., and Ginsberg / Tony Trigilio.
        p. cm.
    Includes bibliographical references and index.
    ISBN 0-8386-3854-6 (alk. paper)
        1. American poetry—20th century—History and criticism. 2. Apocalypse in literature. 3. Apocalyptic literature—History and criticism. 4. Blake, William, 1757–1827—Religion. 5. Ginsberg, Allen, 1926—Religion. 6. End of the world in literature. 7. Prophecies in literature. 8. Religion and literature. 9. Prophecy in literature. [1. H. D. (Hilda Doolittle), 1886–1961—Religion.] I. Title.

PS310.A57 T75 2000
811'.509382—dc21   00-034048

PRINTED IN THE UNITED STATES OF AMERICA

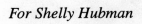

For Shelly Hubman

Contents

Acknowledgments

Gratitude is extended to the following publishers and organizations for permission to quote from the poetry and prose of H. D. and Allen Ginsberg:

By H. D., from *Trilogy*: Copyright ©1944, 1945, 1946 by Oxford University Press, renewed 1973 by Norman Holmes Pearson; reprinted by permission of New Directions Publishing Corporation and Carcanet Press Limited. By H. D., from *Tribute to Freud*: Copyright ©1974 by Norman Holmes Pearson; reprinted by permission of New Directions Publishing Corporation and Carcanet Press Limited. By H. D., from *The Gift*: Copyright ©1982 by The Estate of Hilda Doolittle; reprinted by permission of New Directions Publishing Corporation and Carcanet Press Limited. By H. D., from *Bid Me to Live*: Copyright ©1960 by Norman Holmes Pearson; reprinted by permission of New Directions Publishing Corporation and Carcanet Press Limited. By H. D., from *Notes on Thought and Vision and The Wise Sappho*: Copyright ©1982 by The Estate of Hilda Doolittle; reprinted by permission of City Lights Publishers.

By Allen Ginsberg, from *Kaddish*, in *Collected Poems, 1947–1980*: Copyright ©1959, 1984 by Allen Ginsberg; reprinted by permission of HarperCollins Publishers, Incorporated, and Penguin Books Limited. By Allen Ginsberg, from *Howl: Original Draft Facsimile*: Copyright ©1985 by Allen Ginsberg; reprinted by permission of The Wylie Agency, Incorporated. By Allen Ginsberg, from *Indian Journals*: Copyright ©1970, by Allen Ginsberg; reprinted by permission of Grove/Atlantic, Incorporated.

Special acknowledgment is extended to Gary Snyder and to the Stanford University Libraries for permission to quote from Snyder-Ginsberg correspondence in the Allen Ginsberg Papers (M0733), Special Collections, Stanford University Libraries. Copyright ©1999, Gary Snyder. Thanks to Stephen Mandeville-Gamble, Linda Long, and the staff of the Green Library Department of Special Collections for their assistance during my research in the Ginsberg Papers.

A version of Chapter 4 appeared in *American Literature* 71 (December

1999) as "'Strange Prophecies Anew': Rethinking the Politics of Matter and Spirit in Ginsberg's *Kaddish*."

I wish to thank the Columbia College Chicago Department of English for its assistance during the completion of this manuscript. I owe deep gratitude to Guy Rotella, Mary Loeffelholz, and Stuart Peterfreund for their careful readings of this manuscript and their invaluable revision suggestions. I also would like to thank Donald M. Hassler and Thomas Davis for their mentoring as my earliest scholarly role models, and Diana Culbertson for introducing me to poetic prophecy and encouraging my enthusiasm for the genre. I owe special gratitude to the late Douglas Radcliff-Umstead, whose high standards are, I hope, everywhere in this manuscript.

I would run out of ink before I could list all the friends and colleagues who have helped this project along. I wish to single out several whose intellectual and emotional support was vital, and who read or discussed portions of this manuscript with me: Diana Hume George, Rick Hilles, Jeremy Earp, Sharon Hannigan, Kevin Cassell, Andrew Wilson, Dennis Gouws, and Ven. Geshe Tsultrim Chöpel. I would like to thank my parents, Margaret and Frank Trigilio, for identifying and nurturing my love of language. To Michael Trigilio—gratitude for blurring the boundaries between art and criticism, friendship and family. I especially wish to thank Shelly Hubman for helping me untangle these ideas while they were in their most fragmentary stages, and for her inexhaustible love and patience.

1

Blurring the Line of Vision:
Estrangement and the Prophetic Tradition

God is the same God, always and everywhere. . . . In him are all things contained and moved. . . . He is utterly void of all body and bodily figure, and can therefore neither be seen, nor heard, nor touched . . .
—Isaac Newton, *Mathematical Principles of Natural Philosophy*

Therefore God becomes as we are, that we may be as he is.
—William Blake, *There is No Natural Religion [b]*

[L]ibido is invariably and necessarily of a masculine nature, whether it occurs in men or in women and irrespective of whether its object is a man or a woman. . . . [A]n instinct is always active even when it has a passive aim in view.
—Sigmund Freud, *Three Essays on the Theory of Sexuality*

We can read my writing . . . as a suppressed desire for forbidden 'signs and wonders,' breaking bounds, a suppressed desire to be a Prophetess, to be important anyway . . . a hidden desire to 'found a new religion' . . .
—H. D., *Tribute to Freud*

Do the homosexuals, like the Communists, intend to bury us?
—*Life* magazine, 26 June 1964

Moloch whose love is endless oil and stone! Moloch whose soul is electricity and banks! . . . Moloch who entered my soul early! Moloch in whom I am a consciousness without a body! Moloch who frightened me out of my natural ecstasy! Moloch whom I abandon!
—Allen Ginsberg, *Howl*

13

1. INTRODUCTION: SITES OF APOCALYPTIC THEORY

William Blake, H. D., and Allen Ginsberg created a heterodox tradition of prophetic language in response to the pressures of scientific, industrial, and religious orthodoxies. In *Poetics of Imagining: From Husserl to Lyotard*, Richard Kearney offers important categories from which to assert and interrogate those creations and their implications.[1] Kearney conceives the imagination as a site circumscribed by an "ethics of alterity" (210). Kearney constructs a theory of the imagination located between universalism and radical freeplay, a version of imagining that eludes "both the prison-house of mirrors and the cheerless conformity of Grand Theory" (210). Kearney's introduction considers the tension between reason and inspiration that, I would argue, is at stake in the prophetic poetry of Blake, H. D., and Ginsberg. He writes that "a critical poetics of imagination transcending both the empire of reason and the asylum of un-reason has become an urgent concern for a number of thinkers in our century" (9). Kearney's remark indicates his own position: a commitment to the ethical potential of the notion of "imagination" marked by dissatisfaction with both sovereign metaphysical humanist and fragmented postmodern versions of it.

Kearney's introduction raises several questions I want to engage in this book. The poetics of modern prophecy that emerges from the work of Blake, H. D., and Ginsberg asks how such a poetics can maintain an impulse to transcend the "empire of reason" while avoiding the trap—the "asylum"—of a thoroughgoing dependence on "un-reason." This poetics of prophecy questions whether reason or "empire" can be transcended at all, and suggests that "un-reason" can be cast as something more meaningful than an "asylum" standing in opposition to reason. Blake, H. D., and Ginsberg redirect this empire's language for power. For these poets, imagination is a product and producer of reason and un-reason, reconstructing "empire" (Logos) and "asylum" (divine madness) according to historical variance.

For Blake, H. D., and Ginsberg, an excess of reason dominates the episteme of each poet's particular era, and this excess is legible as a form of empire-building. In Blake's time, Enlightenment science sought to render the natural world mathematizable and thereby wholly knowable, defining and extolling nature as the sum of human learning. Blake's response was to look inward to the imagination of Poetic Genius and to create there a mathesis of imagination, as in his epic poem, *Milton*. H. D.'s prophetic imagination in her epic poem of World War II, *Trilogy*, responded to an era when the natural world was geometrized by war and the inner life of the psyche was systematized by Freudian thought. H. D. created a language for prophecy whose anagrams of "un-reason" reconfigure the relationship of science, religion, and mind so that the three recall and revise the authority of the "empire of reason." As in Blake's *Milton*, *Trilogy*'s circumscribing imagination is unruly and sustained by ambivalence. Meanwhile, the prophetic imagination in H. D.'s poem is "[n]o poetic fantasy / but a biological reality."[2] H. D.'s Freud was a "Professor" who "was not always right"; despite his being, for H. D., a Janus facing both "empire" and "asylum," Freud used nature in a way that colonized "un-reason" in the name of the empire-building of reason. Ginsberg's interest in fusing psychic maladaptation with visionary experience emerged within cultural contexts related to those *Trilogy* evokes: the Cold War antipsychiatry movement and worldwide shifts in scientific research and treatment. These shifts sought to decolonize "the asylum of un-reason" and explore the possibilities of installing "un-reason" as king. In an era when Cold War juridico-medical discourse dammed the flows of the mind, mediating representations of twentieth-century culture, Ginsberg was concerned in *Howl* and *Kaddish* with charting those flows, and even privileging them. Like H. D.'s response to Freud and patristic religion, Ginsberg's revision of divine madness is crucial to his development of a language for prophecy that would fuse transcendent and immanent forms of representation.

Faced with coercive official discourses of science, industry, and religion, Blake, H. D., and Ginsberg crafted a tradition that revises its own authorizing power. To account for their revisionary responses during two centuries of industrialization, the following chapters recontextualize the lineage of Western prophetic poetry, arguing that in industrial cultures, where productivity and utility demand modes of consciousness antithetical to traditional ideas of prophetic inspiration, modern poet-prophets create a language for prophecy based on a continuation and reinvention of past prophetic models. My readings of texts and contexts maintain the vexed but sustaining intertextual paradoxes that suffuse this countertradition, and these readings examine how modern poetic prophecy constructs a rhetoric of vision through a process of inspiration by estrangement from past models of prophetic language. The following chapters argue that the language Blake, H. D., and Ginsberg create for modern prophecy transforms *observation* into *vision* by blurring the boundaries between prophet and God, prophet and tradition, and prophet and audience.

In tracing the construction of a language for modern prophecy in the work of these poets, I demonstrate how each poet conceives consciousness in terms of apocalypse. To shore the potentially tenuous boundary separating apocalypse (as cessation of being) and consciousness (as continuity of being), the link between apocalypse and consciousness in Blake, H. D., and Ginsberg must be addressed.

Apocalypse as both destruction and unveiling—as both the end of old forms of thought and being and the beginning of a new end/purpose—is represented by these poets in language that forecasts the turn from teleology to ontology in critical theory and cultural studies in the West. The logic of apocalypse in Revelation stresses a millennial cleansing that once and for all seals a boundary separating the wicked from the holy: the obedient reside in the New Jerusalem, while forever outside the city "are dogs, and sorcerers, and whoremongers, and murderers, and idolaters, and whosoever loveth and maketh a lie" (The Holy Bible, King James version; Revelation, 22:14–16). A hidden revelation is unveiled, and the human will is redeemed as history ends. The following chapters demonstrate that Blake, H. D., and Ginsberg construct revisionary redemptive narratives that, by contrast, do not cut off the ambivalent productivity of the psyche. They multiply the production of meaning rather than reduce it to logocentric unity. Revelation for them is a moment of consciousness represented by the Satanic conversationalism of Blake's *Milton*, the "corrosive sublimate" of heretical, self-replicating anagrams in H. D.'s *Trilogy*, and the "hymnless" heresy of endless revision in Ginsberg's *Kaddish*. Each poet attempts to conceive an apocalypse without fatalism, to proffer declamatory narratives of redemptive pilgrimage without recourse to foundationalism, and to construct a prophetic poem within Judeo-Christian eschato-teleology without succumbing to the imperial asylum of closure.

To accomplish those tasks, Blake, H. D., and Ginsberg variously reconceive apocalypse as a mode of consciousness—paradoxically redemptive and self-annihilating—rather than of past and future history. Their reconceptions ask significant questions about the relationship between poetics and critical theory, especially about the possibilities of imagination's totalistic relevance in the localized narratives characteristic of the postmodern episteme. My final chapter seeks to close with disclosure, suggesting how the discursive realms of religion, history, poetics, and postmodernism might be affected by the strategies crucial to Blake, H. D., and Ginsberg's conception of apocalyptic consciousness in modern poetic prophecies. This final chapter assumes that these poets contribute significant strategies for negotiating the competing claims of local and global knowledge-making without surrendering to the nihilism of asylum or the absolutism of empire.

At the close of Blake's *Milton*, "Self-annihilation" stages prophetic redemption. Woven garments become the clothes of a new imagination, a reconceived frame of reference that combines immanent and transcendent modes of consciousness to "cast aside from Poetry, all that is not Imagination."[3] Blake's emphasis on "Self-annihilation" does not embrace obliteration; instead it represents an expansion of consciousness by means of a language that collapses distinctions among subject, object, vision, and word. Blake occupies a moment in radical Protestantism when material language and metaphysical vision combine, when the modern prophet confronts the Bible and, as Robert Alter has said of Blake's prophetic legacy, forces biblical language "into radically new contexts" rather than responding with orthodox exegesis.[4]

Similarly, H. D.'s construction of an apocalyptic consciousness in *Tril-*

ogy emerges from her blurring of the boundary between materialist and visionary modes of psychic representation. The condition I describe at different moments in chapter 3 as "visionary consciousness," "prophetic consciousness," and "resurrective consciousness" depends upon H. D.'s locating the immanent in the apocalyptic and the apocalyptic in the immanent. The Magdalene's un-weaving in *Trilogy* stages her visionary conversation with Kaspar, both as a revision of the role of desire and divinity in prophecy and as a (re)weaving of the patristic textual lineage of Western prophecy. Conversing in "visionary forms dramatic," to recall Blake's *Jerusalem*, Mary and Kaspar reconceive Snell's Law from classical physics as a matter of apocalyptic consciousness. Their conditional exchange culminates in the final image of the poem, a gender-ambiguous Christ child held as if the child were myrrh in the arms of the modern poet-prophet.

Similar tensions of provisionality appear in the rhetoric of vision in *Kaddish*, where Ginsberg constructs a language for prophecy within a paradoxically urban-pastoral landscape of New York as "a flower burning in the Day."[5] Poised between apocalypse "and what comes after," Ginsberg charts a pilgrimage that blesses "Death on us all" within a "beginningless, endless" fusion of immanence and transcendence: the final call and response of "caw" and "Lord" from *Kaddish* (209, 212). Although the poem is a life-affirming elegy, its primary referents are death, doubt, and madness. Inspired by Dwight Goddard's translation of the Buddha's remarks on "annihilation," Ginsberg portrays in *Kaddish* what Buddhism's discourse on the Four Noble Truths terms the "extinction of consciousness."[6] Ginsberg's study and practice in Buddhism, from his reading of Goddard onward, is discussed in greater detail in chapter 4. My aim in this chapter is to introduce the correspondence between Buddhism and Western prophecy in Ginsberg's poetry. In the Four Noble Truths, consciousness is defined as the delusional belief that human subjectivity and its environment are essentialist phenomena outside of human history and lived experience.[7] For Ginsberg, "the *shunyata* aspect" of persons and things—the "extinction" of belief in an essentialist consciousness—"gives almost everything its sacred quality."[8] This "*shunyata* aspect," roughly translatable as the aspect of emptiness (and discussed further in chapter 4), stages from a paradoxically decentering center what Ginsberg terms the "prophetical sharpness" of the East-West conjunction in his prophetic poetry. Specifically, for Ginsberg, the *shunyata* of the world becomes the foundation for the antifoundationalist pilgrimage of Naomi and the young Ginsberg in *Kaddish*: his apocalypse without the fatalism or the empty fragmentation of asylum.

Thus, Blake, H. D., and Ginsberg each conceive a strategy for representing apocalyptic consciousness in language without surrendering to the traditional implication that apocalypse is the transcendent end to history, language, and the generation of meaning. It is in terms of those efforts that

I want now to foreground the tension disclosed by my earlier remarks on the subject of apocalyptic consciousness. Like Richard Dellamora's *Apocalyptic Overtures: Sexual Politics and the Sense of an Ending*, the following chapters rely on the notion that deconstruction "is a site of apocalyptic theory."[9] But, again like Dellamora, I am hesitant to leave the matter there. The tension between the provisionality of deconstruction and the closure suggested by traditional notions of apocalypse might lend itself to fatalism; as Dellamora reminds us, the "pervasive tendency to structure individual and group experience in apocalyptic terms can be easily abused" (3). Any reticence from me on the subject of apocalyptic consciousness would threaten to reproduce a critical silence that I seek to avoid: that is, a silence which confronts claims for the visionary yet refuses to theorize beyond the limits of material perception—a silence which considers the asylum briefly, then turns back to the boundaries of empire.

Harold Bloom's 1961 response to *Kaddish* can represent the quite noisy silence I have in mind. Bloom sorrowfully complains that the content of Ginsberg's poetry "is largely and increasingly out of control."[10] Bloom's evaluation of Ginsberg's control—indeed, his desire to evaluate Ginsberg in terms of control—recalls Eliot's injunction against Blake's "formlessness" in *The Sacred Wood*. Bloom declares in his unenergetic reading of *Kaddish* that Ginsberg "is hardly a biblical poet"; instead, Bloom argues, Ginsberg writes "a kind of religious poetry" (214). No demonstration of how or where Ginsberg fails the test of biblical poetry in *Kaddish* is offered, nor is the "kind of religious poetry" Ginsberg writes defined. Moreover, Bloom fails to concretely distinguish biblical from religious poetry in his evaluation. He traces Ginsberg through Blake to Smart, then back to the King James Bible. Yet readers might be left to wonder where Ginsberg fails—his *one speech-breath-thought* poetics, his cultural and religious revisionism, his self-proclaimed ecstatic content?

Bloom's commentary suggests to me that he measures Ginsberg's failure in terms of the poet's distrust of referentiality, a distrust that the following chapters argue is a crucial point of contact between religious certainty and antifoundationalist skepticism in modern prophetic poetry. Noting Ginsberg's echoes of *Adonais* in *Kaddish*, Bloom points up the romantic humanist background of Ginsberg's work. He argues that those echoes produce "in the reader some expectation that all this pathos and sorrow [in *Kaddish*] have been evoked toward some imaginative end" (214). Perhaps because of Ginsberg's polyvocal sense of endings in *Kaddish*, the last section of the poem apparently fails the test of imagination for Bloom, just as *Kaddish* itself fails the test of biblical poetry for him. Referring to the panoptic Lord and howling crows of this final section, Bloom writes, "[a]ll that is human about these lines is the circumstances of their incoherence" (215). Ginsberg's revised Kaddish prayer for his mother declares, "Lord O

Grinder of giant Beyonds my voice in a boundless field in Sheol"; Bloom concludes that "Ginsberg's voice . . . will at this rate soon enough constitute a boundless field of Sheol."[11] Yet this boundlessness is precisely the point, as the discussions of Blake, H. D., and Ginsberg's countertradition of modern prophecy in the following chapters will show. The "imaginative end" that Bloom desires is produced through an emphasis on a language for prophecy constructed on the boundary between romantic humanism and apocalyptic consciousness. The close of Ginsberg's poem is similar to those of *Milton* and *Trilogy*: the prophetic imagination that redeems in each poem becomes the site for an apocalypse without end, here a "Lord" and "caw" coupled in continuous and "endless" revision.

Bloom, then, is descriptively correct, but not evaluatively so. His certitude leads him to silence: "[a]ll that is human" about the final lines of the poem "is the circumstances of their incoherence." But Bloom is merely derisive, for Ginsberg's closing *affirms* that he has "nothing to say."[12] As an instance of apocalyptic representation—much like Blake's literal/littoral word in *Milton*, or H. D.'s anagrammatic cultural revisionism in *Trilogy*—Ginsberg's combined "Lord" and "caw" articulate nothing. That is, they articulate not *one* thing that could be fixed into absolutist structures of representation and meaning. Instead, Ginsberg's focus, like Blake's and H. D.'s, is on creating a language for prophecy that is both apocalyptic and unending. *Self-annihilation* (Blake), *self-out-of-self* (H. D.), and *shunyata* (Ginsberg, through his Buddhist study and practice) declare then unweave self-centered consciousness in favor of a continual reweaving and reassertion portrayed as redemptive in its process rather than in its final result. Indeed, as *Kaddish* suggests, this process or reweaving and reassertion is "boundless" in its efforts to reconfigure meaning and identity as situational, performative border conditions rather than as emblems of ontological certainty. As an ongoing revision of religious orthodoxy and the classical human sciences, this countertradition of prophecy is "boundless" in "Sheol" precisely because of its position outside of the lawlike, legitimizing frames of reference constituted by systems of referentiality. That is, for Blake in *Milton*, prophecy renders heaven unhappy; for H. D. in *Trilogy*, prophecy burns a "corrosive sublimate" that transforms verity to variant; for Ginsberg in *Kaddish*, prophecy is "hymnless" heresy. For these poets, the emptiness of referentiality creates the conditions for more language rather than for silence. As the following chapters demonstrate, this rhetoric of prophecy culminates in endings that conceive redemptive language as polyvocal, conversational, and continuous.

The apocalyptic consciousness conceived by the prophetic imagination in these poems is a boundary site between the transcendent, metaphysical-imperial certainty of the humanist imagination and the immanent, material-local indeterminacy of the postmodern imagination. Borrowing from

Ihab Hassan's language in *The Postmodern Turn*, I would argue that modern poetic prophecy emerges from a site of "disestablished imagination."[13] This disestablished imagination is enacted, hence established, in the conjunction of apocalypse and conversation in Blake's, H. D.'s, and Ginsberg's prophetic poetry. If revised apocalyptic consciousness reconceives the self as a shifting ground of meaning and agency, then the representation of this consciousness in poetry should enact multiple sites of meaning-making and intersubjectivity. But, as Dellamora has cautioned, such shifting ground is dangerous. To be sure, the essentialist, liberatory perspective of most forms of transcendentalism cannot fully account for historical variance or for the interdependence of power and submission. Yet to answer essentialism with radical relativism is to be locked so squarely in variance that one blocks the possibilities for representing transcendental experience in language. With the integrity of the humanist self threatened by an imagination that is disestablished, these multiple sites might lapse into a powerless cacophony. Rosi Braidotti's valuable work in gender and psychoanalysis may offer an alternative to this risk, and may suggest a vocabulary for engaging empire and asylum without recourse to transcendence. Braidotti conceives of gender identity as a location of *historical essence*, where gender identity is articulated in "the conditional present."[14] The following chapters proceed from the idea that what Braidotti terms "essentialism with a difference"—in her work, formulating gender as historical essence—fuels the prophetic imagination: identity and difference are deployed in the construction of a language for prophecy that is historically contingent and mindful of the transcendental aims of visionary history without subscribing finally to these aims, and without attributing finality to them.

2. APOCALYPTIC AUTHORITY

Unlike premodern prophecy, in which models of biblical authority were mediated by the institution of the church, the prophetic poetry of Blake, H. D., and Ginsberg depends on a relationship between prophet and audience wherein audience is considered to be as potentially "prophetic" as the prophet him/herself.[15] The communal *solidarity* of biblical redemption is invoked by these poets, then is re-envisioned as a revelation of sacred *particularity*. For Blake, H. D., and Ginsberg, the linguistic relationship between poet-prophets and the Bible itself depends on an estranging linguistic conflict: although the poet-prophet claims to receive visions from God, these metaphysical visions must be translated into material language, producing discourse at once both revelatory and fallen.

The prophecy of Ezekiel can offer an example of such a conflict between vision and language. Ezekiel's prophecy is authorized externally:

the "word of the LORD came expressly unto him," an experience initiated once the "hand of the LORD was there upon him" (1:3). At first glance, Ezekiel seems to naturalize the conventional conceptual boundary that separates a presumably fallen humanity from Yahweh. Yahweh inaugurates Ezekiel's prophecy from outside the sense-based parameters of referential language. The Logos is transmitted orally from Yahweh to Ezekiel through a holy scroll Ezekiel is commanded to eat. The noun of direct address with which Yahweh speaks to Ezekiel throughout the book presupposes a hierarchical separation between God and human: "Son of man, eat that thou findest; eat this roll, and go speak unto the house of Israel" (3:1). Ezekiel becomes a living sign whose actions symbolically define the sins of Israel, its punishment, and its promised new covenant. Ezekiel's oral consumption of the scroll, an act which embodies him as a natural sign in accord with the metaphysical chariot vision of Yahweh, corresponds to material actions which also signify orally (literally through mastication): Yahweh transforms the metaphysical scroll into physical food that Ezekiel also must eat, a bread of barley cakes baked with excrement. Yahweh then proclaims: "thus shall the children of Israel eat their defiled bread among the Gentiles, whither I will drive them" (4:13). The heavens of Yahweh are the metaphysical counterpoint to the material world; the Israelites cannot perceive Yahweh directly without the intercession of the prophet, nor can they stop the geographic dispersal which emanates from the metaphysical and into the physical world. In Ezekiel's prophecy, the Logos, then, is the standard by which one determines the symbolic value, and material consequence, of fallen language.

Ezekiel's actions can only symbolize the pure language of Yahweh; Ezekiel's vision challenges the attempt to create a language wholly adequate to the representation of sensory experience. The proclamations of Yahweh are representable only through Ezekiel's body, through actions performed by his body, or through the dispersal of Ezekiel's people. The punishment of Israel, foretold in chapter 9, is communicated through a multitude of signs written on the bodies of Israelites whose faith, it is told, will save them from Yahweh's wrath. Yahweh commands a scribe to "[g]o through the midst of the city . . . and set a mark upon the foreheads of the men that sigh and that cry for all the abominations that be done in the midst thereof" (9:4). Written language, this time in the form of the scribe's marks, communicates the Logos through the bodies of fallen, albeit faithful, Israelites. Unlike Ezekiel, they do not thoroughly consume the written word; but the Israelites nevertheless signify as embodied signs the inability of the Logos to function as universal, unmediated representation in a fallen world. These instances from Ezekiel seem to construct a familiar metaphysical paradigm: because the language of Yahweh cannot function as universal language in a fallen world, it must instead exist in the form of symbolic representations in nature itself.

The poetic prophecies of Blake, H. D., and Ginsberg recall and re-envision this familiar split between Logos and fallen language, creating a revised apocalyptic representation of vision. This confluence of continuity and rupture is a defining feature of the role that apocalypse plays in the poetic prophecies of Blake, H. D., and Ginsberg. The shared concerns of these poets can be situated in the history of Western apocalyptics, in what Frank Kermode terms the "sense of an ending," Dellamora "apocalyptic overtures," and Jacques Derrida "the ends of man."[16] The prophetic poetry of Blake, H. D., and Ginsberg enacts prophetic forms that resemble the "apocalyptic tone" of recent philosophic, deconstructive, and psychoanalytic approaches to literature. These poets are distinguished from their particular eras by a persistent concern for apocalyptic representations—a turn toward epics which culminate in endings that could be said to be apocalyptic, insofar as the meaning of the word ranges from catastrophe, to destruction, to mystical revelation, to vision, to prophecy. Blake, H. D., and Ginsberg attempt to conceive representations outside of what each perceives as the limitation of material forms; yet none of them wishes to escape those forms, nor to build systems that neglect to engage them. In their poetry and prose, these poets enact prophetic forms that are linguistically and semantically estranged from prophetic tradition without wholly surrendering the claims of prophecy and apocalypse. By considering how the work of these poets reflects the shift in contemporary critical discourse from teleology to ontology, the following chapters map a poetics of modern prophecy—a rhetoric of vision, a conceptual framework from which these poets engage in a continual assumption and revision of identity and meaning, with the finitude at the foundation of apocalypse continually kept in the offing.

Blake's, H. D.'s, and Ginsberg's language of prophecy crucially revises apocalyptic vision in terms of conversational language. Blake's *Milton* and *Jerusalem* end with an apocalyptic cleansing of language and the birth of language-as-conversation. As H. D.'s *Trilogy* ends, the apocalyptic conversation between Mary and Kaspar culminates in a physical birth that echoes Christ's. The final section of *Howl* consists of a conversation in a mental institution in apocalyptic forms of language that seem mad to those outside its frame of reference; an addendum, "Footnote to Howl," celebrates the "holy" cleansing that follows the apocalyptic representations of the poem. The narrative of *Kaddish*, too, ends in apocalypse and conversation: Ginsberg speaks to a new world as a self-proclaimed prophet, and Naomi speaks back to him in her final letter, delivered after her death. Blake, H. D., and Ginsberg revise the familiar idea of apocalypse as the end of history and meaning. Distinguished from referentiality by their insistence on polyvocality, continual transferences of meaning, and conversation, their revised apocalyptic representations serve as a site for the performance of mediated language and vision.

The following chapters describe how these poets' emphasis on revelatory conversationalism defies the monovocal authority of the Logos, an authority that would cast redemption in terms of the obedience and collective salvation of the faithful consolidated under the authority of God. Though by definition the prophet is a dissenting figure, premodern prophets operate as the means toward social redemption through religious consolidation. Blake, H. D., and Ginsberg, however, seek inspiration in a countertradition of religious dissent that openly resists the consolidation of religious feeling into social institutions. This countertradition owes a significant debt to Gnosticism; *gnosis*, wisdom and self-knowledge, frames the religious and historical tendency toward revisionism in modern prophecy. The so-called heresies of Gnostic Christianity, an early Christian movement eventually driven underground by the Catholic Church, appealed to the revisionary sensibilities of Blake, H. D., and Ginsberg. These heresies will be discussed in greater detail in succeeding chapters, but their essential feature can be stated briefly here: a distrust of power relations underwritten by belief in Judeo-Christian monotheism—specifically, power relations that privilege matter over mind, observation over vision, men over women, and Judeo-Christian theodicy over individual revelation. This countertradition, which I term "New Gnosticism" in chapter 5, borrowing from Ihab Hassan, offers each poet a ground from which to draw on ancient heretical dissent. Each then uses such countertradition as the means of conceiving revised apocalyptic representations. Blake, H. D., and Ginsberg borrow from streams of thought either explicitly or implicitly Gnostic. By placing their borrowing alongside the similar concerns of thinkers such as Michel Foucault and Derrida, chapter 5 explores the possibilities of locating the apocalyptic-religious in postmodernism, and the postmodern in the apocalyptic-religious.

Jan Wojcik, Raymond-Jean Frontain, and Joseph Anthony Wittreich, Jr., have shown that the relationships of prophet to God direct the relationships of prophet to audience, and prophet to prophet, in the lineage of prophecy from Chaucer to the present. Wojcik's and Frontain's investigation of a "quarrel between audience and prophet" concludes that without the sovereignty of the Bible, prophecy risks a chaotic, ineffectual relationship with both the culture it addresses and with scholars who take on the task of exegesis.[17] For Wojcik and Frontain, the study of poetic prophecy necessarily begins with the early Christian exegetes who gave prophecy its "orientation" as a lineage (15).

If, as its etymology suggests, prophecy combines "telling" and "foretelling," then the orientation of this lineage could be destabilized from the start—combining the time line of a lineage with both telling and foretelling, and thereby disrupting the construction of a diachronic orientation based on strict demarcations among past lineage, present telling, and foretelling. Wojcik and Frontain demonstrate that, as a result of historic exigency, the stylistic concerns of Western prophetic texts may also shift in any given era

from translations of vision, to passionate arguments for the primacy of inspiration, to calls for social revolt. Nevertheless, Wojcik and Frontain argue, the transformations prophecy undergoes as a result of historic necessity
are stabilized by a solid continuity originating in the Bible: "one tradition
[the Bible] can stand for all in showing how prophecy changes" (15).

Wittreich identifies a stabilizing, continuous prophetic tradition in his
introduction to *Milton and the Line of Vision*, a collection that substan-
tively explores the fundamental role of Milton in Anglo-American prophetic poetry. For Wittreich, the Anglo-American prophetic tradition— "one
is tempted to call it *the Milton tradition*," he writes—is comprised of a
lineage of "intrapoetic relationships" of shared "interconnectedness."[18]
Wittreich's conception of a single Anglo-American prophetic lineage presupposes that prophetic texts cannot be written without recourse to the
intrapoetic authority—connecting prophet to prophet, and prophecy to
prophecy—of this prophetic line. Like Wojcik and Frontain, Wittreich traces
this authority to a stable ground in the prophecies of the Bible. The prophet
is "speechless" outside the lineage of prophecy (xv). Once the prophet enters into the intrapoetic relationships of this lineage, "he becomes articulate, even to the point of engaging . . . in corrective criticism" (xvi). The
tendency of prophets to undertake such correctives does not render the so-
lidity of the lineage unstable: "This corrective function is validated by the
fact that, while prophets communicate with one another, they all derive
their vision from Christ; they are all ministers of the Word" (xvi). Wittreich
argues that the poet becomes the poet-prophet precisely when touched by a
metaphysical vision that positions the poet-prophet in a lineage "authenti-
cated by scriptural prophecy" (xviii).

The arguments of Wojcik, Frontain, and Wittreich clarify the dynamics
at work in the tradition of Anglo-American poetic prophecy, and both collections trace the efforts of scholars and poets who have helped frame poetic prophecy as a single and singular lineage from Chaucer to the present,
a lineage given speech and orientation by the Bible. However, such arguments do not explain sufficiently those poet-prophets who doubt or deny
that the prophetic texts of the Bible represent unified, semantically coherent (therefore authoritative) visions. Furthermore, conventional trust in a
universal lineage originating in biblical prophecy cannot account for those
poets who position themselves within a prophetic lineage—and claim an
authority—precisely by questioning the universal authority of poetic, prophetic, and biblical traditions themselves. For these poets, the authority of
prophecy crucially involves its own attempt to heal the God-prophet/meta-
physical-material rupture, while paradoxically maintaining the rupture itself as a source of continuity.

3. THE PROPHET READING THE BIBLE

The urge of Blake, H. D., and Ginsberg to create prophetic poetry that simultaneously abides by and transvalues the Western prophetic lineage violates conventional presumptions about biblical revisionism. For the first Hebrew scholars, and later for the fathers of the Christian Church, biblical "interpretation" precluded originality. For early Hebrews and Christians, the truth of the Logos was immune to revision. According to Gershom Scholem, the orthodox conception of exegesis demands that the scholar "develops and explains that which was transmitted at Sinai."[19] Biblical exegesis therefore does not consist "in having new ideas"; instead, as an exegetical scholar one assumes the task of "subordinating" oneself "to the continuity of the tradition of the divine word and . . . laying open what [one] receives from it in the context of [one's] own time" (289). Therefore, the exegete responds not with an original "system," but instead with "commentary" (289). As bearers of orthodox tradition, prophets thus would explain how "revelation unfolds in the course of historical time—but only because everything that can come to be known has already been deposited in a timeless substratum" (289).

By contrast, and using several discourses at once, Blake, H. D., and Ginsberg layer multiple traditions, all as part of revising the originary discourse and tradition that initializes prophecy. Yet each poet shares a substantial familiarity with the Hebrew Bible and the Christian New Testament. Each reads biblical sources through what seem markedly different religious traditions: Blake through eighteenth-century versions of Antinomianism and the tradition of radical dissent, H. D. through southern Pennsylvanian Moravianism, and Ginsberg through a Western and Eastern continuum that includes his upbringing in Judaism, his study of Blake, and the Bodhisattva vows he took as a Tibetan Buddhist. Ginsberg's tradition includes Blake as a significant component; and H. D.'s Moravianism descends from the Moravianism that influenced Blake.

The heritages all three poets bring to the Bible are different, and these differences contribute as much to the continuities of prophetic poetry as do the conjunctions among these poets. The Muggletonian and Antinomian traditions that influenced Blake also constitute an important component of H. D.'s Moravian heritage. The Kabbalistic and Hermetic traditions that interested Blake are significant components of H. D.'s retranslation of biblical prophecy. In addition, the manner in which Blake and H. D. read the Bible is analogous to Ginsberg's own reading of the Bible. The disjunctions and similarities of influence together constitute revised apocalyptic forms of language and meaning.

Of course, Blake's areas of influence, as E. P. Thompson notes, "shade into each other."[20] Thompson and others have observed, however, that this shading also is characterized by a marked divergence among Blake's religious, literary, and philosophical sources. He is correct to note a divergence in the original source material—Milton was no Kabbalist or Hermeticist—but it is important to note that Blake's prophetic reading of the Bible brought all divergent sources into a recognizable convergence. Thompson later examines the divergences as part of Blake's collective "stance" against British hegemony (109). That Blake could revise the same metaphysics of authority that authorized his counterhegemonic poetry is no mere contradiction for Thompson, nor for the study I undertake here. Thompson's book proceeds from the notion that Blake's engagement with material culture cannot be explained wholly within the evidentiary milieu of traditional historical scholarship:

> [T]here are readers of Blake who . . . dismiss as a *jeu d'esprit* a statement as flat and as challenging as that Christ
>
> His Seventy Disciples sent
> Against Religion & Government
>
> For a certain kind of scholar, these lines offer room for a textual commentary upon why (from what obscure source) Blake should have chosen the number *seventy*. If he looks at what is actually being *said* in those two lines, then it seem altogether too disturbing: it is either wrong, or mad, or it requires the rewriting of history. Blake requires the latter. (20)

I do not mean to suggest in the following chapters that only one thing "is actually being *said*" in the continuities of modern prophecy, nor do I mean to suggest that modern prophets "rewrit[e]" history by facile exchange of one hegemony for another. Instead, modern prophets re-envision history to include many meanings, including the visionary, that seem at first to be outside of historical discourse but that actually are crucial elements of the same. The visionary history of modern prophecy is not revisionist, in the sense that the term is used in reactionary, late-twentieth-century discourse; i.e., representing violations of a presumed historical objectivism. It is instead a stance toward history that expands the definition of history to include those psychological and social practices that are placed alongside the material and termed "visionary."

Blake reads the Bible through the lenses of tradesman and artisan class dissent, where the Logos is not cast as solely the province of state religion. Seen this way, the Bible is the "Word of God" in Blake's original annotations, though later he qualifies this by adding the adjective "peculiar." *Peculiar* may seem only a hesitant qualification, yet its root in the Latin word (*peculium*) for *private property* may remove much doubt as to Blake's "peculiar" stance. As Blake writes in his annotations to Watson's (1776) *An Apology for the Bible*: "The Bible or <Peculiar> Word of God" is "exclu-

sive of conscience or the Word of God Universal."[21] Blake links "conscience"
and "the Word of God Universal," and thereby distinguishes biblical authority from modern prophetic authority by marking the former as an
"abomination" that hinders the production and reception of modern visionary language. Once biblical authority is "removed"—recalling Blake's "firm
perswasion," the prophetic power to "remov[e] mountains" in *The Marriage of Heaven and Hell* — "every man" might "converse with God & be
a King and Priest in his own house" (615). This goal is, for Blake, nothing
more than conversing with oneself (God) and assuming social and religious autonomy (King and Priest). For Blake, Being is not represented
fully by the church, but instead by "one's own house." But that house is not
conceived as a habitus for a transcendental, individual subject; instead, the
house is figured by Blake as one of many "houses"—often symbols of
states of consciousness—one passes through "each according to his genius" (*The Marriage of Heaven and Hell*, plate 22).

Blake's annotations to Watson offer a useful introduction to how Blake's
vocabulary and philosophy are mediated through particular ways of reading the Bible, ways that reflect the history of religious and social dissent in
Enlightenment Britain. For Blake, the disentangling of crown and church
holds the possibility of the restoration of a forgotten truth, the Godhood of
humanity, with a primal language that Blake would see as unloosed from
what "London" describes as the self-imposed, "mind-forg'd manacles" of
the world. The closing lines to "There is No Natural Religion" (series [b])
conceive of spiritual restoration, in the form, ironically for Blake, of a redundancy: "Therefore God becomes as we are, that we may be as he is."
The Godhood of the individual human being is "manacled" by the human
propensity to reify Godliness as institutions such as the Church. Blake's
effort to distinguish the Bible as the "peculiar" word of God, distinct from
and lower than individual poetic genius, is for him a necessary redundancy.
"God becomes as we are, that we may be as he is": the statement itself
asserts a truth that for Blake is always already given, but one that the prophecies seek to unbind from a material world where spirit is reified as matter.

"Christ died as an unbeliever," Blake writes in his annotations to Bishop
Watson (614). In *The Marriage of Heaven and Hell* Blake's Christ lives much
the same way. The centrality of Christ as both prophet and lawbreaker in Blake
reflects the diffusion of seventeenth-century Antinomian rhetoric into the discourse of eighteenth-century religious dissent. The Voice of the Devil in *The
Marriage of Heaven and Hell* proclaims that Christ "was all virtue" because
he broke the Ten Commandments and called forth a new way of perceiving
law and social justice: "One Law for the Lion & Ox is Oppression" (plate 24).
Such words echo the Antinomian sentiments of Leveller preacher William
Walwyn, who wrote in his 1649 *Just Defense* that he was "not a preacher of the law,
but of the gospell . . . of [the] doctrine of free justification by Christ alone."[22]

Inspired by Ranter doctrine, Blake counters biblical portrayals of transcendent Godhood with the idea of an immanent God, a supreme being wholly inside human consciousness. Of course, the major narrative conflict in Blake's prophecies occurs when this immanent, internal God is perceived as external by self-manacled minds that conceive a God only in fragmented forms of fallen representation. Thus, in *Milton*, "the fallacy of Satan's churches" consists in the mistaken belief that the natural world is the fallen sum of all that is not Godly. This "fallacy" is seen "outside," within the natural world but outside of the frame of reference—Blake's, through the Ranters—that posits the natural world as comprised of both the immanent (matter) and the transcendent (God). The force of Satan is the force that has, in effect, *thought itself out of* the fullest possible conception of the natural world. The fourfold human divine is "seen in fallacy outside," and this fallen vision is "a fallacy of Satan's Churches" (plate 40). As often is the case, Blake's annotations, this time to Bacon, state the case even more explicitly: "The Devil is the Mind of the Natural Frame" (*Complete Poetry and Prose*, 625).

The interplay of both continuity and restraint that results from Ranter influence on Muggletonianism finds an analogue in the relationship between Ranterism and later Quakerism. Both Ranterism and Quakerism maintained belief in a materially perceivable concept of divinity, although Quakers often portrayed themselves as the sober opposition to perceived Ranter excess and extremism. Here Thompson quotes Alexander Ross's 1653 *A View of All Religions* for confirmation of Ranter-Quaker continuity; Ross observes that Quakers proclaim "some of them are Christ, some God himself, and some equal with God, because they have the same spirit in them which is God."[23]

The continuities of Blake's religious influences are vital to an understanding of the influences Blake and H. D. share. Blake's tradition includes continuities among Ranterism, Muggletonianism, Quakerism, and Moravianism. H. D.'s Moravianism descends from the eighteenth-century Moravianism that survived as a vector of inner-light traditions such as Muggletonianism and Quakerism. Thus, H. D.'s earliest religious tradition—significantly for the crucible of *Trilogy*—shares common root with the core of Blake's tradition.

H. D.'s Bethlehem community was founded by a group of Moravians who settled southern Pennsylvania in the early eighteenth century. The Moravians who first arrived in the colonial United States were followers of Austrian Count Nickolas Ludwig von Zinzendorf, who provided refuge in 1722 to Moravians escaping persecution in England.[24] Zinzendorf was not motivated by altruism; Moravians were allowed to settle on his estate in Saxony because Zinzendorf wished to convert them to Protestant Pietism. The Moravians instead converted Zinzendorf, who later would be remembered as the man who revivified Moravianism and became its spiritual leader.

Despite their ties to Saxon nobility, Moravians did not follow codified, institutionally based modes of authority. Gillian Lindt Gollin notes that Moravian church hierarchy was "bound to no creed," nor did it develop "a logically cohesive body of doctrine."[25] Generations of Moravians instead bequeathed to each other a shared set of beliefs, foremost of which were notions of universal grace and of a dependence on emotion over doctrine.[26] The latter, as Gollin notes, led Zinzendorf to propound a God who defies human logic and reason. Zinzendorf influenced Moravian communities toward such strong belief in a God of direct perception that in these communities "[r]eligious ritual was so interwoven with communal decision-making that it becomes almost impossible to make clear-cut distinction between sacred and secular activity" (Gollin, 20). Moravian communities were not totalizing theocracies, either; Moravian resistance to unified, rational doctrine welcomed differing manifestations of religious practice in these communities.

Ginsberg's prophetic poetry is rooted, like Blake's and H. D.'s, in a method of reading biblical prophecy that blurs the boundary between the immanent and the transcendent, and brings both immanence and transcendence together in revised forms of apocalyptic representation. What Ginsberg names in *Howl* as the *hallucination* of "Blake-light tragedy among the scholars of war" seems an unreal, hallucinatory image only if perceived by sense-bound reason.[27] Instead, Blake's work offers a vocabulary of resistance to Cold War institutions that naturalize, through overdependence on sense-bound encounter, rhetoric that upholds warfare.

This "light" of prophecy might be mere hallucination if perceived from a vantage that sets the material and the metaphysical against each other as binary opposites. Ginsberg spent nearly fifty years explaining (to others and to himself) his 1948 auditory vision—his "illumination," as he has called it—of Blake reciting "Ah! Sunflower." Both *Howl* and *Kaddish* blur materialist and visionary modes of perception; in doing so, they transvalue this blurring so that the hallucinatory might be revelatory. Those in *Howl* "who thought they were only mad when Baltimore gleamed in supernatural ecstasy," become those who perceive the precise, nonhallucinatory sound of the "eli eli lamma lamma sabacthani saxophone cry" which at the end of section 1 of *Howl* "shiver[s] the cities down to the last radio" (26, 77). In *Howl* Ginsberg locates the prophetic in the hallucinatory, and thereby seeks to demonstrate that the hallucinatory can be real. *Kaddish* also fuses materialist and metaphysical representations in its language for redemption. The prophetic poet builds a "Heaven in darkness" from conjoined utterances of "caw" and "Lord" coupled in continuous revision of each other.[28]

In *Howl* and elsewhere in Ginsberg's work, the direct inspiration of "Blake-light tragedy" creates a counterhistory to resist the language of a world portrayed as overdependent on reason—a dependence which, for

Ginsberg, is manifested in the postwar university research mobilized to support the anticommunist Cold War "military-industrial complex." In his 1988 *Your Reason and Blake's System*, Ginsberg constructs a Blake precisely suited to his own prophetic impulse. Blake inspires Ginsberg's own impulse to begin with the metaphysical authority of biblical prophecy; then, as Ginsberg writes, Blake initiates his own project to revise this authority, to "tur[n] the Bible upside down."[29]

Ginsberg's affinity with, and estrangement from, biblical authority does not culminate solely in the urgent importance of Blake to his work. Ginsberg's reading of the Bible through Blake is mediated by Ginsberg's Buddhist practice. Indeed, Ginsberg abandoned his attempt to re-create his 1948 Blake vision only at the urging of Buddhist teachers whom he consulted during a 1963 journey to India. Barry Miles's interpretation of the trip to India is useful here, insofar as it dramatizes Ginsberg's eventual renunciation of his quest to relive the original vision as an embrace of what I have suggested is an "immanent transcendent" impulse in his own poetry: "Now he felt he had been wrong, that maybe he had even misunderstood Blake and that Blake's 'Human form divine' meant completely living *in* the human form."[30] The affirmative rhetoric of *Howl* (1956) and *Kaddish* (1961) anticipates what Ginsberg realized in 1963: both poems might be said to be based in the syntax of Blake's statement, in which the "human" (immanent) and the "divine" (transcendent) are united in one "form."

The form of Ginsberg's prophetic poetry extends from this immanent-transcendent content. Ginsberg's insistence on the breath-unit as a foundation for poetic form is the culmination of his reading of biblical prophecy through Judaic tradition, through the content and form of Blake, and through the meditative practice of Tibetan Buddhism. The breath-unit is the original breath of life of Yahweh, the Blakean breath of inspiration, and the elemental "Ah" of Buddhist meditative practice.

The divinity of breath historically has been of great importance to so-called heretical Christian traditions, all of which appeal as countertraditions for Blake, H. D., and Ginsberg. The Gnostic tradition is of special note here, where the Gnostic Mother Goddess breaths life unto the formless world, creating a world circumscribed by gnosis which is later co-opted by the jealous, intellectually blind god Ialdabaoth. Ialdabaoth's struggle resembles the triumph of Urizen in Blake's prophecies. Blake's Urizenic principle is at work in H. D.'s revisionary cosmogony, yet she crucially extends the gynocentric roots of gnosis, and condenses these roots in the Mary of *Trilogy*. Ginsberg's Buddhist influence also echoes the divinity of breath in so-called heretical traditions. In *The Gnostic Gospels*, Elaine Pagels demonstrates that Hinduism and Buddhism influenced Gnosticism, thus placing Hinduism and Buddhism at the origins of early Christianity.[31]

4. INTRAPOETIC AUTHORITY, IMMANENT TRANSCENDENCE

In *The Marriage of Heaven and Hell*, Blake claims to dine with the prophets Isaiah and Ezekiel; their conversation suggests that the authority of vision lies in contentious, dialogic relationships between subjects and objects
of vision. In *Tribute to Freud*, H. D. describes seeing visions forming on a
wall, and explains that her effort to follow these visions eventually caused
her to collapse from mental exhaustion; Bryher continued when H. D. fal-
tered, watching visions form themselves upon the same wall that, crucially,
was blank to her until H. D. had looked away. Later, in analysis with Freud,
H. D. continues the work of vision begun with Bryher. Her vision is not
solitary; the truth of the *seen* is mediated through multiple *seers* who do
not unanimously agree on a unitary meaning for what is seen. In interviews
and journal entries, Allen Ginsberg has offered multiple descriptions of the
day in 1948 when he was overcome by the voice of Blake reciting "Ah!
Sunflower." The visionary experience was solitary—he was alone and had
been masturbating—but the experience itself drew him closer to the people
and products of the world. Staring out his window, he collapsed the subject-
object distinction between himself and the external world. As he said of the
vision in a 1966 *Paris Review* interview with Thomas Clark, "some hand
had placed the sky but . . . the sky was the living blue hand itself. . . . God
was in front of my eyes—existence itself was God."[32] Later, in a bookstore,
subject and object melded in his observations of fellow customers. Ginsberg
told Clark that he, the clerk, and the customers "all had the consciousness,
it was like a great *un*conscious that was running between [*sic*] all of us that
everybody *was* completely conscious" (interview, 216).

I begin my examination of Blake's, H. D.'s, and Ginsberg's poetic prophecies at a blurred line between their languages of *seeing* and *seen* because
this blurred line is a site where these poets draw on biblical authority yet
presume a reciprocal, not authoritarian, relationship between subject and
object (between prophet and God, prophet and prophet, and prophet and
audience). The following chapters demonstrate that the prophetic poems of
each resist the univocality of naming while engaged in a process that enacts polysemous naming as part of social and cultural resistance. The traditional lineage presupposed by scholars of poetic prophecy, in which the
authority of the Bible creates the authority of prophecy, may limit critical
understanding of these poets, insofar as these poets engage the universality
of the Logos in order to enact polysemous versions of naming and making.

a) Blake: Visionary Materialism

Much of what is at stake in modern prophecy can be illustrated in the dining scene in plates 12 and 13 of Blake's *The Marriage of Heaven and Hell*. Plate 12 contains Blake's own version of a countertraditional sacred meal:

> The prophets Isaiah and Ezekiel dined with me, and I asked them how they dared so roundly to assert that God spake to them; and whether they did not think at the time, that they would be misunderstood, & so be the cause of imposition.

Three important issues emerge from the dining scene, each reflecting why poet-prophets might estrange themselves from, yet simultaneously embrace, prophetic tradition. First, and perhaps most crucial for the tradition of prophecy, Blake recounts a *vision* in which physical and metaphysical representations coexist in a relationship that resists uniform hierarchization, possibly including even the sort of linguistic and logical hierarchization that guarantees the conveyance of vision. Blake's encounter with Isaiah and Ezekiel is one of the many instances in *The Marriage of Heaven and Hell* where sense-based language faces the difficulty of interpreting extrasensory visionary experience. Though Blake's questions to Ezekiel focus on the ability of language to both create and convey a "reality"—whether or not "God spake to them"—plate 12 places greater emphasis on the visual components of Isaiah's and Ezekiel's prophecies. "I saw no God, nor heard any, in a finite organical perception," Isaiah responds, "but my senses discovered the infinite in every thing." Blake uses the trope of the sacred meal actually to legitimate a countertradition: here, the sacred meal authorizes a divinity that resists metaphysical hierarchization and does not assert an institutionally sanctified, apostolic authority. As Blake asserts in his annotations to Watson: "Every honest man is a Prophet, he utters his opinion both of public and private matters" (*Complete Poetry and Prose*, 617).

Yet for Blake—and for H. D. and Ginsberg—prophecy and opinion are not equivalent. Indeed, each poet is committed to uncovering what amounts to a contextual language for prophecy that also is primal. As committed to contingency as these poets are, they believe that relationships between imaginative minds produce an inspired discourse distinct from mere opinion. Just so, Blake's questions during the dining scene might constitute a search for a uniform, authoritative interpretation of Isaiah's and Ezekiel's visions. As the dialogue proceeds, however, they emerge more clearly as an argument against the reification of divine vision by the authority of the Logos. Isaiah claims that once convinced — "perswaded"— of the authority of his vision, he "cared not for consequences but wrote." Blake asks of Isaiah the question all visionary writers must answer: "Does a firm perswasion that a thing is so make it so?" Isaiah answers that prophetic validation exists in the language of poetry, which "in ages of imagination . . . removed mountains." Isaiah's response, voiced as a component of Blake's own initializing prophetic vision, confirms *poetic* language as the interpretive authority of visionary perception. For Blake, H. D., and Ginsberg, prophetic poetry is a special province of the imagination, one that creates and conveys a language and empirically verifiable world suffused with vision.

Blake first asked why Isaiah and Ezekiel "dared" claim their visions to be prophetic, and hence pointed to the possibility that the truth-value of prophetic vision might reside in visionary relationships that resist consolidated modes of religious, metaphysical, and epistemological authority. Blake next asked by what methods anyone might represent the making of vision into prophetic knowledge. To both questions, the answer, for Blake, lies in inspired utterances that exist both inside and outside of the boundaries of metaphysical discourse. For Blake, if poetry is to be the most suitable medium of the veracity of prophecy, then poetry must resist the religious and metaphysical doctrine upon which it initially depends. As in H. D.'s anagrammatic revisionism and Ginsberg's "elemental" language of continually mobile utterances, modern poetic prophecy is sustained both by the faith in a primal language for prophecy and, paradoxically, by a trust that such a language depends on contextual, indeterminate modes of making knowledge.

Blake's first question was not answered completely, however. Neither Isaiah nor Ezekiel fully addressed the possible misunderstanding of their messages by audiences. Blake's request for metaphysical validation, which Blake's Isaiah answers by pointing *away from* a metaphysically perceived God and toward "the infinite in every thing," also highlights the resistance prophets produce in audiences. Blake asked if Isaiah and Ezekiel "did not think at the time, that they would be misunderstood, & so be the cause of imposition." Blake risks as much himself.[33] Whereas Blake's first two questions confronted prophetic authority and representation, his third can suggest one more significant characteristic of modern prophetic poetry: the strangeness of prophetic utterance suggests a vision only interpretable by the mad. Vision, Blake asserts, is best performed in the language of poetry that resists metaphysical authorization; only those deemed mad are best fit to receive such resistant poetry at all. Inspired discourse, then, requires an audience willing to resist the very authoritative lineage that is the ground for inspiration.

Blake's questions regarding prophetic lineage, prophetic authority, and the language of madness culminate in a final question that argues, crucially, for the urgency of that which is deemed mad. The question is not one of simple inversion, where the mad become sane and the sane mad, but rather of how these categories are conceived by audiences, and of how audiences come to trust the universal veracity of these categories:

I then asked Ezekiel why he eat dung, & lay so long on his right & left side? he answered, "the desire of raising other men into a perception of the infinite: this the North American tribes practice, & is he honest who resists his genius or conscience only for the sake of present ease or gratification?" (Plate 13)

According to Blake's narrative, prophecy encompasses a lineage that extends from Israel through England and North America—an instance of the same Enlightenment universalism his prophetic poetry revises. Authority resides not in the metaphysics of vision, where language represents presumably fallen forms of an originating unity; instead, authority derives from a cultural practice that furthers—universally—individual perception.

b) H. D.: The Prophetic Unconscious

In the following chapters, I suggest that from Blake forward the modern prophet continues and resists the coercive language of wholly metaphysical and wholly material authorization. For these poets, *renaming* is the language situation where the metaphysical and the physical are conjoined to remake and convey poetic prophecy. Given this emphasis on renaming, Hilda Doolittle's prophetic poetry already seems disabled from the start by the insistent repetition of the coercive name *H. D.*, assigned to her paternalistically by Ezra Pound during the imagist phase of her career. From the outset, H. D. is named by an authority that would be inscribed in her work throughout her entire career.[34] Yet H. D.'s career is marked by resistance to models of authority that naturalize the devaluing of feminine cultural codes in favor of masculine cultural codes. The language of H. D.'s prophecies foregrounds the coerciveness of phallic naming from the start, and conceives of strategies for resistance that are revelatory and prophetic.

H. D. locates visionary language at the intersection of culturally coded gender identity and what she terms her "suppressed desire to be a Prophetess." However, an understanding of H. D. is incomplete if her work is seen only as an attempt to answer a male-dominated poetic establishment with a feminine poetics, as if the semiotic value of *masculine* and *feminine* were as easily discernable as the biologic forms that originate the naming of these terms. Gynocentric perspectives on H. D.'s work are valuable; the importance of quest-heroines in her feminist revisions of Western mythology, at the least, attests to the need to understand her emphasis on the experience of female subjects within cultural formations—family, medicine, military, mythology, and poetry—dominated by male subjects.[35] H. D.'s role as a prophet is not separate from her feminist poetics. H. D. revivifies Western prophetic prophecy at the intersection of Western apocalyptics and feminism. The transformative urge of *Trilogy* seeks to replace an overdependence on sense-bound forms with a prophetic vision that is "not poetic fantasy / but a biological reality." This "biological reality" is only real insofar as it is based on metamorphosis rather than the laws of static, sense-bound reason. Metamorphosis is crucial to the alchemical combination of female divinities in the poem; in H. D.'s crucible, patristic religious traditions are transformed by the contentious voices of dissenting, predominantly female-centered, religious traditions. When *prophecy* and *body* commingle here, the result is a sense of prophetic vision whose own metaphysical authority is decentered, "disentangle[d] / from its art-craft junkshop / paint-and-plaster medieval jumble / of pain-worship and death symbol" (*Walls*, 18.2–5).[36]

The most suggestive locus in H. D.'s work of both materiality and vision—or "biological reality" and "poetic fancy"—is in the account in *Tribute to Freud* of her visionary experience in 1920 on the Greek island of Corfu. The experience itself, her "writing on the wall" vision, inaugurates the prophetic impulse of her later career. Yet her analysis with Freud, and specifically her thinking through the vision itself during analysis, actually served as the catalyst for her creativity during the 1930s, and thereby helped her compose the visionary poetry of the 1940s and after. Of course, her analysis with Freud also brought with it her most explicit confrontation with coercive language structures and the subordination of the feminine, themes important to her later, visionary work.

Two contradictory issues surrounding vision and gender politics emerge in the account of the vision in "Writing on the Wall," later published with her Freud journals in *Tribute to Freud*. First, it seems that the vital, final image of the vision—what H. D. speculates is the "determinative" of the hieroglyphic on the wall—represents a subsuming of H. D.'s sexual identity into a unity that otherwise maintains the inaccessibility of the polarities of female and male, represented by the Niké and Apollo figures she perceives coming together on the wall. On the other hand, female and male signs converge here within a narrative circumscribed by unfixed frames of reference: her account of a dialogic analysis contains at least two different interpretations of a vision (interpretations that are mystical, material, and some combination of the two), a vision originally mediated through a person not present during the crucial "translation" of the vision in analysis. This exhausting catalogue of who "sees" and who "reads" the vision actually questions the durability of fixed gender identity; it becomes a "determinative" instead for the polyvalent role of vision, gender, and sexuality in H. D.'s prophetic poetry. After Bryher "carries on the reading where [H. D.] left off," Bryher sees an image of a man "reaching out to draw the image of a woman (my [H. D.'s] Niké) into the sun beside him."[37] If H. D.'s subjectivity in her poetry is bisexual, it is not bipolar, insofar as the feminine and masculine are "beside" each other—and at work as signs concurrently, attempting no subordination of the feminine to the masculine—as are Niké and Apollo in her Corfu vision.

c) Ginsberg: Bardic Hysteria

The countertraditional prophetic poetics of Blake and H. D. are "continued" in the work of Ginsberg. Ginsberg hailed Blake as a prophetic influence since his 1948 auditory vision, the catalyst for Ginsberg's transformation of his poetics and epistemology; he cites this vision as necessitating his move from a poetics of precise, materialist localizations inspired by William Carlos Williams to a prophetic form and content traceable to Blake and the Bible. Ginsberg directly incorporated Blakean images, symbols, and themes in his poetry, and in explanations of his poetry, from the publication of *Howl* in 1956. As recently as 1986, he claimed the Blake vision to be "[t]he only authentic experience I feel I've had, something that seemed like a complete absorption of all my senses into something totally authentic as experience."[38]

In a letter to Richard Eberhart, Ginsberg claims that the element of the visionary in *Howl* functions to unite rather than separate the protagonists of the poem. He tells Eberhart that "the poem itself is an act of sympathy, not rejection." He describes *Howl* as an expression of "sympathy and identification with the rejected, mystical, individual"; the poem, he writes, "pay[s] homage to mystical mysteries in the forms in which they actually occur here in the U.S. in our environment."[39]

Like Blake's and H. D.'s poetic prophecies, Ginsberg's prophecies are written against reified institutional exemplars of science, religion, and reason. In *Howl* and *Kaddish* he specifically targets the harrowing effects of institutions such as schools, the family, orthodox Western religion, Western legal and medical establishments, and the postwar military-industrial complex. The range of Ginsberg's critique of the postwar United States, along with his mainstream fame as a founder of the Beats, tends to distract from an understanding of precisely how his poetry might be called visionary or prophetic. Ginsberg's own construction of his public persona contributes as much to the suspicious reception of his work in mainstream literary circles as does anything purportedly unorthodox in the work itself.[40] His explanation of *Howl*, the poem that helped break the New Critical stranglehold on modern poetry, and that above all contributed to Ginsberg's fame, makes few rhetorical concessions to a scholarly audience, and seems at first glance not suited to be taken seriously: "*Howl* is an 'affirmation' of individual experience of God, sex, drugs, absurdity, etc. . . ."[41] Within the same passage, however, Ginsberg attests that the poem offers in its "private, individual acts of mercy" an alternative to "merciless" postwar culture. Here, as in the troubling of "affirmation" with quotation marks, it becomes clear that for Ginsberg the experience of God and the experience of absurdity inhabit the same spiritual and intellectual spaces, the embodiments of which in the poem are, at the least, sex and drugs. The motion of the poem, with its emphasis on what seems like random stylistics, utter spontaneity, and entropic structure, actually represents what Ginsberg has termed a statement of "basic human virtues": a carefully conceived moral stance that the poem celebrates as a collective "force" which "comes from positive 'religious' belief and experience."[42]

Ginsberg has described the seemingly spontaneous, ragged lineation of *Howl* and *Kaddish* as an attempt to transcribe the authenticity of interior consciousness, here identified with the visionary, into an embodied mode of communication—a technique he says is rooted in biblical prophecy. This mode of communication is an attempt to merge consciousness, speech, and writing into a language that can represent the metaphysical and material concerns of prophecy. The language in Ginsberg's prophetic poetry reflects a desire to "captur[e] the inside-mind-thought," a desire to transcribe what he terms "the unspoken visual-verbal flow inside the mind."[43]

Ginsberg's outspoken defenses of *Howl*, such as those above, were not universally well received. On the one hand, Ginsberg's experiments with lineation and language were assimilated so quickly into postwar American culture that imitators adopted the surface qualities of his poetics without an awareness of the literary and prophetic substance behind this aesthetic. On the other hand, academic critics trained in the High Modernist mode generally dismissed the prosody and themes of *Howl* as, at best, sloppy prose and, at worst, drugged incoherence.[44] Ginsberg's liner notes to the recorded version of "Pacific High Studio Mantras (Om Ah Hum Vajra Guru Padma Siddhi Hum)" exalt mantra chanting as "an extension of shaking your ass or raising your voice in joyful exaltation," and at the same time warn of the "vanity of mystical consciousness."[45] Chapter 4 proceeds from the premise that the former "exaltation" and the latter, cautionary "vanity" occupy positions of equal importance in the poetry, though often only the former is emphasized by the critical community.

Ginsberg's revisions of the poem reflect an attempt to craft language which would accurately reflect internal, "natural flow." In addition to crafting the opening lineation of *Howl* to resemble the structure of Hebraic prophecy, Ginsberg revised the language of the first line itself to represent a visionary form and content that would adumbrate the "mystical" in material language. The original line characterized his protagonists as "mystical"; he later renamed them "hysterical":

I saw the best minds of my generation destroyed by madness,
   starving hysterical naked. . . .

In his 1986 annotations to the poem, Ginsberg describes the change from "mystical" to "hysterical" as a "crucial revision" that constitutes "a key to the tone of the poem" (*Howl: Original Draft Facsimile*, 124). Ginsberg's protagonists enact mysticism and *hysteria*, a term rooted for twentieth-century readers in the material practices of psychoanalysis.

Ginsberg's emphasis on the breath-unit is an attempt to fuse the vision-ary consciousness of biblical prophecy with human consciousness. As *"one speech-breath-thought,"* this combination of the metaphysical and mate-rial paradoxically does not attempt to minimize the social practices of the physical world, nor to reify the prophetic urgency of the transcendental. Ginsberg's use of this paradox in his poetry continues the prophetic mode shared by Blake and H. D. Ginsberg, like Blake and H. D., "anchors" this paradoxical fusion of immanent and transcendent representation in the polyvocal language of his poetry itself. The revisionary strategy Ginsberg brought to the first utterance of a *"speech-breath-thought"* in *Howl* reflects the poem's structural concern to combine the immanent and the transcen-dent—or, more specifically, to emphasize the "mystic" qualities of his pro-tagonists without eliding their "hysterical" historical conditions.

My readings of the visions of Blake, H. D., and Ginsberg seek to illus-trate that in certain versions of Western prophecy the supposed durability of the terms *transcendental* and *material* is questioned by prophetic texts that collapse the dichotomous signification of these terms. Blake's *vision-ary materialism*, H. D.'s *prophetic unconscious*, and Ginsberg's *bardic hys-teria* all are responses to eras when the efforts of scientific reason defined the boundaries between the immanent and transcendent, delineating a split between observation and vision to which these poets responded with (re)visionary language. Enlightenment reason created conceptions of knowl-edge in which the world was considered wholly knowable, and in which this knowledge was based on natural observation; the Enlightenment episteme was dominated by a "mathesis" of knowledge, as Foucault terms it in *The Order of Things*. This mathesis is generated by Newton's image of "Lord God Pantokrator," a conception of God in Whom "are all things contained and moved."[46] The "Pantokrator" was a logocentric ideal that sought to order all language and knowledge under what Jean-Joseph Goux terms "the *paternal metaphor*," where God is seen as "the central and cen-tralizing metaphor that anchors all other metaphors."[47] In *Milton*, Blake responds to "Newtons Pantocrator," as he termed Newton's image of a mechanizing God, with a language of transference—a language of con-tinual displacement and metaphoricity whose mobility dramatizes a dis-mantling of the "Woof" of science that, for Blake, encloses the world with a mathematized conception of language. According to Newton, the percep-tions of God are not accessible to humans: "As a blind man has no idea of colors, so have we no idea by which the all-wise god perceives and under-stands all things."[48] For Blake, the "Woof" of natural science must be re-vised because it renders inaccessible to human understanding that which is outside of nature and of measurement in time.

H. D.'s realization of her "suppressed desire to be a Prophetess" can be traced to the effect of her work with Freud. Her construction of a public voice for prophecy equally depended on revising dualistic splits between material and metaphysical representation on the one hand, and between supposed feminine passivity and masculine activity as defined by Freud's science of the mind on the other. In his *Three Essays on the Theory of Sexuality* (1905), Freud assigns to the libido the role of activity. While gesturing toward a combined feminine-masculine conception of active desiring, Freud ultimately theorizes desire as the exclusive province of male subjects. In a footnote, he first admonishes the reader that it is "essential to understand clearly that the concepts of 'masculine' and 'feminine,' whose meaning seems so unambiguous to ordinary people, are among the most confused that occur in science."[49] Yet, as Freud says in the footnote, the use of "masculinity" and "femininity" to signify activity and passivity constitutes "the most serviceable" meanings for the terms "active" and "passive" in psychoanalysis; thus, he reproduces the same "ordinary" misconceptions he claims to clarify. As much as Freud seeks to clarify the ambiguities in the terms, and explain their "serviceability," the text to which this footnote refers assigns the libido "invariably and necessarily" to masculinity, explicitly because "an instinct is always active even when it has a passive aim in view" (85). H. D.'s poetry revises Freud's gesture as a means of positing an embodied divinity. For H. D., desire generates a prophetic unconscious whose revisionary language creates immanent conditions for transcendent experience. In her prophetic poetry, desire is the province of both male and female subjects, and female subjects shift from (passive) objects of discourse to (active) speaking subjects as part of a continuity and revision of authorizing sources.

Ginsberg's prophetic poetry responds to an era when homosexuality was cast by psychoanalytic science as a form of deviance, and was equated with threats to national security. Ginsberg crafted a language of prophecy suffused with homosocial desire and interconnected with his mother's language of madness and her avowed communism. For Ginsberg, *hysterical* is a more accurate translation of the condition of his protagonists than is *mystical*; the revision is, he writes, "dictated" by "common sense" (*Howl: Original Draft Facsimile*, 124). However crucial the revision might be, Ginsberg himself realizes the danger of the connotations of *hysterical* in a poem focused on "mercy" and "affirmation": "The word 'hysterical' is judicious, but the verse is overtly sympathetic" (*Howl: Original Draft Facsimile*, 124). *Hysterical* re-envisions the mystical with the materiality of language and desire; and this revision contextualizes psychiatric debates over whether mental illness might be a pathological or visionary condition. Moreover, as a sign for a transgressive femininity, *hysteria* ("wandering womb") survives as a colloquial pejorative for homosexuality and bisexuality, a pejorative Ginsberg remakes in *Howl*. Ginsberg's "affirmative" aims in *Howl* are enacted in his revision of pejorative hysteria, and his transvaluation of

psychoneurotic hysteria. This revision of the divinity of madness is continued in *Kaddish*, where Ginsberg constructs schizophrenia as a model for
prophetic consciousness. In *Kaddish*, he revises the "Backroom metaphysics" of Cold War language that otherwise "zones" identity through the in-
ternalization of discipline (216–17). Ginsberg incorporates the popularized
fusion of homosexuality with national and familial threat in order to create
a revelatory language to represent his mother's communism and her madness. From discourses of reason that would fix language and identity into
zones of sexual-political normativity and transgression, Ginsberg creates a
continually mobile language of prophecy that in *Kaddish* "blesses" the
margins with a "Heaven in darkness."

5. FROM OBSERVATION TO VISION

In order to forecast the methods by which these poets operate from sites of
continuity and estrangement, I want to call attention to how Ezekiel's chariot
vision highlights the possibilities of recollection and revision in ways that
would appeal to Blake, H. D., and Ginsberg. As I discussed earlier, the
representability of Ezekiel's vision might seem to rest wholly on a familiar
metaphysical split between the language of the prophet and the word of
God. However, certain elements of Ezekiel's vision seem to call for frames
of reference that presume indeterminacy, rather than the essential order of
the Logos, as a significant category of understanding. As an intertextual
model for poetic prophecy in the modern world, the prophecy of Ezekiel
suggests that the texts of biblical prophecy themselves may not adhere to
an authoritative, uniformly coherent vision of the natural world.

Michael Lieb's remarks are useful in this context: "Ezekiel is as much a
poet as he is a prophet, and many of the texts that his prophecy engendered
represent to a great extent creative reformulations of an essentially poetic
substratum."[50] The following chapters explain how the conjunction of the
poetic and the prophetic in Blake, H. D., and Ginsberg both engenders and
limits poetic prophecy. These poets operate on the premise that the lineage
that authenticates their prophecies becomes coercive if invoked without
each poet's active effort to estrange him/herself from the line of prophecy.
To help understand how these three poets paradoxically place themselves
both within and outside of the tradition of prophecy and its apocalyptic
implications, it might be useful to think of a significant contrary example.
In *The Waste Land* Eliot invokes the prophecy of Ezekiel to recall the power
of an authoritative past. In "The Burial of the Dead," for instance, Ezekiel
"know[s] only / A heap of broken images." For a contrast to Ezekiel's "broken" knowledge, Eliot's footnote to this passage refers the reader to the
valley of the dry bones in chapter 37 of the book of Ezekiel, where Ezekiel

is asked by Yahweh if the bones can live: Ezekiel responds, "O Lord GOD, thou knowest" (37:3). Unlike the prophetic poetry of Blake, H. D., and Ginsberg, the prophetic impulse of *The Waste Land* presupposes that the authoritative knowledge of a transcendent being supersedes the immanent authority of the human prophet. However, the continuities of prophecy in Blake, H. D., and Ginsberg presume that, as Lieb has said of Ezekiel, prophecy crafts a creative reformulation of the "essentially poetic substratum" of the Bible. Traditional Western prophecy reveals knowledge that is known to be "deposited in a timeless substratum," to recall Scholem; however, Blake, H. D., and Ginsberg see this substratum as "essentially poetic" and thereby subject to continuous revision and historical variance (Scholem, 289; Lieb, 306).

According to Lieb, Ezekiel's intricate description of the wonder of the throne-chariot, the foundation of the visionary experience itself, demonstrates that Ezekiel's vision represents "an artifact that cries out for *objectification* . . . for the bestowal of a name" (34). Lieb suggests that it is naming that allows for exegesis at all. By implication, then, the standard by which one measures the vision of Ezekiel is not the metaphysics of the vision but the *account of* the vision in the text itself: "Ezekiel's vision has no referent—no 'source'—but itself"; the vision "cannot be reduced to any *thing* that might tempt one to substitute the object for that which it is meant to represent" (33). Denying the universality of material representation of the vision does not negate the power of representation; instead, it intensifies the need for some form of language sufficient to the visionary experience. Indeed, as Lieb observes, "[n]aming the vision represents the first step in performing an exegesis upon it" (34). This interdependence between naming and interpretation implies that the observer who renders unstable the name of a cultural artifact or concept multiplies the potential meanings of the artifact rather than negates them. Yet the presumption that language does not wholly represent the world does not render *meaning* null and void. Blake, H. D., and Ginsberg demonstrate in their prophetic poetry that a distrust of totalizing language encourages a new language adequate to the representation of a polysemous mode of vision. For each, seer and seen combine to enact languages of literal/littoral polysemousness (Blake's *Milton*), anagrammatic revisionism (H. D.'s *Trilogy*), and an "elemental" language that moves continually between nonreferential sound ("caw") and referential language ("Lord") (Ginsberg's *Howl* and *Kaddish*).

Lieb also demonstrates that Ezekiel's prophecy hinges on moments when language does not depend on a metaphysical correspondence between the natural and supernatural worlds, in which the former presumably would serve as a fallen version containing only traces of the latter. To be sure, Ezekiel's vision presupposes for the orthodox exegete a familiar metaphysics of vision, where Ezekiel experiences not Yahweh but the "likeness" of Yahweh (1:28). Nevertheless, Lieb's claims for the vision and the metaphysical explanation of it remain plausible, rather than contradictory, within the boundaries set forth by Ezekiel's language. Ezekiel's account states that the object of the vision (the chariot) returns the gaze of the subject who sees: Yahweh's chariot is a vision that also *sees*. Ezekiel describes the wheel rims as "full of eyes round about them" (1:18). Ezekiel's vision conceals a metaphysical frame of reference (the hidden face of Yahweh) at the same time that, remarkably, it dramatizes this frame of reference (the wheel rims). As Lieb argues, the vision "confounds both by defying full perception and by seeing back"; the object "which is beheld also beholds" (39). From Lieb's claim that the vision blurs any absolute distinction between subject and object of vision, one might infer that the presumed metaphysical separation between God and seer cannot be asserted with certainty. The hierarchical opposition between the supernatural world of *vision* and the natural world of *seer* (sayer) collapses into a relationship which mediates between vision and seer. Both see and are seen. For Lieb, the implications of this visionary relationship profoundly affect biblical scholarship; this "new awareness of the vision as a literary event" revitalizes Judaic and Christocentric understanding of biblical prophecy. Ultimately, he maintains, "[e]very effort at analysis becomes an exercise in self-exegesis" (40).

Lieb's discussion bears significantly on the question of how biblical prophecy becomes an influence in the figurations of poet-prophets in the modern era. If the metaphysical authorization of prophecy by supernatural vision can be questioned in the original source material—that is, if Yahweh and Ezekiel mediate the vision together—then metaphysical authorization of the lineage of poetic-prophecy might be subject to revision. Nor must it be assumed that the language of prophecy represents a fallen form of transcendental language.

As with standard readings of biblical prophecy, Lieb's approach to the question of authentication initially assumes that vision exists outside of the natural world, that issues of coercion and resistance in prophecy bypass nature in favor of the relationship between God and humanity. Lieb, however, extends this standard approach to nature, vision, and language to raise further questions about where the authority of *meaning* is located in texts of the visionary. The vision of Ezekiel is represented as an object that both sees and is seen. As that which is seen, it is external to the natural world; as that which sees, it is inside of the natural world. The vision, then, is accessible to human understanding, a view that presumes that in the natural world meaning is made from more than just fallen traces of an originary essence.

I do not mean to repeat debates over the efficacy of postmodern literary studies in the chapters that follow. Nevertheless, a clarification of the relationship between postmodernism and my subject matter is necessary, because the following chapters draw on postmodernism to illuminate how issues of agency, subjectivity, and cultural authority affect our understanding of the traditional lineage of poetic prophecy. These chapters will locate the visionary in postmodernism's approach to history, and the historical in modern prophecy's approach to vision. In so doing, I will show that Blake, H. D., and Ginsberg conceive of resistant cultural forms that can be clarified with recourse to postmodern theories of the unstable relationship between language and culture. The paradoxes of prophetic language and vision are best understood by contemporary critical approaches to politics and identity that value the role of indeterminacy. Because they offer an institutional framework for discussing the linguistic openness of indeterminacy, the vocabularies of postmodernism and poststructuralism best suggest modes of representation for poems that resist authoritative vision in their attention to revision and a polyvocal alterity.

Blake, H. D., and Ginsberg embrace polyvalent representations as part of a response to what each perceives as the coercive unity of representation in the industrial world. Each responds to coercive language with apocalyptic representations of visionary language. As I have discussed above, apocalyptic representations of modern prophecy are antimetaphysical, even anti-apocalyptic. Though each poet is a careful, industrious builder of systems, each nevertheless distrusts the logic of systematization itself. Their resistance to the authority of unity that governs scientific reason leads each poet to commit to a rhetoric of revision that seeks to unsettle the logic of narrative discourse, even to the extent of embracing discourses of madness.

For Freud, such mental processes resemble psychosis, and are as fruitful for creativity as they are dangerous for mental health. In *The Order of Things*, Foucault separates the discourses of madness and poetry: the mad speak signs whose meanings "never ceas[e] to proliferate," while the poet conversely "brings similitude," and hence representability, to such signs. Gilles Deleuze and Félix Guattari, writing within the revisionary post–World War II antipsychiatric movement, find in such "asyntactic, agrammatical" representation politically productive means of resisting an absolutist relationship between literature and industrial culture.[51] Freud warns of psychosis; Foucault finds the languages of madness and poetry oppositional; Deleuze and Guattari conclude (with hope) that "literature is like schizophrenia" (133). For Blake, H. D., and Ginsberg, discourses of madness and paradox offer a means for constructing new languages for vision and apocalypse— and for each, divine madness demands the same re-envisioning urge as does vision and apocalypse. Of course, my affinity for Lieb's presumption that all "analysis" could become "self-exegesis" may threaten to confine religious language and meaning only to matters of textual production. This threat weighs productively on the following chapters without, I hope, constraining the power of religious language with postmodern textualizing, or quashing the insights of postmodern textualizing with divine essentialism.

2

The "Moment Satan Cannot Find": Blake's Transferential Language of Vision in *Milton*

1. A LANGUAGE FOR PROPHECY

The title figure of Blake's *Milton* first appears in a pathetic, fallen form. "Unhappy tho' in heav'n," the poet wanders "the intricate mazes of Providence," as uninspired as any Urizenic character from the prophecies. In this context, the figure of Milton who frames the action of Blake's poem labors under the same delusions Blake attacks in *The Marriage of Heaven and Hell*, where "The Voice of the Devil" characterizes Milton as the "fettered" poet who composed *Paradise Lost*. Of course for Blake, the fallen "history" Milton composed "in fetters" authorizes the usurpation of imagination by reason in the natural world. But if Blake believed *Paradise Lost* valorized the role natural religion plays in the "history" of "reason usurp[ing] its place" to "gover[n] the unwilling"—where Milton's Messiah is lawgiver rather than lawbreaker—then Blake may have perceived the Milton who authored *Paradise Regained* as a figure representative of the prophetic counterbalance to this history. Blake's *Milton* is predicated on the need to find a language sufficient to describe a journey away from the religious solidarity of *Paradise Lost* and toward the mediated language of selfhood that characterizes *Paradise Regained*.

The figure of Milton in *Milton*, paradoxically, is redeemed yet fallen. His suffering stages the major tension of Blake's prophetic poem: Milton, the pilgrim-prophet, must revise the conditions of his own redemption, and must create a language sufficiently revitalized to express this revision. The enormous influence of the historical Milton is not enough for Blake to create a model for conceiving apocalyptic change in an era of human history when consciousness is shaped by the productions of industry, and religious discourse is framed in monologic contexts. Milton's attempts to enshrine free speech and "justify the ways of God to man" are efforts at religious cohesiveness, attempts to bring his English audience into a solid religious tradition based on the Hebrew prophets' concerns with redeeming the collective social whole. Blake, however, represents the moment in radical Protestantism that turns the corner toward something that looks like a secular vision, where material language combines with the metaphysical futurism of prophecy. Or, as Blake writes in *A Vision of the Last Judgment*, combining the material with his vision of apocalyptic representation, "When the Sun rises do you not see a round Disk of fire somewhat like a Guinea O no no I see an Innumerable company of the Heavenly host crying Holy Holy Holy is the Lord God almighty" (565–66).

These issues of biblical authority, religious community, and material language are taken up in important ways by Alter in *The Art of Biblical Poetry*. Alter traces the "inner congruence" existing between poet and biblical precursor.[1] Alter points to Blake as a figure who generates ruptures in this "ideal community" of poets and biblical precursors. Alter writes that beginning with Blake, "it became much more common for writers engaged in the Bible to wrestle with it . . . forcing pieces of language into radically new contexts, riding with the poetic momentum of the biblical texts toward ends that might be intermittently in consonance with them but more often at cross-purposes with them" (209). The intent of this chapter is to demonstrate how Blake created "radically new contexts" for sacred language. As Alter explains, emerging discontinuities between later-poet and biblical-poet "are not just arguments with an idea or creed but also imaginative responses to a way of saying something, often indeed acts of poetic emulation in the midst of argumentation or ironization" (209).

The religious community Milton envisions in *Paradise Lost* and *Paradise Regained* is revised in Blake's *Milton* as a community equally broken away from and beholden to the authority of biblical prophecy. For Blake, Milton himself must be rewritten. The figure of Milton is the means by which Blake recalls past models of prophetic language, and by which these past models then become the basis for conceiving, in the present, representations of an "apocalyptic" future. Blake's use of eighteenth-century biblical and scientific discourses in describing the inward journeys of Christ in *Paradise Regained* and Milton-Blake in *Milton* emphasizes individual revelation over the material forms of the natural world. Those journeys are represented by linguistic structures in which meaning is created from nonhierarchical relations. Blake draws from the authority of the prophetic Milton to create in *Milton* a language for prophecy that paradoxically both expands and fixes the meaning of individual utterances. Milton's conception of a religiously cohesive audience for prophecy is countered by Blake's insistence on a rupture and continuity within the Miltonic line of prophecy. "Would to God that all the Lords people were Prophets," Blake writes, in the preface to *Milton*, quoting from the Book of Numbers; prophets, yes, but within a community where insistence on lawlike identity is overcome by Blake's conception of a mediated selfhood in which seemingly irreducible measurements of the body in time are overcome by measurements of the imagination, by "moment[s] that Satan cannot find" (*Milton*, 35:42).

Blake scholars generally agree that the prophetic path to redemption in Blake is inward, and that for Blake an overvaluation of the natural world must be overcome in any redemptive discourse created by the imaginative mind. However, not all commentators concur on the means by which an alternative to the natural may be brought into existence within a poetic structure mindful of history and consistent with Blake's insistence on the "renovation" of the natural world.

The responses of critics to issues of mind and nature in Blake's prophecies can be grouped into two differing perspectives, both of which are strongly influenced by the psychological dimensions of *Milton*. For Andrew Cooper, Paul Youngquist, Northrop Frye, and Harold Bloom, Blake's response to what he sees as an overvaluation of the natural world is an effort to liberate the mind from the fetters of nature and fallen representation. As evident as is Blake's distrust of language and nature, a second group of critics is less inclined to close off the possibilities Blake would find in nature. For these critics, especially Diana Hume George, Mark Bracher, and Nelson Hilton, Blake's emphasis on mind over matter is precisely a problem *of* language, one which admits not of closure but of continual revision.

For those critics who see Blake attempting to liberate the mind from nature, the Blake-Milton relationship in *Milton* dramatizes Blake's private quarrel with Milton, or it represents a solipsistic attempt by Blake to refine the particulars of his mythology, where Blake's revision of Milton is a metaphor for his struggle to mend warring aspects of himself. Cooper argues that *Milton* is primarily, for Blake, an attempt at self-control; the poem chronicles Blake's attempt to conquer the incipient madness continually present in his poetry. Along similar lines, Youngquist sees the poem as a recuperative response to the seemingly maladaptive symptoms of Blake's life as a poet and painter. Frye's extensive commentary on the poem culminates in a conventional Christian interpretation of Blake's preface, noting that *Milton* pivots on the desire to "buil[d] Jerusalem. / In Englands green & pleasant Land" (*Milton* 1:15–16) and thus represents Blake's vision of the second coming of Christ.[2]

Milton is Harold Bloom's exemplary dramatization of the anxiety of poetic influence. Bloom convincingly explains the reasons for privileging the psychological dimensions of Blake's quarrel with Milton, and for emphasizing that this quarrel is a major component of Blake's self-representation as a poet-prophet. My own focus on attachment and estrangement—on continuity and rupture—among poets in the Western lineage of prophetic

poetry could call to mind Bloom's theory that the solidarity of poetic tradition depends to a large extent on how poets incorporate their own anxieties
about tradition and lineage into their work. I share Bloom's insistence on
understanding prophetic influence through an emphasis on psychic processes. For modern poet-prophets, however, psychoanalysis is not an end
in itself; it is instead a means by which a greater understanding of the relationship between prophecy and culture can be achieved. The unconscious
processes of the human psyche perform a necessary function in the cultural
and mythological systems of Blake, H. D., and Ginsberg. However, none
of those poets is satisfied with normative models of psychic life, just as
none accepts the cultural tendency to transform social norms into models
of psychic hegemony.[3] The differences between Bloom's approach and mine
might best be characterized by our dissimilar approaches to ruptures within
prophetic lineage.

Bloom's frequently cited psychological model of poetic lineage presupposes that individual poet-prophets resist their place in the chronologically
hierarchical arrangement of tradition, where antecedent poets exert the pressures of their influence on new generations of poets who must struggle
against their ancestors to attain the "right" place in the tradition. Despite
the contentiousness in Bloom's model, the poets in his system ultimately
do form a "visionary company," a solid if not unified compact. Bloom's
model is important because, at best, it emphasizes the psychosocial tensions of poetic prophecy. At worst, however, Bloom's exploration of these
psychosocial tensions tends to de-emphasize the historical exigencies that
help underwrite the specific impulses of this tradition, and tends to take for
granted the solidarity of tradition as part of proving the psychological sche-
mata he uses to *create* this tradition. Equal attention must be given to those
instances where prophetic poets never quite square themselves with the
tradition of prophecy itself. The prophetic poetry of estrangement is fraught
with psychosocial tension, but the consequences of this tension do not point
solely toward a means of understanding the process of making a tradition,
as they do for Bloom. Instead, a persistent re-envisioning of the value and
composition of tradition arises from this tension, providing a usable current on which prophets draw when rewriting the authority of tradition.

For critics such as George, Bracher, and Hilton, this usable current is
exemplified by Blake's effort to create a language for visionary experience
based on continual revision. For these critics, Blake's privileging of psychic conflict is not an escape from materiality, nor is it a fall into madness;
instead, it is part of an effort to collapse the boundaries between psyche
and nature, language and vision, and humanity and God. George reveals
this effort in *Blake and Freud* by highlighting "the poet in Freud and the
psychoanalyst in Blake." She shows how Blake anticipates Freud, and how
Blake's "mapping of psychic processes actually subsumes Freud's" in

areas that anticipate the revisionary responses to Freud of contemporary psychoanalytic theory.[4] I recognize the potential danger of adding Freud to a discussion of Milton and Blake's re-envisioning of nature, especially insofar as natural experience provides a crucial foundation for Freud's theories of mental life. However, George observes correctly that although the natural did offer Freud the best material for systematizing the psyche, his later writings are marked by a "bemoaning" of "natural limitation" (85). Of this later Freud, George notes that "his was a system in which the 'natural' was both the valley and the summit of human possibility" (84). Though others, particularly Youngquist, portray Freud's work as the very empiricism that Blake would attack, I would argue that the Freud of chapter 7 of *The Interpretation of Dreams*—like the post–1921 Freud to which George refers above—offers useful analogies for understanding Blake's attempts to re-envision the natural world as locus and limit of prophetic imagination.

Blake critics mindful of Freud have applied the tension between fragmented and unified subjectivity in Freud to Blake's ideas of identity and language, exploring how Blake's complex psychological systematizing of being and lack might anticipate Freud's. Indeed, for Bracher, the Blake-Milton quarrel emerges from Blake's desire to "ungird" self-presence from language in favor of a mediated conception of language and subjectivity, of "mediated presence."[5] Milton's pilgrimage, then, is for Bracher a movement from a metaphysics of presence to a mediated presence.

As Hilton observes, Blake's movements between sense and non-sense are as much an engagement with language as they are a representation of dissatisfaction with the limits of language. In *Literal Imagination: Blake's Vision of Words*, Hilton's discussion of Blake's poetic language eschews psychopathological conclusions to examine how Blake's language reflects his conception of a visionary imagination. "Blake's words are the foundation of his work, which is an explanation of . . . how directly the Poetic Genius can speak," Hilton observes, with regard to the importance of language to Blake's vision.[6] For Hilton, Blake's language is "multidimensional," his words open to dimensions of thought that cannot be perceived through univocal discourse (11). George and Bracher portray Blake as a poet dissatisfied with a dichotomous split of the mind from nature, a split other critics argue leads to madness or liberatory promise. Hilton shows that Blake's conception of nature as visionary follows from polysemous representation in his work, from a language of both systematized structure and fragmentary context: "The polysemous word is 'economical' in that it permits a condensed vocabulary and expression, and contextually dependent . . . in that it relies on the speech situation to point up the pertinent *seme*, or unit of meaning" (10). Blake's language consists of littoral boundary conditions that create "Litteral expression" (*Milton*, 42:14).

Blake's language for prophecy seeks revisionary possibilities in the relationship between desire and language. The figure of Milton suffers in both body and mind at the beginning of *Milton*; and this suffering becomes the occasion for Blake to call forth a revision of Milton's line of prophecy at the levels of desire, inspiration, and language. Milton reacts to the inspirational Daughters of Beulah with "burning thirst and freezing hunger"; their prophetic power is his "terror" and "torment." The opening lines are both a call for epic inspiration and a representation in miniature of the action of the poem, which is itself a representation of "right" prophetic inspiration: "Unhappy tho in heav'n," Milton can redeem the "torment" of his "fettered" frame of reference if he embraces "The Eternal Great Humanity Divine," which is "planted" in the "Portals" of the prophetic poet's mind (2:7–8). What moves Milton is an image of his own restrained desire, as Blake would say in *The Marriage of Heaven and Hell*. This, then, is the terror the Bard's song in *Milton* can vanquish: though in heaven, Milton is unhappy because he has allowed his desire to become muted. The Bard's song tells how the body in chains of mind utters a chained world in its own image; the "history" of this restraint of desire, as Blake says in *The Marriage of Heaven and Hell*, "is written in Paradise Lost. & the Governor or Reason is call'd Messiah" (plate 5). The productions of the unredeemed Milton are the muted "False Tongue" of a desire "weak enough to be restrained." Milton "obey'd, he murmur'd not. he was silent" (*Milton*, 2:18).

Unable to speak, Blake's Milton can only watch the fragmenting image of prophetic inspiration, his Sixfold Emanation, "scatter'd thro' the deep" (2:19). Once moved to prophecy by the Bard's song, the pilgrim-poet Milton seeks to redeem his prophetic power, first at the level of inspiration. Inspiration is represented by the individual power of the poet-prophet, whose individual desire is greater than the authority of the church. Milton's choice of prophetic inspiration over church authority depends upon a perception of his audience as prophetic:

> The loud voic'd Bard terrify'd took refuge in Miltons bosom
> Then Milton rose up from the heavens of Albion ardorous!
> The whole Assembly wept prophetic, seeing in Miltons face
> And in his lineaments divine the shades of Death & Ulro
> He took off the robe of the promise, & ungirded himself
>   from the oath of God. . . .
>
> (14:9–13)

Milton detextualizes himself: his prophetic "ungirding"—where *textus* comes from the Latin *tessere*, "to weave"—produces a prophetic response in the Assembly of Albion. The "loud voic'd" Bard's song moves Milton away from the univocal language of a fallen world, where "[o]pacity was named Satan, Contraction was named Adam" (13:21).

Milton's desire owed its restraint to "the oath of God," the belief in a metaphysical, eternal selfhood separate from immanent human experience. As a sense of Godliness which stands in opposition to Blake's conception of Poetic Genius, this "oath of God" resembles the utterances of the Gnostic creator-god Ialdabaoth, whom Blake recasts as the Urizenic/Satanic creator God of the Christian creed, the God who commands a law of obedience and silence toward His unwavering oneness.[7] "I am One God, Father Almighty" is reconceived in *Milton* as the stubborn self-presence of Satan's Moral Law: "I am God alone / There is no other" (9:25–26). Satan's monovocal Law transforms prideful self-presence into "principles of moral individuality" that reproduce themselves each time they are uttered, a self-repetition responsible for Satanic power in the poem (9:26). "[T]he Unutterable name," Yahweh, is "worship[ped]" as a God who instead "mak[es] to himself Laws from his own identity": "[Satan] Compell'd others to serve him in moral gratitude and submission / Being call'd God: setting himself above all that is called God"(11:11–12).

Milton's journey begins with an attempt to craft a prophetic language of mediated subjectivity that will unbind him from reified church authority. Blake's desire in *Milton* to speak beyond the limitations of his own "gross tongue" echoes Milton's similar desire in *Paradise Regained* (20:15). Stanley Fish, Leonard Mustazza, and Steven Goldsmith have explored how the antidramatic narrative of *Paradise Regained* implies a struggle between materialist and prophetic discourse.[8] What is missing in these discussions of prophecy is a conception of how an alternative vision of language attempts to re-envision a fallen world without lapsing into silence or the solipsism of private language. Both Mustazza, in "Language as Weapon in *Paradise Regained*," and Fish, in "Inaction and Silence: The Reader in *Paradise Regained*," argue that the drama of Milton's poem turns on Christ's attempt to go beyond language and find redemption in the absence of words. Presumably, in the absence of a redemptive language that would exist outside of nature, the only option available to Christ is the repudiation of postlapsarian language. Goldsmith argues, instead, that *Paradise Regained* does not privilege wordless "silence" at all, that the poem is in part a defense of poetry, a defense of inspired linguistic expression. However, Goldsmith does not explore what this "inspired silence" implies for the otherwise public role of the prophet, thus rendering wordless the constructed nature of prophetic language, the language that "mov'd Milton" and his prophetic audience in *Milton*. For Blake, such a problem would be severe: if Milton himself must be rewritten, then Blake must find a way to reconceive language in terms that avoid reification and silence.

If Blake is to redeem the natural world with prophecy, it seems he must do so either with a fallen language, therefore binding himself to paradox, or with no recognizable language at all. I would argue that paradise is regained, both by Blake's Milton and by the Milton of *Paradise Regained*, once ideologies of the natural, exemplified in Blake's time by discourse produced and limited by established authorities such as state religion and science, are exposed as reductive and constraining, a recognition that permits the poet to construct a language sufficient for a visionary conception of nature. For Blake, "redemption" requires an apocalyptic language, in which the poet refers back to multivalent representation written in the past in order to envision a polyvocal language for an apocalyptic future.

In both poems the redemptive language of imagination is "transferential" rather than reificatory; that is, the remembered reality of nature is rejected in favor of a polysemous language of mobile representation. Here, a word on transferential language is necessary, since this chapter explores Blake's use of a transferential language as an immanent representation of divinity. As Stuart Peterfreund argues in "Blake and the Ideology of the Natural," a language of transferential relations is for Blake one in which "refigured unending metalepsis" is "metaphorized as a versing or walking or flowing together, or conversation."[9] Transferential language for Blake depends upon an understanding of the fullest sense of the English verb *transfer*, "to bear, or carry across": to recall Peterfreund, transferential language can be defined as "a cognitive and linguistic process" linked to a "spatiotemporal displacement or deferral in which one moves out of one term . . . into the other, and does so endlessly" (94). Peterfreund describes Blake's continuous displacement or deferral as a performative principle of the poet's conception of divine language, a mode of representation based on the "enactment, through the medium of language, of the sacramental" (94). In *Jerusalem*, such language takes the form of a "convers[ing]" in "Visionary forms dramatic," which creates "Visions / in new Expanses" (98:28–30). Transferential linguistic forms in *Milton* culminate in "the Divine Revelation in the Litteral expression" (42:14).

Blake's Milton and the Milton of *Paradise Regained* both privilege a relationship between imaginatively inspired minds and the natural world in which speakers embrace, through artistic encounter, a mobility of representations in the natural world, rather than mitigate these pluralistic representations through sense-bound encounter. In a world of multiple signification, *meaning* is negotiated through transferential, inspired discourse; in a fallen system in which oscillating semantics are reified into stable matter, however, *meaning* is calculated from the remembered reality of the natural world. *Milton* and *Paradise Regained* make it clear that the unsatisfactory alternative to this transferential vision of nature is a world in which relations between human beings and nature have been reified into an alienated, fallen state perceived, mistakenly, to be "natural." A radically reconstructed language seeks to redeem humanity in both poems—a language in which meaning is localized in the unfixed boundary between the material and spiritual worlds. Ultimately, the prophetic "Fountain of Light" (4.289) with which Christ answers Satan's final temptation in *Paradise Regained* becomes in *Milton* the prophetic light of multivocal language, the necessary state of contrariety in Beulah that must be experienced before Blake's messianic Milton collapses the boundary between mind and spirit in his pilgrimage toward redemptive self-annihilation. Blake's Milton ungirds a presumably "natural," immutable selfhood on his pilgrimage; this process of ungirding is one of self-annihilation, insofar as the protagonist's fixed notion of self is transferred into a mobility of selves that are represented in a language of relations and contexts, of multiplicitous conversation and redemptive vision.

My purpose in this chapter is threefold: first, to demonstrate not only that the "natural" is attacked by both *Paradise Regained* and Blake's *Milton*, but that the critique in both instances is similar; second, to show that in both poets the alternative to ideologies of the natural can be expressed in language that is at once inspired and mindful of the human propensity to "fix" the inspired by reifying it; and third, to show that both poems call for a strategy that counters the propensity to reify by establishing a transferential relationship between subject and language.

2. A MOBILE MOMENT: BLAKE AND BIBLICAL LANGUAGE

In crafting a language sufficient for prophecy—which includes representing revelation as immanent vision—Blake's work draws on eighteenth-century biblical criticism, especially the mode of criticism that attempted to systematize the visions of biblical prophets. Blake's desire to engage and revise Milton is inseparable from his desire to do the same with eighteenth-century biblical interpretive tradition. In *Biblical Tradition in Blake's Early Prophecies*, Leslie Tannenbaum observes that for eighteenth-century writers, "the influence of Milton was as strong as that of the Bible and . . . Milton's poetry became so engrafted to the biblical tradition that the distinction between the two traditions is often difficult to maintain."[10] Blake used biblical tradition to revise both exegetes and poets; for him, to rewrite Milton's "False Tongue" was also to rewrite the exegetical tradition of his own era.

Blake's project, combining poetry and exegesis under the rubric of *inspiration*, draws to some extent from Bishop Robert Lowth's *Lectures on the Sacred Poetry of the Hebrews*, first published in 1753. Lowth, best known for his discovery of biblical parallelism, would have appealed to Blake primarily for his claim that the linguistic foundation of the Bible is poetic. Lowth also maintained that biblical prophecy exhibits particular qualities, "which, although poetical . . . do not properly belong in the species of poetry."[11] Biblical prophecy is unique in that it consists of a commingling of multiple genres, "complete poems of different kinds, odes as well as elegies" (Lowth, 168). Lowth's evaluations of biblical poetic genres also would have appealed to Blake, especially in terms of his contrast in *Milton* between the "False Tongue" of the language of memory and the "Litteral" voice of the language of inspiration. Lowth argues, for instance, that the alphabetic poetry of the Bible is distinct from biblical prophecy on the grounds that alphabetic poetry is the result of "study and diligence, not of imagination and enthusiasm" (148). Alphabetic arrangement of verse, according to Lowth, is "a contrivance to assist the memory, not to affect the passions"; and such a structural mechanism is "utterly repugnant to the nature of prophecy" (148). Blake's *Milton* distinguishes inspired language from the language of church authority in much the same way. Milton's quest to ungird Christ from the church is described as a quest "To cast off the rotten rags of Memory by Inspiration" (41:4). Blake's Christ, too, is the desiring, lawbreaking alternative to the wandering Milton who opens *Milton* afraid of the image of his own inspiration.

Although Lowth's emphasis on the "enthusiasm" and "passions" of the prophet seems to underwrite Blake's wrathful Rintrah, Lowth's remarks also can easily be adapted to the notion that the prophet is only divinely mad. Hence, both prophets and their exegetes risk being cast as ineffectual, raving outsiders, especially in an age when Augustan poetic ideals of decorum, wit, and finish still held sway. For Lowth, the prophet is "seized" by the effect of the "very violent agitation of the mind" caused when he is chosen by God to speak the Word (150). Thus, when Blake's Milton "ungirded himself from the oath of God" and provoked the Assembly of Albion to "we[ep] prophetic," Blake risks reproducing Ion's bewitched response to reciting Homer: both Milton and the *Ion* point to a rhetoric of prophecy in which true prophets persuade their audiences and exegetes to prophetic responses; in Platonic and Augustan discourse, however, the audience that "we[eps] prophetic" is an audience rendered dangerous because it has gone mad. Indeed, the Greek word from which *prophet* derives is *mántis*, which also designates *mania*.

For Lowth, the potential mania of prophecy is contraverted by the metaphysical authority of God. Even though in Hebraic tradition the word *prophet* (*nabi*) had multiple meanings, Lowth argues that all were held together by the common notion that the prophet is "chosen by God himself" as an instrument of revelatory inspiration (Lowth, 148). Lowth's orthodox assertion of a metaphysical God who chooses to bestow the authoritative voice of revelation on a separate person in the presumably fallen world would not appeal to Blake's sense that Poetic Genius is the immanent principle of metaphysical Godliness found in all people: "The desire of man being Infinite the possession is infinite & himself Infinite" (*There is No Natural Religion* [b]). No need, then, exists for the authority of prophecy to emanate externally from a metaphysical source; for Blake, the source of prophecy instead is Poetic Genius, the constitutive presence in human desire. Blake's use of critical and historical tradition was flexible enough to meet the needs of his own system. Thus, though Blake would have found inspiration in Lowth's influential remarks on the poetic nature of biblical prophecy, he would have disagreed that prophecy nevertheless is nothing but an exertion of inspired passions, a manifestation of "divine madness," specifically caused by an unnatural commingling of metaphysical and physical states of consciousness. For Blake—and as I will argue later, for H. D. and Ginsberg— the ideal audience does keep the conceptual implications of apocalypse in the offing during the act of reading; yet for the modern poet-prophet, prophecy is a mode of consciousness shared by prophet and audience, not disseminated from God to fallen prophet to a wholly resistant audience.

Blake's eclectic use of tradition brought about aesthetic choices that placed him on the boundary between, as Foucault would term them, the classical and modern epistemes.[12] Blake's role as a hinge between the two epistemes will be discussed further at the end of this chapter; for now, though, his revision of Lowth's emphasis on prophetic "passions" can help outline the epistemic choices at Blake's disposal. Lowth observes that biblical prophecy makes use of composite poetic genres and narrative incoherence more than any other mode of biblical poetry, and he extols prophets for such borrowing: for him it is proof of the sacred foundation of biblical language (though for many moderns composite forms become an example of the groundlessness of the word). Lowth's reduction of prophetic impulse to Platonic divine madness implies a need to shore up eclectic models of representation as soon as they are named as such. He borrows from Augustan aesthetics when faced with generic inconsistencies or structural fragmentation. Poet-prophets, according to Lowth, maintain a contentious relationship with poetic form because they are "[n]aturally free, and of too ardent a spirit to be confined by rule"; the forms of poetic prophecy, then, are "usually guided by the nature of the subject only, and the impulse of divine inspiration" (170).[13] For Lowth, the inspired language of the Bible can be understood in terms of an authoritative linguistic structure that makes the material forms of the world wholly representable; in Foucauldian terms, Lowth's project extends classical mathesis—"a universal science of measurement and order"—to the manic articulations of biblical prophecy.

For Blake, the material forms of the world suggest divine representability, inasmuch as those forms point away from material structure and toward the imaginative structure of Poetic Genius. In *Milton*, prophetic language "identifies" and thenceforth rejects the "Eternal Death" of the Bacon-Newton-Locke "Woof"—the web of linguistic and conceptual limitations spun by ideologies of the natural—in favor of the Blakean fourfold lineament of the human form divine. Yet Blake does not sever his link with classical mathesis. The attempt to craft a language for revelation is not necessarily the divinely mad opposite of mathesis. Foucault states in *The Order of Things* that "the fundamental element of the Classical *episteme* is neither the success or failure of mechanism, nor the right to mathematize, or the impossibility of mathematizing nature" (57). Instead, he argues, such a science of order represents a continuity, "a link with the mathesis which, until the end of the eighteenth century, remains constant and unaltered" (57). Blake's order of things is an order of the imagination; not a rejection of mechanism, but a revision of it. Blake's conception of a divine language in *Milton* revises Newton's coinage of a mechanistic, totalizing "Lord God Pantokrator"—for Newton, "[i]n him are all things contained and moved"— so that "Newtons Pantocrator," as Blake vilifies him, is subject to a language of Blakean "minute particulars," visionary moments measured against the standards of imagination, not against those of a mathematized natural world.[14]

Lowth's argument that the Bible, and especially biblical prophecy, is *poetry* would have been most influential in Blake's revision of biblical poetry and biblical exegesis; and Lowth would have been important for Blake's recasting of imagination as an instrument of redemption and revelation crucially present in human desire. Even here, at the level of biblical aesthetics, Blake used his concurrence with Lowth as a component in the countertraditional aims of his prophecy. Lowth's efforts to aestheticize the Bible aimed at proving the Bible's religious superiority to countertraditions otherwise deemed paganistic or heretical. As Tannenbaum observes, such a move is consistent with the rhetorical strategies of eighteenth-century biblical commentators who used emerging disciplines—the growth of the human sciences—to espouse the superiority of the Bible while demonizing countertraditional belief systems: the Bible, "when compared with the literature and beliefs of the pagans, was vindicated on the basis of aesthetics, philology, psychology, and history, rather than primarily on the grounds of natural law or natural analogy."[15] For the orthodox, such a rhetorical strategy confirmed the sanctity of the Bible, whereas for the deists this turn to the "sciences of man" emptied the Bible of the sacred.

Blake chose a different approach, and his method is the basis of prophetic language in *Milton*. His adaptation of eighteenth-century sciences sanctified what he perceived as the Poetic Genius of the Bible: this "sublime of the Bible" exposed the ideological effects of biblical and deistic approaches to nature and language, thereby promoting Blake's own conception of humanity speaking, as in *Milton*, with the voice of "Litteral Expression," thereby bringing about through such apocalyptic representation "the Great Harvest & Vintage of the Nations" (43:1). To generate this revision of biblical poetry and exegesis, Blake revised Milton. Milton's significant turn away from medieval and Renaissance prophetic models is revised by Blake at the level of the relationship between language and nature, and

is enacted in Blake's *Milton* in his revision there of *Paradise Lost* and in his
continuation and revision of *Paradise Regained.*

Eighteenth-century biblical commentary poised itself between Augustan
models of order and a prevailing belief that the works of poet-prophets
defied linear narrative and traditional poetic form. The Bard's song in
Milton—a figure for Blake's epic itself, and thus a figure for that which
moves Milton to revise himself in *Milton*, and for Blake's impulse to revise
eighteenth-century prophetic tradition—lies between two similar poles. For
Blake, the Bard's song both draws on linear conceptions of universal order
and adheres to a construction of imagination that cannot be fully systematized by fallen perception. Stating the case for an unfettered imagination,
Blake's Bard decries Los's move "from Particulars to Generals," a moment
that subdues inspiration and gives birth to Satan, the "Miller of Eternity,"
whom Los characterizes as "Newtons Pantocrator weaving the Woof of
Locke" (3:37, 42; 4:11). At the same time, the Bard's song is circumscribed
by a repeated command—"Mark well my words, they are of your eternal
Salvation"—that would commit the song to the orders of memory and repetition that serve the technical concerns of oral prophecy and the historical
aesthetics of Augustan ideals of order and hierarchy. Los's movement "from
Particulars to Generals," a Satanic move for a poet committed to the divinity of "minute particulars," creates a world imagined as a pantograph, a
device for making copies: "Newtons Pantocrator," then, displaces with
mechanical reproduction the idea that "Every Mans Wisdom is peculiar to
his own Individuality" (4:8).

If the Bard, as the combined form of Los-Palamabron-Blake-Milton, is
eventually to redeem the natural world, then (according to the Blakean
model) he must speak outside of the naturalized parameters of language.
Although inspired by Christ's distrust of the natural in *Paradise Regained*,
he constructs a language that resembles Satan's mode of prophecy in *Paradise Regained*, where the multivocal is privileged over the univocal. Such a
language must be formed in Beulah, and must in turn give visionary form
to the natural world. Once Milton descends to the fallen world to enter
Los-Blake's tarsus—connecting Blake's physical movement with the spiritual motion of his pilgrimage—he initiates the reconstruction of nature,
beginning first in the dimension of time-measurement:

> But others of the Sons of Los build Moments & Minutes & Hours
> And Days & Months & Years & Ages & Periods; wondrous buildings
> And every Moment has a Couch of gold for soft repose,
> (A Moment equals the pulsation of the artery)
> And between every two Moments stands a Daughter of Beulah
> To feed the Sleepers on their Couches with maternal care.
>
> (28:44–49)

F. B. Curtis notes that Blake was aware of the controversy surrounding Newton's use of the word *moment* to calculate the precise velocity of moving bodies. For Blake, the *moment* is an "imaginative instant" that does "not denote any time-unit, but rather the moment of poetic inspiration and creation."[16] The distinction is important, insofar as the re-creation of the natural world in *Milton* begins here, in the dimension of what Curtis terms the "time-unit." Moreover, it must be remembered that the combined form of Los-Palamabron-Blake-Milton is itself a moving body—a body on a pilgrimage—and were one able to calculate the exact velocity of this moving body, one would localize the body in the world of sensation and memory rather than in the redemptive space of imagination. Blake's sandal, which figuratively binds Blake's moving body to his pilgrimage as it physically binds itself to his foot, represents the movement in the poem from the vegetable world of clock-time to the spiritual realm of the "imaginative instant." The sandal represents the boundary state between materiality and spirituality, and signifies a privileging of becoming over being, inspiration over memory; the sandal commences the movement from nature to vision in the poet's "walk forward thro' Eternity" (21:14).

Curtis affirms the difference between Newton and Blake on the issue of this "mobile" moment, noting that "Newton had equivocated on the mathematical 'reality' of these 'moments,' whereas Blake desired to show their imaginative or spiritual 'reality.'"[17] In *Milton*, then, the task of the poet-prophet begins in earnest once the sandaled Los- Palamabron-Blake-Milton reconstructs natural representation outside of the constraint of clock-time:

> Every Time less than a pulsation of the artery
> Is equal in its period & value to Six Thousand Years.
> For in this Period the Poets Work is Done: and all the Great
> Events of Time start forth & are conceivd in such a Period
> Within a Moment: a Pulsation of the artery.
>
> (28:62–29:3)

The *eternal* moment can be estimated by the "Six Thousand Years" of the Judeo-Christian theodicy set forth by Bishop Ussher's chronology; but in its greatest potential, this "imaginative instant" is measured by the individual, apocalyptic moment of artistic inspiration, recapitulated in the human pulse.

Just as the reconstruction of the naturally authorized world in *Paradise Regained* begins once Christ "unobserved / Home to his mother's house private returned" (4.638-39), so too in *Milton* the prophetic act of an individual in a private moment (Blake engraving in his garden) sets in motion the events that lead to global redemption. The inspirational potential of the moment ultimately is realized in Blake's visionary reconstruction of nature, where the prophetic Milton creates a natural world that is "a Vision of the Science of the Elohim" (29:65). Once the figure of Milton "annihilates" his belief in a univocal language of memory and embraces the oscillating semantic potential of the inspirational word, he creates the necessary pathway in *Milton* for the re-envisioning of the natural world in terms of apocalyptic representation.

3. SPOKEN FROM THE "SPECULAR MOUNT": ABSOLUTE TEMPTATION IN "PARADISE REGAINED"

Given what he represents of eighteenth-century biblical tradition, Milton is the key third term for Blake between memory and inspiration, between mathematized language and prophetic language, and between clock-time and the imaginative instant. *Paradise Regained* operates both as a continuity and a revision of *Paradise Lost*. As most commentators on the poem have noted, it is significant that Milton chooses the decidedly undramatic representation of Christ's temptation in the wilderness to tell the story of Christ's transcendence.[18] Milton conceptualizes the infinitude of Christ not through the drama of crucifixion and resurrection, but instead by emphasizing Christ's redemptive re-envisioning of ideologies of the natural. In describing the baptism of Christ to his council of demons in Book 1 of *Paradise Regained*, Satan delineates the naturalized boundaries of his kingdom. Christ, he tells the demons, represents a threat to "our freedom and our being / In this fair empire won of Earth and Air" (1.62–63). The Satan of Paradise Regained rules the "empire" of the natural world; he is, as Blake writes in his annotations to Bacon's *Essays*, "the Mind of the Natural Frame" (625). Indeed, in *Milton*, when Milton in the course of his redemption recognizes that "Eternal Death" is actually salvational "Self annihilation," Blake's Satan reveals himself as the God of natural representation: "I [Satan] alone am God & I alone in Heavn & Earth / Of all that live dare utter this" (38:56–57). Seen through Satan's fallen frame of reference, God is represented by the monovocal utterance, against which all other forms of religious and linguistic meaning are rendered unnatural. Blake's Urizenic God is a singular figure "alone in Heavn & Earth."

At the opening of *Paradise Regained* Milton appeals, as Blake's Bard does in the opening lines of *Milton*, to a linguistic force beyond the natural world. Milton asks his Spirit to "bear" him "through heighth or depth of Nature's bounds, / . . . to tell of deeds / Above heroic, though in secret done" (1.13–15). The paradise that at one time seemed lost might now indeed be found, but only, as Blake takes up the point in *Milton*, once ideologies of the natural are revealed as they "truly" are: constraining. The linguistic force of multivocality—seen in the contrast between Satan's sin-

gular God and the Tetragrammaton, YHWH, the original for Blake's fourfold being—is central to this process of prophetic reconstruction of natural
representation.

Satan's command of nature, on the contrary, depends on a belief that the
world is only the sum total of its material parts, and that this "cavern'd"
state, closed to desire by the five senses, is natural.[19] Having asked the muse
to carry him "through heighth or depth of Nature's bounds," Milton proceeds to contrast the *natural* and the *visionary*—for Blake the *Satanic* and
the *inspired*—in the first temptation of *Paradise Regained*, where Satan
demands that Christ perform a miracle on the natural world:

> "But if thou be the Son of God, command
> That out of these hard stones be made thee bread;
> So shalt thou save thyself and us relieve
> With food, whereof we wretched seldom taste."
>
> (342–45)

Satan's words can be seen as an intertextual anticipation and enacting of
two major themes in Blake's use of nature in his own poetry. First, Satan
emphasizes the sensory experience of tasting a food wrought by the Son of
God and owing to his dominion over nature. Blake, whose allegiances
leaned, at the least, toward the Gnostic account of creation rather than the
authorized King James Version, would have disagreed with Satan's implication that Christ holds such dominion over the natural world. Blake writes
of the Christological principle of Poetic Genius in *There is No Natural
Religion* [b]: "He who sees the Infinite [signifying both non-finite and in-
ward-seeming] in all things sees God. He who sees the Ratio only sees
himself only" (3). Indeed, countering Satan's request for Christ to turn the
stones to manna is Blake's closing to *There is No Natural Religion* [b],
where, having proclaimed that the "Infinite" is to be chosen over the "Ratio," he concludes that the fixed boundary between the individual and God
is self- imposed by humanity. Blake conceives the incarnation as a mutable
boundary condition subject to redemptive revision at the level of the individual: "Therefore God becomes as we are, that we may be as he is." Blake
would concur with Milton's portrayal of the failure of Satanic perception
in *Paradise Regained*: infinity cannot be perceived, nor represented, by a
mind unwilling to venture beyond the natural world.

The second implication for Blake of Satan's temptation is perhaps the
most obvious. Yet because this temptation speaks to Satan's unwavering
reliance on sensory perception in the natural world, it offers a further look
at how Milton's conception of prophecy and language likely influenced
Blake's in *Milton*. Satan demands that Christ turn the stone to bread; such
a miraculous transformation of the natural world would prove that he is

indeed the Son of God. For Blake, the temptation would demonstrate that
Satan's acts are based on sensory memory rather than artistic encounter,
which results in an alienation of the imaginative mind from its need to
"make it new." Simply to transform natural objects into other natural objects (Satan's understanding of incarnation) seems more the role of science
than art, particularly given that the science of Blake's day accepted as its
precondition the existence of a stable, remembered reality: a reality which
naturalizes clock-time at the expense of the "imaginative instant," and in so
doing names empirical knowledge as necessary knowledge. It should come
as no surprise that the figure of Satan and the figure of the Enlightenment
natural scientist conjoin in Blake's work in contexts where both Satan and
science presuppose a privileging of memory over inspiration. As Blake says in
his annotations to Boyd's *Historical Notes*, "Nature teaches nothing of Spiritual Life but only of Natural Life" (*Complete Poetry and Prose*, 634).

As I have indicated, Blake's desire for a comprehensive system of prophetic representation demonstrates a continuity with classical thought; a
gap in this continuity emerges, however, from Blake's revision of empirical measurement and observation. Blake seeks to recast what he sees as the
coerciveness of *observation* with the multivalent potential of *vision*. Blake
is inspired by the authority of the Milton tradition; yet Blake revises this
same tradition to reflect an era when Milton's cohesive Christians are disciplinary figures of efficiency and productivity. As discussed in chapter 1,
the Bible is, for Blake, the "<Peculiar> Word of God, exclusive of conscience or the Word of God Universal"; the Bible is meaningful within the
continuity of mathesis only, paradoxically, at the discontinuous level of the
imaginative instant, the moment of the individual pulse.[20]

Christ in *Paradise Regained* proclaims that he has been sent by God to
live "In pious hearts, an inward oracle / To all truth requisite for men to
know"—that he is the figure *spoken again* by God, spoken *in* humankind
(1.462–64). For Milton, the incarnation is a force of the Logos. For Blake,
to make an inward journey, and to transcend the boundaries of the natural
world, potentially draws forth Poetic Genius—the immanent divinity Blake
conceived to be inside us all and subject to our own desire: "The desire of
Man being Infinite the possession is Infinite & himself Infinite" (*There is
No Natural Religion* [b] 3). "Infinitude" emerges from prophetic perception and representation; thus Blake maintains that any person "who sees
the Infinite in all things sees God" (3).

Blake might understand Christ's self-representation in *Paradise Regained*
(as an "inward oracle") to mean that God speaks again, through Christ, the
physical embodiment of Poetic Genius. But the converse is true as well: if
the embodied infinite is there waiting to be beheld, then the capacity to
perceive the human form reductively, in terms of a mere embodied nature,
also exists. In short, if one understands the irreducible in terms of naturally

stable entities, such as Newton's *corpuscles*—"little bodies"—then there can be no such thing as an infinite, an inward or non-finite, corporeality. Blake's struggle as a prophet in an emerging industrial world is to craft a prophetic language that describes the natural world, and cannot be reduced to the univocal—e.g., to corpuscles, to one body, to "One God, Father Almighty, Maker of heaven and earth." Blake's revision in *Milton* conceives of prophetic language as a polysemous, moving body, one as multiplicitous as the many contextual meanings of the word used to describe its journey. Just as Los's initial perception of the natural world in *Milton* causes the condition wherein he "became what he beheld" (3:29)—a condition Blake sets out to repair—Milton's rewriting of *Paradise Lost* in *Paradise Regained* dramatizes the fall of Satan, and also changes the colorless Son of *Paradise Lost* into the inward-seeking Christ of *Paradise Regained*.

At the close of Book 1 of *Paradise Regained*, Christ identifies himself to Satan as an "inward oracle" (463), and in so doing distinguishes true from false prophets: Christ speaks from an oracular position beyond nature, whereas Satan attempts to negate any discourse not reducible to categories of natural sensory perception. Christ, in turn, negates Satan's natural language with a gesture of finality: "And thou no more with pomp and sacrifice / Shalt be inquired at Delphos or elsewhere, / At least in vain for they shalt find thee mute" (1.457-59). Fittingly, as possessor of the natural world, Satan disappears into it, "Into thin air diffused" (1.499)—a flight to a naturalized interiority, and an act that, for Blake, epitomizes the contrast between the redemptive potential offered by Christ and the "same dull round" of nature (*There is No Natural Religion* [b], 3) that marks Satan in *Paradise Regained*.

For Blake, though, the fallen condition of the world is not perpetuated solely by the "thin air" of the natural frame. Nature alone does not sustain false prophets. In *The Marriage of Heaven and Hell*, Blake implicates the role of natural law, underwritten by natural religion, in the reduction of potentially prophetic perception: "One Law for the Lion & Ox is Oppression" (plate 24). Responding to Belial's suggestion that he tempt Christ with beautiful women, Satan declares that the second temptation in the wilderness must consist of "manlier objects" of heroic, Homeric value, with material consisting of:

> "more show
> Of worth, of honor, glory, and popular praise,
> Rocks whereon greatest men have oftest wrecked;
> Of that which only seems to satisfy
> Lawful desires of nature."
>
> (2.225-30)

As I have discussed, the first temptation conflated what Blake would term the natural and the infinite. The second temptation contributes a third, and for Blake, equally distressing term: the lawful. The second temptation presumes that once having descended into himself, Christ might there find Satan (in the guise of Moses the Lawgiver, he who names the forbidden and unforbidden), instead of encountering and embracing Poetic Genius. Blake likely would read the potential effects of Satan's second temptation in much the same way that he portrays the conventionally Puritan Milton at the opening of *Milton*: his desire would be muted, his pilgrimage turned to wandering, his body and mind tormented.

Insofar as the natural world plays a crucial role here, it is fitting that preceding the second temptation, Christ begins to feel the bodily hunger brought on by his fast. Having spent forty days without food, and without the need for food, Christ capitulates momentarily to his natural senses: "But now I feel I hunger, which declares / Nature hath need of what she asks" (252–53). Like Blake's Ezekiel in *The Marriage of Heaven and Hell*, however, Christ's allegiance in *Paradise Regained* ultimately is to "the desire of raising other men into a perception of the infinite," and not merely to fulfill "present ease or gratification" (*The Marriage of Heaven and Hell*, plate 13). Blake would have concurred with Milton's conception in *Paradise Regained* of Christ as a prophetic figure, one who resists the temptation of naturalized values—those values that signify the crucial, evaluative difference between true and false prophecy in *Paradise Regained*—in favor of the values of an interiority at once immanent and transcendent. Blake's revision of Milton conceives prophetic interiority as an infinite principle that finds its materialist counterpart in the Poetic Genius of every human being.

Satan counters prophetic representation with appeals to visions of the natural world to convince Christ to heed his offers. Before tempting Christ to satiate his hunger with a bountiful table of food and drink, Satan reminds him that he has a naturalized privilege to partake of "all created things." As he spreads out the food and drink for Christ, Satan proclaims that nature has become "ashamed" and "[t]roubled" that Christ does not take advantage of what he terms Christ's natural dominion over the otherwise fallen world (332–33). He continues:

> "What doubts the Son of God to sit and eat?
> These are not fruits forbidden, no interdict
> Defends the touching of these viands pure
>
> . . . .
> All these are spirits of air, and woods, and springs,
> Thy gentle ministers, who come to pay
> Thee homage, and acknowledge thee their Lord."
> (368–70; 374–76)

For Blake, no "interdict" indeed would prevent Christ from "these viands," these "ministers" of the natural, fallen world; the Bible of the Urizenic world authorizes Christ to feed his naturalized hunger, by virtue of the "gentle ministers" of natural religion and natural law.

Blake's portrayal of natural religion—State Religion—as a constraining force authorized by natural law in the Urizenic world finds its way into Blake's own reading of *Paradise Regained*, as shown especially in his illustrations to the poem. Blake's illustrations to *Paradise Regained* confirm what he saw as the significant role natural religion plays there in legitimizing, and authorizing, natural law. In "William Blake: Illustrator-Interpreter of *Paradise Regained*," Joseph Anthony Wittreich, Jr., explains that Blake's illustrations were ideologically consistent with the eighteenth-century notion that textual illustration was a mimetic form of criticism.[21] According to Wittreich, an illustration served as "a mode of explanation and enlightenment" for its text (94). An examination of Blake's illustration to the second temptation demonstrates that Blake's illustrations are consistent with eighteenth-century mimesis. However, Blake's illustration also is an attempt to coauthor and thereby re-envision the poem, to redeem Milton in the same way he revises him in *Milton* itself.

The illustration to the second temptation, titled "Christ Refusing Satan's Banquet," shows Christ turning from enfolded, nymph-like creatures (likely a visual condensation of Belial's suggested temptation), with the figure of Satan above the scene spreading forth his banquet, a crown held in his left hand. Geoffrey Keynes remarks that this crown does not appear in *Paradise Regained*, and in fact "has been added by Blake's imagination."[22] Added, indeed, by the imagination; of course, imagination in Blake is the crucial stage for the prophetic character in humanity, and prophecy is essential to his own revision in *Milton*: "Would to God that all the Lords people were prophets." The Law stabilizes fluctuating matter, naming fixed boundaries between the lawful and unlawful. Blake's Milton "annihilates" these boundaries in favor of mediated boundaries—relationships among imaginative minds—and Christ does the same in Blake's illustration of the second temptation in *Paradise Regained*, turning away from, as Blake terms it in *There is No Natural Religion*, the "same dull round" of an imagination circumscribed by the absolute authority of material kings and armies.

This scene, as Blake envisions it in his illustration, demonstrates the prophetic figure of Christ shunning both the natural world of sense experience and the authorization of this sensory sphere by natural law, metonymized by the crown. Christ declares that he turns down the sensory delight of the lawful feast in favor of a "truth" that in fact "Is yet more kingly" (476). Or, to allow Blake's coauthoring of the text, Christ turns down the feast because it privileges materiality over Poetic Genius *and* because the feast is circumscribed by the kingly crown in Satan's left hand.

Christ says as much in the Book of Matthew, the inspiration for *Paradise Regained*, where his response to Satan's temptation becomes his own re-envisioning of Deuteronomy: "Man shall not live by bread alone, but by every word that proceedeth out of the mouth of God" (Matthew 4:4).

Even though the prophecies of both Milton and Blake are underwritten by the authority of the Bible, Blake rewrites this authority in *Milton*, recasting in a language of relational values and mediated presence Milton's "law" that "Governs the inner man" (*Paradise Regained*, 2.477). Whereas Milton seeks to justify a solid community of Christians in his prophecy, Blake asserts the authority of individual Poetic Genius. Milton's conception of a Christian community shapes internal pilgrimages that end in obedience to biblical authority. As Christopher Hill has observed, for Milton Blakean desire would be an unfettered condition "tending to anarchy, unless . . . tempered by a recognition of God's purposes."[23] Blake's tormented portrayal of Milton at the beginning of the poem is an attempt to dramatize Milton's belief that, as Hill writes, "[d]iscipline must be internalized."[24] Blake rewrites Milton's disciplined Christ, turning the antidrama of *Paradise Regained* into the theater of *Milton*, and fusing Christ's turn away from nature with Satan's embrace of conversationalism.

Indeed, it is Milton's Christ in *Paradise Regained* who would cease the mobility of language that Satan proposes. As much as He rejects Satan's naturalized language in *Paradise Regained*, Blake's Christ also shares Satan's impulse for "answers" that lack disciplined finality, as Milton's Christ perceives them (1.434). Blake's Christ combines the inward-seeking Christ and the conversational Satan of *Paradise Regained*: the crucial effect of redemptive language in Blake's *Milton* is its production of, as Milton's Christ says of Satan's words in *Paradise Regained*, "dark, / Ambiguous" effects and its dependence upon a polyvocal "double sense deluding" (1.434–35).

For Blake's conception of the public role of the prophet, the most significant of the temptations Christ resists would be the final one, in Book 4, where he is offered not only the power of natural law—the kingdoms and armies proffered in Book 3—but also the power of natural knowledge. The particularly Hellenic composition of natural knowledge in *Paradise Regained* finds an echo in Blake's *Milton*. As the messianic Milton of Blake's epic undertakes his battle with Urizen to redeem the human form, Urizen attempts to draw Milton away from repairing the Four Zoas by virtue of making precisely the same offer that Satan makes to Christ in Book 4 of *Paradise Regained*. Urizen urges Milton not to persist in his quest to save what he perceives as the eternal, but instead to "Come bring with thee Jerusalem with songs on the Grecian Lyre! / In Natural Religion! in experiments on Men" (19:46–47).

Satan urges Christ toward much the same in *Paradise Regained*, tempt-

ing Christ with an "empire" of "wisdom" (4.222) that would render the
world wholly knowable:

> "All knowledge is not couched in Moses' Law,
> The Pentateuch or what the Prophets wrote;
> The Gentiles also know, and write, and teach
> To admiration, led by Nature's light."
>
> (4.225–28)

Such knowledge, Satan adds, would "render" Christ a "king complete"
(283). For the purposes of this temptation, Satan's language is multivocal,
combining the knowledge of Moses and the Gentiles. Christ renders Satan's
terms dichotomous, in effect separating into oppositional terms those concepts that together would be crucial to the redemptive pilgrimage in Blake's
Milton: Christ in *Paradise Regained* conveys redemption as a choice between "The Stolen and Perverted Writings of Homer & Ovid: of Plato &
Cicero" or "the Sublime of the Bible" (*Milton*, plate 1). In *Paradise Regained*, Satan famously conceptualizes the "natural" choice in terms of a
Hellenic ideal:

> "Look once more, ere we leave this specular mount,
> Westward, much nearer by southwest; behold
> Where on the Aegean shore a city stands
> Built nobly, pure the air, and light the soil,
> Athens, the eye of Greece, mother of arts
> And eloquence, native to famous wits
> Or hospitable, in her sweet recess,
> City or suburban, studious walks and shades;
> See there the olive grove of Academe,
> Plato's retirement, where the attic bird
> Trills her thick-warbled notes the summer long . . . ."
>
> (4.236–46)

Satan inverts Christ's inner pilgrimage into an outward voyaging and
westering vista of Hellenic culture—an attempt to naturalize the world of
outward appearance. The "rules" of naturalized power and knowledge, Satan
argues, will complete for Christ a kingship "Within thyself, much more
with empire joined" (283–84). However, like the figure of Milton in Blake's
Milton, Christ in *Paradise Regained* not only must turn aside natural objects, he also must construct a proper prophetic frame of reference to bring
about redemption.

The "specular mount" of *Paradise Regained* resembles, in effect, the
"Moment in each day that Satan cannot find" in *Milton*. Though it seems a
natural space (a mount), its inspirational potential can only be seen

(specularized) by a mind "governed" by Poetic Genius. Christ's reliance on inward-seeking divinity is constructed according to Hebraic models of knowledge, not in terms of "the olive grove of Academe," the site of Plato's academy. The problem, foremost, is in language, according to Christ. Those who communicate with the authorization of Hellenic models, Christ argues, speak

> "Much of the soul . . . but all awry,
> And in themselves seek virtue, and to themselves
> All glory arrogate, to God give none. . . ."
>
> (313–15)

Christ answers Satan's speech by negating Satan's model of discourse analysis and production, one that resembles the notion of "infernal" reading Blake propounds in plate 24 of *The Marriage of Heaven and Hell*, a model where polysemic language might produce an inspirational relationship between audience and text that decenters the "natural" authority of the speaker. Christ's rejection of Socratic models of naturalized, dialectical knowledge in Milton's poem, then, seems to anticipate a negation of Blake's vision of a prophetic discourse model:

> . . . "[M]any books,
> Wise men have said, are wearisome; who reads
> Incessantly, and to his reading brings not
> A spirit and judgment equal or superior,
> (And what he brings, what need he elsewhere seek?)
> Uncertain and unsettled still remains,
> Deep versed in books and shallow in himself,
> Crude or intoxicate, collecting toys
> And trifles for choice matters, worth a sponge,
> As children gathering pebbles on the shore."
>
> (321–30)

Only with "spirit and judgment equal or superior" to the writer does an audience inspirationally rather than mnemonically enter discourse. For Milton's Christ, this judgment is the incarnation of the Logos. For Satan, it is rhetoric. Satan says to Christ:

> And with the Gentiles much thou must converse,
> Ruling them by persuasion as thou meanest;
> Without their learning, how wilt thou with them,
> Or they with thee hold conversation meet?
>
> (4.229–32)

Satan conceives of language as conversational, in the sense that Blake intends in such contexts as the discourse of Isaiah and Ezekiel in *The Marriage of Heaven and Hell*, or the end of Book 4 of *Jerusalem*. Prophetic consciousness is constructed by Milton in terms of what Christ terms "our native language" (333), that is, a language whose originary precedence infuses it with greater authority, for Milton, than Socratic models of discourse production and analysis. Here, Milton is extending a conception of language and nature whereby Hebrew maintains what Foucault terms the "lost similitude" between the name and that which is designated by the name: "Hebrew . . . contains, as if in the form of fragments, the marks of that original name-giving."[25] Blake's revision of nature and language demands that the inspired mind not "gathe[r] pebbles on the shore"—not simply re-collect these "fragments"—but instead negotiate this littoral boundary as a means of shaping a multivalent language sufficient to the task of representing prophetic vision.

4. BEULAH: STAGING INSPIRED INDUSTRY

Given the Satan-Christ dialogue in *Paradise Regained*, redemption for Blake occurs in a "moment" that is found only by those who embrace multiplicitous meaning, an understanding that renders fluid the conventional Judeo-Christian separation between the absolute authority of a transcendent God and a fallen populace. The mobility of the Blakean moment, anticipated and enacted on Milton's "specular mount," reconstructs the Christ of *Paradise Regained* as a figure that resembles the Satanic Spectre of Negation in *Milton*. When one negates, one maintains a condition of stasis that does not allow for "equal or superior" frames of reference, a condition that silences the multivocal opposition Satan propounds while on the "specular mount." Negation inverts the system in *Milton* whereby *states* are preferable to *individuals*, and it authorizes instead a system in which contraries do not result in progression. To live in stasis, for Blake, is to live Satanically. The linguistic choice of mobility over stasis creates in Blake's rhetoric of prophecy a frame of reference that guides the relationships between prophet and God, prophet and prophet, and prophet and audience in the following three ways: through a language that reconceives transcendence as an immanent principle of imagination; through a reconception of biblical prophetic authority that calls for the authorization of prophetic speech by God and the tradition of past prophets so that the authority of biblical tradition may be revised in favor of the individual prophet's imagination; and through a language that is (Satanically) conversational rather than monologic.

Prophetic language in *Milton* is characterized by multiple meanings; and the most important staging area on the path toward redemption in the poem is the twofold domain of Beulah, the setting where "Contrarieties are equally True" (30:1). Blake's revision of mathematized language begins in Beulah, where the univocal sign—the structure and blueprint of fallen human experience—is emptied of its naturalized value. Once Milton's emanation, Ololon, unites with the poet-pilgrim in Beulah, the potential exists for a redeemed Natural world where "the Rose . . . bursts her crimson curtaind bed / And comes forth in the majesty of beauty" (31:56-58).[26] Moreover, a re-envisioned nature redeems Milton's frame of reference as prophetic, just as the redemption of contraries in Beulah re-envisions global perception in the poem. Beulah, then, represents a means to conceive of prophetic language for both prophets and their audiences. No longer does Milton's pilgrimage seem to lead only toward Eternal Death; now he sees that Eternal Death represents the end of a belief in immutable selfhood and the beginning of an identity mediated by apocalyptic representation. Milton's transformed perception of Eternal Death—as a beginning rather than end—becomes his call to action, first inspired by the voice of the Bard's song.

By localizing the notion that contraries are not oppositional, that reality is grounded in a relationship between terms that from a fallen perspective *seem* to be oppositional, Beulah offers a physical space in nature where the prophetic transformation of Milton's frame of reference can be staged. Just as in *The Marriage of Heaven and Hell*, where Aristotle's *Analytics* helps to underwrite the either/or epistemology of Satan's mills, Blake's Milton, too, faces a world divided by natural knowledge and religion. In this world frozen by oppositional relationships that negate rather than unite, "Differences between Ideas" divide the world in such a way that "Ideas themselves" are "slain in offerings for sin" by the "dreadful Loom of Death" (35:5-7). This threat to inspiration is not the "Eternal death" that Milton perceives as he comes to Beulah. The "Loom of Death" suggests the sacrifice of inspiration—an offering authorized by the natural world—in which for Blake "One Law for the Lion & Ox" ought to be recognized as "Oppression."

Of course, Blake's project is complicated by the fact that he must construct a prophetic language while remaining wholly within presumably fallen language, specifically within poetry. Blake's awareness of this paradox represents the major conflict of his prophecies, and is the premise behind the creation of Beulah as a staging ground for confronting the paradox. Blake sees English as "the rough basement," where language is a "stubborn structure" of "dumb [speechless] despair" (*Jerusalem*, 36:58-60). Blake's project, of course, depends on his unwillingness to accept the silencing of the imagination as a result of mathetic representation: "I must create a system or be enslav'd by another Mans / I will not Reason & Compare: my business is to Create" (*Jerusalem*, 10:20-21). The rhetoric of prophecy Blake creates depends on Blake's building from this "rough basement" a polyvocal rather

than "stubborn" structure, one that uses past models of inspired language—
rather than just English—to conceive of forms of representation suited for
his apocalyptic conception of prophetic consciousness.

Blake seeks a primal language for prophecy that paradoxically depends
on both the globalizing authority of originary precedence and the localized
particularity of context. In *Paradise Regained*, Milton reaches back to Hebraic discourse to reconceive a language for redemption, yet his conversational Satan appeals to Blake's urge toward a divine language of
multivocality. Blake's language for prophetic inspiration draws on these
models from *Paradise Regained*, but also on a fusion of psyche and language that anticipates Freud's theories of unconscious representation and
primal language.

In *The Interpretation of Dreams*, Freud writes that the commingling of
otherwise opposing ideas finds its "similar attitude" in the process of "poetic creation."[27] As in *Milton*, where "Reason is a State / Created to be
annihilated" (32:34–35), the unconscious process of dream-life described
by Freud is such that contradictions are "simply disregarded," that "'No'
seems not to exist as far as dreams are concerned."[28] Inasmuch as dreams
themselves are a map of unconscious processes for Freud, his remarks on
the mind's privileging of contradiction echo Blake's own redemptive pilgrimage in *Milton*. That is, the inability to precisely measure the "natural"
truth of a statement, an effect that Freud suggests occurs in the unconscious, actually resembles the power Blake draws on in order to transform
the Newtonian moment in *Milton* from reificatory to transferential—and,
for Freud, countertransferential—representation:

> There is a Moment in each Day that Satan cannot find
> Nor can his Watch Fiends find it, but the Industrious find
> This Moment & it multiply, & when it once is found
> It renovates every Moment of the Day if rightly placed[.]
> In this Moment Ololon descended to Los & Enitharmon
> Unseen beyond the Mundane Shell Southward in Miltons track.
>   (35:42–47)

As Curtis observes, Satan's "Watch-Fiends" correspond to the Newtonian
vision of clock-time that Blake reconstructs in Beulah.[29] The Blakean moment is "found" when the speaker is reunited with the prelinguistic voice,
here signified by Ololon, whose name derives from the Greek root that
gives us *ululate*. Blake's imaginative instant, the standard by which one
distinguishes prophetic language from other modes of representation, moves
classical designation away from formal artifice and toward a conjunction
of context and, in Foucault's terms, "the primitive moment in which it was
pure designation" (104). For Blake, the problem is larger than the familiar

opposition of reason and imagination. *Milton* instead asks which of the two is originary: the efforts of the "Watch Fiends" are thwarted by the "Industrious" labor of poets and prophets, who return inspiration to a "rightly placed" origin where an authentic linguistic voice is represented better by ululation than analytic reason—where, that is, the howl of ululation "multipl[ies]" rather than negates polysemousness. In the Blakean moment, as on Milton's "specular mount" in *Paradise Regained, meaning* is a border condition between matter and spirit, and is mediated by a meeting of imaginative minds—Los and Ololon, or prophet and God, or prophet and audience. Blake attempts to conceive a mathesis where the order of things is located in the imagination rather than in the remembered reality of the natural world.

The Watch-Fiends also correspond to Freud's notion that the psychoanalytic session becomes "redemptive," so to speak, as analyst and analysand together produce a "relaxation of the watch upon the gates of Reason."[30] For Blake and Freud, the inspirational moment is accessible, then, but not by the watchful eye of Aristotelian reasoning. Instead, the mind is best open to inspiration when one enters into an intersubjective relationship in language. Freud's remarks in "Negation" can be extended to a discussion of polysemy, where intersubjective relationships (here, Blakean transferential language suggests Freudian transference and countertransference) are both a means of repressing multiplicitous meaning—to protect ego boundaries— and a means of satisfying the contrarietous productions of the unconscious. In "Negation," Freud writes that polysemic language is repressed by the time ideas reach consciousness, even though in the unconscious the process of negation simply does not occur: "This view of negation fits in very well with the fact that in analysis we never discover a 'no' in the unconscious and that recognition of the unconscious on the part of the ego is expressed in a negative formula."[31] According to Freud, dreams, like the unconscious, "show a particular preference for combining contraries into a unity or for representing them as one and the same thing" (*The Interpretation of Dreams*, 353). He suggests in "Negation" that the process of moving from conscious negation to unconscious polysemy begins in the transferential relationship between analyst and analysand: "Perception is not a purely passive process" (238).

What Blake propounds in Beulah of course could not be fully explained by recourse to its anticipation of the analytic context of Freudian psychoanalysis. I have reached forward from Blake to Freud to understand the nature of prophetic language in Milton; Freud himself reaches back to ancient Egypt for a primal language of both originary precedence and localized contextuality. In "The Antithetical Meaning of Primal Words," Freud revises his earlier assertion, in *The Interpretation of Dreams*, that contraries are unified in the unconscious. From his later reading of philologist

Karl Abel's "The Antithetical Meaning of Primal Words," Freud concludes that the unconscious linguistic process he describes in *The Interpretation of Dreams* "is identical with a peculiarity in the oldest languages known to us."[32] Freud stresses Abel's identification of a foundational, prehieroglyphic Egyptian language where there exists, as Abel puts it, "a fair number of words with two meanings, one of which is exactly opposite of the other."[33] Abel identifies words in this language that are compounds of oppositional words, such as "'old-young,' 'far-near,' 'bind-sever,' 'outside-inside' . . . which in spite of combining the extremes of difference, mean only 'young,' 'near,' 'bind,' and 'inside' respectively."[34]

As a prehieroglyphic language, this tongue most closely resembles the ululating, prelinguistic moment implicated in Blake's Ololon, where meaning is not fixed by "the extremes of difference," and where the "Industrious" construct from these differences an inspirational moment of transferential language that cannot be found by the static-Satanic. Ultimately, neither ululation nor pictorial representation claims unmediated perception of reality. Blake's image of a language for prophecy echoes the method of ancient Egyptian language also described by Abel: both forms of representation recognize that the truth-value of any linguistic or textualized representation of experience is contingent upon the transferential relationship among multiple, distinct meanings. Thus, in Beulah the "Industrious" seek not to differentiate the natural world, but instead to multiply its semantic potential, an expansion of meaning that stages in *Milton* the conception of a performative, prophetic discourse.[35]

Blake's emphasis in Beulah on a prophetic language that resembles hieroglyphic modes is consistent with rhetorical models of prophecy that were readily available to him in his day. Tannenbaum writes that, of the terms used to describe the rhetorical strategies of prophetic language in Blake's era, *hieroglyph* "had widest currency and was often connected to theories about the origin and development of language."[36] Blake's use of prehieroglyphic and hieroglyphic modes of language emerges from available eighteenth-century biblical commentary, which proffered the idea that the prophetic books of the Bible used hieroglyphics—or, at the least, pictorial language—as a middle term to negotiate the dichotomous demands of material and metaphysical modes of representation. The visual components, moreover, of eighteenth-century ideas about prophecy would have appealed to Blake as a painter and engraver. The care with which letters had to be cut into plates—backwards—and the fact that the plates themselves were organized first by the size of the picture, allowing the pictures to be more than mere gloss, attests to Blake's enacting through the mechanics of his trade the "industrious" moment of visual-verbal prophetic discourse.

Eighteenth-century biblical commentary drew commonly on the notion that prophetic discourse combined the visual and verbal in order to bypass

the limitations of material representation. Blake's engraving and his use of
visual tropes—his language of "visionary forms dramatic"—work together
in the service of his conception of a divine language, constituting what
Tannenbaum terms a "literal application" of eighteenth-century conceptions of biblical prophecy.[37] In his multivolume *The Divine Legation of
Moses Demonstrated* (1738–1741), the Bishop of Gloucester, William
Warburton, argued that biblical prophets constructed their language for vision in a mode analogous to that of Egyptian hieroglyphics.[38] Available in
Blake's time in several editions, Warburton's *Divine Legation* was widely
cited and translated by eighteenth-century scholars. Warburton maintained
that just as the Egyptians used hieroglyphics to overcome the inability of
ancient language to communicate abstraction, prophets used visual signification to overcome the inability of nature-based, material language to convey the extra-natural, visionary phenomena of prophecy. Ancient language,
Warburton argued, "was at first extremely rude, narrow, and equivocal," to
the extent that "Men would be perpetually at a loss, on any new Conception, or uncommon adventure, to explain themselves intelligibly to one
another" (2.81–82). Visual signs, then, "arose out of *Necessity*" (2.83).

    In Blake, prophets inherit this problem from antiquity; his task in *Milton*
is to conceive of language that would expand the frame of reference of both
prophet and audience without loss of meaning or descent into madness
(divine or otherwise). Indeed, Warburton argued that for prophets the "mixed
Discourse of Words and Actions" necessarily renders visionary experience
meaningful. The seemingly nonsensical actions of biblical prophets are
recast by Warburton as consequences of a necessity that is anything but
mad: "The true Defence of the *Prophetic Writings*, is . . . that *Information
by Action* was, at this time, and amongst these People, *a very common and
familiar Mode of Conversation*" (2.85–86). Warburton's remarks offer an
important context for Blake's trope of the sacred meal in *The Marriage of
Heaven and Hell*. There, he asks the prophets Isaiah and Ezekiel "how they
dared so roundly to assert that God spake to them"; he asks Isaiah "what
made him go naked and barefoot three years," and asks Ezekiel "why he
eat dung, & lay so long on his right and left side" (plates 12 and 13). Their
replies suggest that "information by action" is dramatized by Blake in his
prophetic books as a "common and familiar mode of conversation," and
that Blake's mode of conversation revises both the Hellenic and Hebraic.
Isaiah answers that his physical "information by action" was caused by
"the same that made our friend Diogenes the Grecian"; Ezekiel answers
that his actions arose from "the desire of raising other men into a perception of the infinite" (plate 13).

    Blake revises Milton's language in a way that resembles Warburton's
description of biblical revisions of ancient language. According to eighteenth-century theories of prophetic representation, biblical prophetic lan-

guage pushed the representational limits of ancient language, and in doing so created a new language out of crucial fragments of the old. Eighteenth-century biblical commentators conceived of ancient language as a mode of representation consisting of a small stock of words burdened, as in Blake's Beulah, by ever-multiplying, "equivocal" meaning (Warburton, 2.83). That this new language might seem absurd—as does, say, Blake's insistence on redemptive contrariety in Beulah—owes more to the perceiver than the perceived, according to Warburton: "the *Absurdity* of an Action, as the very Word shews, consists in its being extravagant and insignificative; but use and custom made these in Question both sober and pertinent" (2.86). Like the polysemous, prehieroglyphic utterance Blake deploys in *Milton*, Warburton's conception of prophetic language combines *seer* and *seen* in such a way as to create a historically essential "significative action" (2.83). According to Warburton, if the hieroglyph is "a picture or image, presented to the imagination through the eyes and ears," then prophetic language is in effect a hieroglyph uttered by the prophet himself. Warburton cites Exodus to designate this fusion of *seer* and *seen,* "the voice of the sign" (Warburton, 2.86).

For Blake, ideas circulating in late-eighteenth-century England about the roots of prophetic language in the hieroglyph contribute to the rhetorical function of prophetic language, staged first in Beulah. Although contrariety is itself a dominant trope throughout Blake's work, the use of contrariety in *Milton* merits special attention. There, contrariety points backward to visual components foundational to Blake's prophetic language, yet is revised significantly to construct a futurist model for the apocalyptic function of Blake's prophecies.

The social and psychological effects of prophetic language are enacted in *Milton* once the combined form of Los-Palamabron-Blake continues its pilgrimage past Beulah and onward into the "Mundane Shell" of the natural world. Here, the primacy of action and performance—Blake's emphasis on motion over stasis—points up theatrical and visual conceptions of prophecy privileged in the eighteenth century and shared by Blake. Tannenbaum's observation that the spectacular nature of poetic prophecy can be traced from Aquinas and Donne through Milton is useful for understanding the source material Blake drew on in his conception of the iconic nature of prophecy and audience reception. The "theater" of Blake's prophecy, as Tannenbaum terms it, is enacted in such a way that prophet and audience collapse into one another: Milton's prophetic "ungirding" produces an audience that "wept prophetic" in Blake's dramatic re-envisioning of the antidramatic *Paradise Regained* (*Milton*, 14:10–11).[39] For Blake, prophecy mediates identity— "annihilates" subject/object distinctions—to the extent that the separation between prophet and audience is untenable: for Blake, and as I will discuss in later chapters, for H. D. and Ginsberg, prophets need prophetic audiences. The test for false prophecy may not be prediction or even audience resistance, two common medieval and Renaissance standards, but instead the ability of the audience to enact, through the process of reading, the coupling of visual and verbal representations that is essential to Blake's construction of a redemptive language.

5. LANGUAGE AND A VISION OF NATURE: A "MOMENT" IN "WILD THYME"

I have argued that the moment of inspiration for Blake partakes wholly of the polysemic nature of language first staged in Beulah; that Blake's construction of prophetic language emerges from scientific and religious debates over language and representation in his own time; and that Blake's conception of a language for prophecy anticipates Freud's own search for a primal language, and reflects seventeenth- and eighteenth-century representations of ancient Egypt as a source for prophetic language. Crucially for Blake, the linguistic power of the non-Urizenic moment of inspiration in *Milton* re-creates nature as a vision:

> In this Moment Ololon descended to Los & Enitharmon
> Unseen beyond the Mundane Shell Southward in Miltons track
>
> Just in this Moment when the morning odours rise abroad
> And first from the Wild Thyme, stands a Fountain in a rock
> Of crystal flowing into two Streams, one flows thro Golgonooza
> And thro Beulah to Eden beneath Los's western Wall
> The other flows thro the Aerial Void & all the Churches
> Meeting again in Golgonooza beyond Satans Seat.
>
> (35:46–53)

Like all other prophetic forces in *Milton*, the "Wild Thyme" (*wild time*) inside this moment appears monstrous or Edenic, depending on the perceiver's frame of reference. The insertion of a singular time-dimension into Milton's pilgrimage, and the localization of a language of contrariety in a space outside of natural clock-time, together constitute a movement from the twofold space of Beulah to Blake's fourfold human form divine.[40] In short, the redemption of contraries becomes "divine" once localized outside of the three-dimensional natural world, in a fourth dimension outside of natural clock-time.

Foucault observes that *progress* was defined within the classical episteme as the ability of language to arrest the chaotic movement of time, to "giv[e] the perpetual disruption of time the continuity of space" (*The Order of*

Things, 113).[41] The classical era, he writes, is distinguished by the belief that language and nature "fitted over each other exactly" (103). If it were true, as the classical episteme set forth, that all sensate reality could be traced back to the material basis of a finite, indivisible form—such as Newton's corpuscles, for instance—then intense labor on the part of science could lead back to a prelapsarian, Adamic language of one-to-one correspondences between words and things. This debate over language and the limits of representation plays an important role in Blake's conception of redemption in *Milton*, which borrows from and revises the classical function of naming. Scientific discourse, Foucault writes, is founded on the authority of naming: "The fundamental task of Classical 'discourse' is *to ascribe a name to things, and in that name to name their being*" (120). The legislative power of onomastics, an effect of naming Blake seeks to expose in his prophecies, is present in Socrates's pronouncements in Plato's *Cratylus* on the nature of naming and representation.[42]

Socrates's remarks contain distinct implications for what Blake undertakes in *Milton*. The *Cratylus* pivots on the question of whether or not naming, connecting the word to the thing, can bring the perceiver to an unmediated perception of reality.[43] Noting that the first name-givers were "the legislators," Socrates concludes that "the art of the legislator" constitutes, indeed, the art of naming (471). The reification of linguistic representation in terms of the natural world finds its equivalent, then, in the construction of *law*, where name-givers become equated with law-givers. The implications for *Milton*, where the prophetic poet is a moving body on a pilgrimage, do not stop here, however. Socrates also characterizes the art of naming in terms of the act of observing bodies in motion. Arguing that "all things are in motion and progress and flux, and . . . this idea of motion is expressed by names," Socrates aims to prove that naming causes motion to cease (470). The act of calculating a fixed representation of the natural world, he says, "indicates, not that things are in motion or progress, but that they are at rest" (471).

What Socrates terms in the *Cratylus* as a desire to find "a standard which shows the truth of things"(472) can be seen in the *Symposium* as a problem of knowledge and desire: a problem of how knowledge is constructed from a dialectical relationship between desire and lack.[44] This problem cuts to the core of Blake's quarrel with Milton. Why would Milton's Christ desire the good when he already has it? Why would Blake's Milton embrace a heaven that he has made "unhappy" through silencing his own desire? In the *Symposium*, Socrates contributes the words of Diotima, the Mantinean wise-woman, to the discourse on love, in order to offer an alternative to natural knowledge. Diotima posits Eros as a figure "halfway between mortal and immortal" and "midway between matter and spirit" (553, 555). Diotima explains the nature of wisdom using the metaphor of procreation, where the lover of knowledge "long[s] not for the beautiful itself, but for the conception and generation that the beautiful effects" (558). Diotima's response would seem to position her theory of desire in a space that conjoins materiality and metaphysicality—partaking, as it does, of both "mortal and immortal"—a site of knowledge-making that would appeal to Blake's revisionary conception of desire and knowledge in *Milton*. Yet, as Luce Irigaray has noted, Diotima's conception of mobility is a mobility upward, toward a familiar "transcendence inaccessible to our condition as mortals."[45] Diotima's discourse would represent, for Blake, one more "standard" of the "truth of things" that requires continuity (a "midway" conception of desire and knowledge, the mortal and immortal) and revision (a transcendence whose inaccessibility must be rectified). Blake's mode of naming and making in *Milton* indeed is mobile, but toward an immanent transcendence, not toward transcendentalism.

Blake's attempt to subvert the Newtonian *moment* of precise measurement of velocity also is a response to the seventeenth-century desire, legitimated by Hellenic models, to extend the mathematization of thought into the search for an Adamic language of one-to-one correspondence. Fish argues that Hebraic language, Blake's textual model for prophetic discourse, "was the most successful candidate" in the seventeenth-century search for the prelapsarian language (*Surprised by Sin*, 113). That Blake would place his own construction of a redemptive language in an Edenic location, Beulah, should come as no surprise, insofar as early attempts to reconstruct Adamic language "were usually tied to the search for the terrestrial Eden" (*Surprised by Sin*, 117). The reconstruction of prelapsarian language involves a re-envisioning of *meaning* itself, a model of language that resembles the mobility of representation in prehieroglyphic Egyptian language that Abel points up in "The Antithetical Meaning of Primal Words." Antithetical words are in perpetual oscillation between opposite poles, and hence resist fixed representation. The "Industrious" indeed "multiply" the multiplicitous Blakean moment, but their labor cannot be characterized in terms of a stable, mathematized reality. Instead, their work is "rightly placed" within a mobility of unfixed representations; their "right" place is paradoxically both primal and contextual.

6. APOCALYPTIC REPRESENTATION AND PROPHETIC IMAGINATION

Blake's re-envisioning of nature as a space "beyond Satans Seat" results from the active, time-bound labor of the poet. For Blake, this labor entails inspired work at his cottage, where "I might write all these Visions / To display Natures cruel holiness: the deceits of Natural Religion" (36:24–25). Prophetic labor—the work of vision—also produces Milton's rewrit-

ing, his use of Christ's inward pilgrimage in *Paradise Regained* to revise
ideologies of nature in *Paradise Lost*. The linguistic labors of both Blake and
Milton, first staged in Beulah, now conjoin in Blake's garden, as the fallen,
"Mundane Shell" becomes transformed into the divine, fourfold world:

> So Milton
> Labourd in Chasms of the Mundane Shell, tho here before
> My Cottage midst the Starry Seven, where the Virgin Ololon
> Stood trembling in the Porch: loud Satan thunderd on the stormy Sea
> Circling Albions Cliffs in which the Four-fold World resides
> Tho seen in fallacy outside: a fallacy of Satans Churches.
>
> (39:56–61)

Through a poetic, polysemous language, in which contraries are the vehicle of prophetic representation, nature is reconceived as a vision into
which the fallen form of Satan/Urizen cannot enter. Satan only externally
circles the re-envisioned land, and his fallen frame of reference likewise
still "see[s] in fallacy." He sees only the outside, only external surface;
inside, his perception extends no further than the natural world.

The apocalypse of the poem is an apocalypse of consciousness, in which
the poet deploys the transferential language of prophecy in order "To cast
off Bacon, Locke, & Newton from Albions covering / To take off his filthy
garments, & clothe him with Imagination / To cast aside from Poetry, all
that is not Inspiration" (41:5–7). Here, as elsewhere in Blake, woven garments signify textual matters (*tessere, textus, text*). In addition, Blake's use
of "covering," "garments," and "clothe" pun on the use of the term "cloth-
binding" for 'bookbinding" in the publishing industry. The puns serve the same
purpose as does plate 15 of *The Marriage of Heaven and Hell*, where Blake's
"Printing house in Hell" offers the "infernal" alternative to libraries of natural
knowledge. Blake, of course, incorporates clothing tropes frequently
throughout *Milton*, with human and divine forms distinguished by what
they wear. Fallen humanity wears the garments of nature, while figures of
inspiration cast aside natural, Urizenic garments for those of the imagination.

Blake's apocalyptic punning culminates when Christ combines with the
Starry Seven to form the Starry Eight in plate 42. William Herschel's surpris-
ing discovery in 1781 of the planet Uranus, the seventh planet—and the first
telescopically discovered in human history—also figures as a possible source
of Blake's use of language and space in *Milton*. Herschel's discovery constituted a significant challenge to the scientific community, not the least because Herschel
was an amateur astronomer at the time. Rather than confine itself to practical application of Newton's work, as had occurred through much of the eighteenth century,
the scientific community now was required to alter the conception of a fixed universe that had dominated through the history of scientific discourse.[46]

Blake makes use of this intellectual sea change, reconfiguring as an apocalyptic shift in human consciousness the conceptual shift occasioned by the discovery of Uranus. When Christ forms the Starry Eight, he becomes, paradoxically, the embodied central principle around which all the other bodies revolve: he is the transcendent son who becomes the system's immanent sun. As the global-personal action of the poem culminates, the garment of this transcendent-immanent body functions as the trope of a redeemed natural world:

> . . . with one accord the Starry Eight became
> One Man Jesus the Saviour. wonderful! round his limbs
> The Clouds of Ololon folded as a Garment dipped in blood
> Written within & without in woven letters & the Writing
> Is the Divine Revelation in the Litteral expression:
> A Garment of War, I heard it namd the Woof of Six Thousand Years.
>   (42:10–15)

The "Litteral expression" of language also might be read as "littoral" expression. As "littoral" expression, Christ's linguistic garment in Milton and the "specular mount" in *Paradise Regained* both occupy a space on the border—on the shoreline—between the "Sea of Time and Space" (the natural world) and the world of inspiration.

"View'd from Miltons Track," from the pathway of inspired language, the Sea of Time and Space constitutes "a vast Polypus / Of living fibres" that grows "monstrous" under the war-banner of Negation (34:24–26). As Hilton observes, the "fibre" in Blake makes up "the root of human physical existence"; and each fiber represents a "*seme*, or unit of meaning" in a polysemous vision of language that, as I have argued, rewrites the natural state of physical existence as visionary.[47] Christ's literal/littoral garment occupies a moment "rightly placed" in oscillating position; thereby, this littoral garment "renovates every Moment of the Day"—and connects the human and divine with the fibers of the redeemed Polypus—with its reconstruction of a *visionary* nature.

As both "the Sea of Time and Space" and a "Polypus" of redemptive Blakean "fibres," the representation of visionary nature in *Milton* is consistent with classical mathesis, a desire for a body of representation that conceives the world as wholly knowable. Onomastics is the process by which mathesis orders the material and human forms of the world into the forms of scientific discourse.

In "Blake, Foucault, and the Classical Episteme," Daniel Stempel argues convincingly that a more accurate portrayal of Blake's historical position than the standard one would see his discourse as classical rather than Romantic.[48] Stempel demonstrates how Blake's discourse fits Foucault's division of the classical episteme into the four vectors of classical general grammar: designation, derivation, articulation, and attribution. Stempel observes that Blake diverges from the classical episteme by revisioning classical attribution into intensional rather than extensional logic. As Stempel notes, Blake blurs the division between *seer* and *seen* by recasting *perception* as *apperception*. Therefore, Stempel writes, Blake must be positioned between classical and modern epistemes: Blake's intensional rewriting of extensional logic marks him as "both the contemporary and the opposite of Alexander Pope" (403).

Stempel significantly extends the scope of Blake's position in literary history. Blake becomes a hinge between Augustan and Romantic thought—as might also be said of his eighteenth-century biblical sources—and more than the figure who bequeaths Romanticism to nineteenth-century British poetry. Stempel concludes that "Blake's rebellion against conventional discourse is not a romantic counterstatement—it is a *re*statement of classical discourse" (403) in terms of a prophetic language that is "not the duplication of the order of the imagination," but instead "the creation of the order of the imagination" (394). The totality Blake posits combines both imaginative and remembered reality; it is not confined to the representational systems of the naturalist, economist, or grammarian. It shares the totalizing impulse of mathesis, yet represents an "order of things" wherein material forms are transformed by the imagination into an organizational scheme beholden to form, matter, and spirit combined: the Blakean fourfold lineament of the human form divine, "The Eternal Great Humanity Divine."

Blake's human form divine is based on an engagement with and revision of natural representation. For Blake, a transferential relationship that mediates rather than negates antithetical poles of meaning produces a vision of nature in *Milton*, where apocalyptic representation transforms the wine-presses of war into a prophetic vision:

> Rintrah & Palamabron view the Human Harvest beneath
> Their Wine-presses & Barns stand open; the Ovens are prepar'd
> The Waggons ready: terrific Lions & Tygers sport & play
> All Animals upon the Earth, are prepard in all their strength
>
> To go forth to the Great Harvest & Vintage of the Nations.
> (42:36–43:1)

The fallen perceptions of the natural world seen earlier in the poem are revisited. Cleansed by apocalypse, they reappear as a vision. "The Last Judgment," as Blake writes in *A Vision of the Last Judgment*, "is an Overwhelming of Bad Art & Science. Mental Things alone are Real what is Calld Corporeal Nobody Knows of its Dwelling Place" (565). Here, Blake

urges the transformation of the Urizenic, natural world into the imaginative, through a transferential vision of language that, in *Milton*, negotiates
the littoral boundary between the Sea of Time and Space and the visionary
world. Modes of thinking that count and catalogue the natural world (as
Foucault describes the functions of the classical episteme) serve the same
purpose for Blake as does throwing sand in the wind in "Mock on Mock on
Voltaire Rousseau":

> Mock on Mock on Voltaire Rousseau
> Mock on Mock on! tis all in vain!
> You throw the sand against the wind
> And the wind throws it blows it back again[.]
> (*Complete Poetry and Prose*, 477)

Nothing imaginative is produced in this wholly material economy governed by mathesis; indeed, the atomistic natural science of Democritus and
Newton is represented at the end of the poem as "sands upon the Red Sea
shore / Where Israels tents do shine so bright" (lines 11–12).

Meaning is the littoral boundary, or Red Sea shore, in *Milton*. The Last
Judgment that closes *Milton* "annihilates" the naturalized antithetical base
on which language and perception rest; moreover, it annihilates a world where
natural law authorizes this epistemology, a world where, as Bracher notes,
"self-presence" has governed as naturalized ruler over "mediated presence"(3).

Milton concludes on the personal level as well as the theoretical—combining the inward and apocalyptic pilgrimages of the poem—with its image of Blake engraving alone in his garden. The vision of language he has
created redeems his own labor as a poet-prophet, especially in works such
as *The Marriage of Heaven and Hell*, where antithetical relationships are
crucial to a method that seeks to subvert the antithetical basis of reality in
the natural world. Indeed, Blake inherits this problem from *Paradise Regained*, attempting to subvert naturalized constructions of language without falling into silence. Both *Paradise Regained* and *Milton* question a
fundamental "natural" assumption concerning language—namely, that what
at first glance seems the nonsense of the polysemic is actually a prophetic
site where a transferential relationship between subjects and language is
enacted. Blake's "Mental Fight" culminates in this moment, conceptualiz-
ing the apocalyptic cleansing of a world otherwise constructed on the basis
of mistakenly naturalized "Stolen and Perverted Writings," on fallen frames
of reference. "Self-annihilation"—apocalypse—is not the vanquishing of
consciousness in *Milton*, but instead the expansion of consciousness through
modes of representation based on transferential relationships among subject, object, vision, and word.

3

The Measure of "Deplorable Gaps in Time": A Language for Visionary History in *Trilogy*

1. INTRODUCTION: "WE GO BACKWARD OR FORWARD"

Responding to received traditions, the contemporary conditions of World War II, and an anticipated apocalyptic future, H. D.'s *Trilogy* revises authorized discourses of redemption in order to create a transformed language for modern prophecy. The revisionary prophetic poetics of *Trilogy* (which comprises *The Walls Do Not Fall*, *Tribute to the Angels*, and *The Flowering of the Rod*) stems from three significant literary and historical factors: the discourses of pacifism available during World War II, the observational languages of Freud and classical science, and the prophetic vocabularies of Moravianism. H. D. transforms each of these discourses in order to formulate a visionary prophetic language that, like Blake's, is transferential rather than reificatory.

H. D.'s narrative conjoins the violence of Golgotha with the rebirth in the manger in order to tell a story in which the relational language of modern prophecy displaces the absolutist language of orthodox prophetic tradition. H. D.'s response to the language of orthodox prophecy revives and reinvents Blake's transformation of Western prophecy in *Milton*, discussed in chapter 2. Like Blake in *Milton*, H. D. seeks to transform biblical verity into variant through a method that reaches backward for authorized models of prophetic language that can be deployed as representations of futurist, apocalyptic modes of consciousness.

If the past offered models, albeit imperfect ones, contemporary paradigms for revisionary prophecy were few during the time H. D. composed *Trilogy*. Nationalism dominated the World War II era, of course, and H. D.'s commitment to pacifism in her prophecy found few companion public voices. Perhaps the only public figure in England at the time who would have shared H. D.'s commitment to prophecy as a vehicle for pacifism was G. K. A. Bell, the outspoken Bishop of Chichester. Bell's mixture of pacifism and prophecy has much in common with H. D.'s, but his insistence on transcendence can help measure the extent of H. D.'s revision of traditional prophetic language in *Trilogy*. Bell's wartime essays and sermons, collected in *The Church and Humanity, 1939–1946*, suggest an important context for the combination of inspiration and threat that the metaphysical authority of prophecy held for H. D. In "The Church's Function in War-Time," first published in November 1939 in the *Fortnightly Review*, Bell affirms that the Church "has the right to prophesy" during war. The Church, he argues, must commit itself "to analys[ing] the issues which lie behind a particular conflict, and to rebuk[ing] the aggressor."[1] Yet Bell argues that the Church must transcend the urgencies of the State. Church prophecy, he writes, "must be disinterested and independent," and "should speak only what the moral law compels it to speak" (27).

The role of the prophet during war is, of course, one of the major questions explored in *Trilogy*. As a prophetic response to the language of war, *Trilogy* shares with Bell's texts a pacifist impulse. Yet as a work of modern prophecy, its revision of the patristic tradition that underwrites orthodox reception of prophecy—including Bell's—places *Trilogy* outside of the "disinterested" (read "transcendent") response Bell seeks to encourage. Bell argues for an ecumenical "Universal Church" that would heal the wounds of nations through a call to religious cohesion, and through a representation of Christianity that is outside of time and history. He claims that the Church is uniquely suited to respond to war because the Church "touches the invisible, the unchanging, the supernatural, and the supernational" (25–26).

H. D.'s prophetic response to the war, in contrast, seeks to represent redemption by collapsing distinctions such as Bell's. In *Trilogy*, H. D. crafts material representations of the transcendental authority Bell otherwise maintains to be "supernatural" and "supernational." To create a language for such a prophecy, H. D. first seeks to revise conceptions of "universal" theodicy.

As a project that would revise prophetic pacifism, a discourse hardly spoken during World War II, H. D.'s effort seems a solitary one.[2] H. D. saw herself as one of the few public intellectuals whose discourse in the years between the wars sought to portray redemption without succumbing to the paralysis of escapism or the limited scope of materialism. Speaking of contemporary intellectuals as either disengaged or ineffectually busy, she wrote: "One refused to admit the flood was coming—the other counted the nails and measured the planks with endless exact mathematical formulas, but didn't seem to have the very least idea of how to put the Ark together."[3]

In analysis with Freud, H. D. concluded that prophecy would be the most urgent response by poets to the "flood" of the impending war. Biblical representation became politically urgent during H. D.'s analysis, necessitating for her a revision of Freud's materialism, especially his resistance to her emphasis on myth and religion. H. D. invokes biblical images of the flood in *Tribute to Freud* in order to describe the self-induced powerlessness she perceived among the artists and intellectuals of her circle: "My brain staggers now when I remember the deluge of brilliant talk I was inflicted with" (57). By contrast, in a 1943 letter to Norman Holmes Pearson she confidently describes the task of the modern prophet as "future world-reconstruction." Despite Freud's materialist assumption that her mythopoeic mind was an escapist symptom, H. D.'s period of psychoanalysis with Freud led her to conclude that the primary role of poetry is prophetic redemption. She tells Pearson that "'Protection for the scribe' seems to be the leit-motif" of *Trilogy*.[4]

H. D.'s revisions of psychoanalytic discourse provide the background for her revisions of prophetic pacifism in *Trilogy*. In *Psyche Reborn: The Emergence of H. D.*, the first major study seeking to recover H. D.'s reputation as a poet, Susan Stanford Friedman discusses in depth the contentious relationship between H. D. and Freud during analysis, and shows how this relationship fueled H. D.'s later poetry. Friedman explains that H. D. added a dialogic, countertransferential element to her work with Freud, whom H. D. termed "The Professor." Taking the lead from Friedman's groundbreaking work, contemporary H. D. scholarship has elaborated Freud's naturalist and masculinist biases, emphasizing the fact that "the Professor was not always right."[5] In *H. D. and Freud: Bisexuality and a Feminine Discourse*, Claire Buck focuses on the split subject of psychoanalysis to reveal H. D.'s revisions of female identity as more complex than they were portrayed in the initial scholarly recovery of H. D. in the 1970s. Susan Edmunds's *Out of Line: History, Psychoanalysis, and Montage in H. D.'s Long Poems* emphasizes historically contingent modes of female identity in H. D., thereby refiguring Friedman's construction of gender identity in *Psyche Reborn* in ways that recognize a more theoretically nuanced sense of identity in H. D.'s longer poetry.[6] Little has been written, however, on how such revision comes to bear on H. D.'s conception of herself as a poet-prophet in the Western tradition, or on how such revision offers H. D. the opportunity to reconfigure, like Blake, the traditional, authorized and authorizing role of the poet-prophet in the modern world.[7]

Following her analysis with Freud, H. D. composed prophetic poetry grounded in immanent and transcendent representations of visionary consciousness. As Friedman and others have shown, Freud's naturalism offered a materialist context for H. D.'s visionary strategies, while Freud's normative models of female desire necessitated H. D.'s revision of psychoanalysis. H. D. describes Freud as Janus, the Roman god of beginnings and endings. H. D.'s Freud-Janus makes meaning on the border between the linearity of the conscious mind and the nonlinearity of the unconscious. Yet he also creates an unbreachable boundary between a presumably active, masculine subject *in* discourse and a presumably passive, feminine object *of* discourse. Because "the Professor was not always right," H. D. sought to revise his materialist and masculinist biases in *Tribute to Freud* and *Trilogy*.

In *Tribute to Freud*, H. D. confirms the need for a new language and a new metaphysics in what might be seen as a statement of her rhetoric of vision in *Trilogy*: "We retreat from the so-called sciences and go backward or go forward into alchemy" (145). Her paradoxical movements both backward and forward constitute no mere neglect of science in favor of aesthetics; her statement is no disavowal of scientific observation for its own sake. Instead, she seeks to rewrite with "new words" the "as yet unrecorded" relationship between the role of prophecy and mind during World War II (145). During H. D.'s second week of analysis with Freud, she already had noted in her journal the conjunction of scientific, religious, and literary discourses vital to her self-representation as a poet-prophet:

> I am on the fringes or in the penumbra of the light of my father's science and my mother's art—the psychology or philosophy of Sigmund Freud.
> I must find new words as the Professor found or coined new words to explain certain as yet unrecorded states of mind or being. (*Tribute*, 145)

Although at the time of this entry H. D. was unsure what might ensue from her analysis with Freud, she was convinced that the need for "new words" would entail an imaginative revision of both science and art. H. D. dramatized these "new words" in terms of the poetic vocation of prophecy during her analysis with Freud, when his co-interpretation of her vision in Corfu led her to characterize her imagination as one rooted in a "suppressed desire to be a Prophetess" (*Tribute*, 51). H. D.'s commitment to endlessly transmutable—and, as I will discuss later, dangerously reiterative—alchemical language in *Trilogy* leads to the creation of a counterhistory poised on the borderline between vision and history, transcendence and immanence, and conscious and unconscious states of mind.

The natural observation of Freudian and classical scientific discourse becomes in *Trilogy* the work of *vision*. "There is a formula for Time that has not yet been computed," H. D. concludes in her diary entry for her second week of analysis with Freud (145), implying that her "new words" would measure those "as yet unrecorded states of mind or being." H. D.'s revision of prophetic authority to recollect and transform all-but-lost traces of prophetic images of women—the Virgin Mary, Mary Magdalene, Venus, Mithra, Pistis Sophia—proceeds from her transformation of the measurements of the natural world into visionary measure. Despite Freud's masculinist bias—and because of his insistence on the nonlinearity of time measurement in the unconscious—the body is re-envisioned in *Trilogy* as visionary, oscillating on a border "between the poles of heaven and earth" (*Flowering*, 11.6). For H. D., the measure of prophecy de-emphasizes clock-time in favor of "the desire to equilibrate // the eternal variant"; here, "the hunger / for Paradise" creates the "demand of a given moment" that re-envisions clock-time as imaginative measurement (*Flowering*, 5.4–5, 7, 9). Eternal verities are replaced by variants; clock-time is replaced by what was in Blake an "imaginative instant," a prophetic "moment" in imaginative time. Her revision of time measurement transforms "merely the will to endure" (as she puts it) into the desire to construct an immanent principle to represent the metaphysics of modern prophecy. What begins in *Walls* as the simple pronouncement that "eternity endures" becomes in *Flowering* the representation of an eternal body "journe[ying] back and forth / between the poles of heaven and earth forever" (5.28; 11.5–6). From this provisional location, the modern prophet's multiplicitous tongues revise monuments of orthodoxy and create a multivocal language for apocalyptic redemption.

Although *Tribute to Freud* and *Trilogy* revise the phallocentric gaze of Freud, these texts also draw on the authority of traditional Freudian analysis. This tradition was for H. D. both materialist and visionary; as noted, H. D. alternately names Freud "the Professor" and a manifestation of the Roman god Janus. For H. D., the prophet makes her language from a backward/forward vision, creating heretical gaps in the residue of tradition. In *Trilogy*, the gaps she creates between linear history and the seemingly ahistorical quest of the poem become measurable—representable and meaningful—at a conceptual border location between scientific observation and prophetic vision.

Crucial to her transformation of Freud and natural science, H. D.'s backward/forward rhetoric is also a critical component in her revision of orthodox Moravian religious language. H. D.'s Moravianism emerged from eighteenth-century British and Austrian migration to the colonial United States, with the most thriving Moravian community located in H. D.'s birthplace, Bethlehem, Pennsylvania. Because of its radical Protestant heritage (discussed above in chapter 1), Moravianism's relationship with religious authority is contentious: Moravian doctrine was not codified; clergy and laity shared a measure of power in interpreting liturgical language; early Moravian economical and social structures were based on communal, rather than hierarchical, models; and Moravian religious practices themselves included embodied sacraments—at least one of which, as I will discuss later, sanctified same-gender intimate contact.

Working with her Moravian past, H. D. conceived a prophetic imagination in *Trilogy* that draws from the same countertradition that informs Blake's prophecies. For Blake, the principle of Poetic Genius is crucial to the "mental fight" that turns mainstream Protestant and classical scientific images of nature into vision. H. D. continues Blake's rhetorical strategies with a difference. As a Moravian, H. D. inherited Blake's radical Protestantism. The Moravian heritage of H. D.'s Bethlehem, Pennsylvania, community is a product of the traditions of dissent from which Blake's reading of the Bible derived. This shared heritage results in similar strategies of representation in their prophetic poetry. The Muggletonianism of Blake's childhood was an extension of Antinomian, Leveller, and Ranter impulses from the previous century. By the eighteenth century, Moravianism represented an established dissenting discourse, one that Blake explicitly incorporated into his work. E. P. Thompson describes Moravianism (with Swedenborgianism) as one of the "specific vectors" of Blake's inheritance from seventeenth-century traditions of dissent.[8] Like Blake, H. D. rejects Protestant insistence on the collective, apocalyptic salvation of the congregation. Like Blake, she draws on countertraditional Gnosticism to enact this split. Like Blake, she conceives a multivalent language to represent such a task.

I will return to a more detailed account of H. D.'s transformation of Moravian representations of divinity below, specifically in terms of Moravian social structures, sacred practices, and power relations. First, in order to understand how H. D.'s countertraditional images of women and desire create representations of female-coded agency, it is important to understand the specific role sexual politics plays in H. D.'s attempt to recast orthodox religious language into prophetic language in *Trilogy*. Sexual and gender politics fuel H. D.'s revisions of divine language in *Trilogy*. H. D.'s revelatory "Marys a-plenty" (*Flowering*, 16.9) are less ambivalent about the role of female prophets than are Blake's conceptions of a passive "femininity" and an active "Female Will." H. D.'s project must revivify a prophetic discourse buried in a public tradition—prophecy—resistant to the voices of women. Her "suppressed desire to be a Prophetess" emerges in *Trilogy* in her speaker's movement from private object of discourse to public agent of prophecy: "Our Lady universally" is reimagined as the Lady who crafts unfixed representations of prophetic women in her "blank pages / of the unwritten volume of the new" (*Angels*, 37.2, 38.11–12). H. D. revives images of female prophets as part of a revision of scientific and religious discourses of nature; this approach to prophecy redeems the body as an immanent principle of divine energy, but without the promise of transcendence characteristic of Bishop Bell's essays and sermons. In H. D.'s revision of Freudian and religious languages, desire serves a dual function: as a sign for the roots of libidinal knowledge-making among sexed subjects, and as a site for enacting sensory representations of prophetic visionary experience informed by her Moravian reception of the Bible.

A look at the Moravian religious and mythopoeic source material H. D. brought to her analysis with Freud can clarify H. D.'s conception of her

role as a poet-prophet. Moravian beliefs inspired H. D. to read authoritative discourses such as the Bible with the confidence necessary for their
revision in *Trilogy*. Gillian Lindt Gollin has shown that the contextual nature of Moravian "doctrine" allows for the same sort of intellectual divergence that characterizes Blake's eclectic use of authoritative tradition:
Moravian ethical standards, paradoxically, "could give no uniform and consistent direction to human conduct"; Moravianism indeed welcomed an
idea of moral law in which "the same religious dogma could be and indeed
was interpreted in such a way as to give rise to different and even opposing
ethical maxims."[9] Working from a religious tradition that resists uniformity
and embraces contrariety in its doctrine, H. D. transforms biblical verity
into variant in *Trilogy*.

Of course, this focus on revisionary language as the key component in
individual redemption was not a strategy limited only to H. D.'s Moravian
community. The Moravian impetus to move away from priestly authority
to the interpretive authority of the individual comes as much from American attempts to separate from England as it does from British radical Protestantism. Ronald E. Martin describes this period of emerging literary
nationalism in American culture as one actually dominated by movements
toward the "destruction of knowledge," in which the linguistic authority of
social and religious institutions was attacked by thinkers who called for its
replacement by the authority of the individual, as in the tendency of
Emerson's "radical relativism" to render "all approaches to knowledge arbitrary."[10] Arguing that this "intellectual frontierism" has been long a part
of America's mythos, Martin states that this mode of epistemology seeks to
produce "an egalitarianism of the life of the mind" (3). Most important to a
study of *Trilogy* is Martin's emphasis on the nineteenth-century culture of
redemption—the desire for an epistemology of egalitarianism—and his
argument that this mode of thinking continues well into the twentieth century. As Martin observes, twentieth-century writers such as Stein, Pound,
Stevens, and Williams shared strategies that "undermined customs of genre,
text, and linguistic representation in ways that foreshadowed subsequent
Deconstructionist thought" (xiii). H. D.'s transformations of Moravianism
and psychoanalytic theory produce in *Trilogy* a mode of prophetic representation that is consonant with the historical context described by Martin.

But however much it reflects a larger cultural pattern, H. D.'s emphasis
on a revisionary language for redemption in *Trilogy* is an effect of Moravian
attitudes toward religious language. Moravian understanding of the Bible
afforded H. D. a model for reinscribing coercive language in redemptive
terms. Moravianism does not prohibit the laity from interpreting the language and the semiotic figurations of the church hierarchy. Janice S.
Robinson writes that in the tradition that H. D. practiced, "[a]ll members of
the faith were permitted to know and use the symbolic language so that it

could not be used against them."[11] This blurring of traditional religious authority, extending to the laity the interpretive function most Western religions reserve for a priesthood, may well have influenced H. D.'s desire to speak as a female prophet. Once self-authorized, however, H. D.'s prophecy extends beyond Moravian exegesis, anticipating a reinvention of apocalypse in her recasting of referential language.

Another shift from authorized to revisionary prophecy can be seen in H. D.'s use of desire as a means of combining immanent and transcendent representation. Moravian religious conceptions of power and language suggest a model for the representation of prophetic vision as a combination of material and metaphysical categories of understanding. Reading the Bible through the lens of Moravian tradition inspired H. D. to craft a representation of divinity that might be perceived as immanent human desire. Claire Buck's argument that H. D.'s poetic language is grounded in a "bisexual discourse" can help sketch how H. D. creates a language for poetic prophecy from Moravian biblical interpretation. Divinity and desire in *Trilogy* are grounded in bisexual signification, another shift from verity to variant. H. D.'s associative and anagrammatical representations of divinity represent differences of identity through techniques of sameness. Following her analysis with Freud, H. D. seems to have returned to Moravian-inspired readings of the Bible, motivated by an interest in connecting Moravian conceptions of same-gender desire to Freud's version.

The Moravian ritual of same-gender foot-washing, an attempt to re-enact John 13, provides an instance in which Moravian hymnals sought to represent transcendence in terms of human sense perception. Here, sensory perception of divinity is based on same-gender desire. During this practice, the leader of the congregation sang a hymn for the occasion. Jacob John Sessler notes in *Communal Pietism Among Early American Moravians* that the chosen hymn was meant to emphasize the sensual aspects of Moravian conceptions of Christ.[12] The following foot-washing hymn, from *The Litany Book*, indicates that human desire was understood to be a necessary element of Moravian faith:

> What did he do, that matchless heart,
> The soul full of desire,
> The body with death pangs and smart
> Pervaded as with fire?
> He did fetch water, and did gird
> A towel round his body,
> And then to lave their feet desired,
> Which he to wash was ready.[13]

The Moravian obsession with images of Christ's wounds shows a similar motivation to perceive the human body of Christ in its fullest physicality;

Christ is thus seen both in his "death pangs" and as someone "full of desire." Moravian faith and practice understood this combination of immanent (sensual) and transcendent (divine) images of Christ to be a component of direct revelation. Sessler observes that Moravian belief in "Christ's immediate presence" was so strong that on 13 November 1756, the congregation at Herrnhut named Christ the Chief Elder of the Church. Christ was elected Chief Elder because the congregation felt the earthly exigencies of the job would be too much for a single mortal. Sessler writes that for Moravians, this focus on Christ as an immanent principle of divinity "gave them almost a sense perception of God" (106). The embodied vision of divinity evident in Moravian foot-washing will be taken up later in this chapter, as I discuss H. D.'s collocation of "Marys-a-plenty" in *Trilogy*, with specific emphasis on H. D.'s revisionary dramatization of Mary's anointing the feet of Christ in the Gospel of John.

The Moravian kiss of peace also enacts an embodied representation of divinity. A sacrament in which members of the same gender kiss each other, the kiss of peace was a practice that conjoined earthly and spiritual love and was more important to Moravian faith than the foot-washing ritual. Moreover, the kiss was meant to symbolize the unity of Moravians with their dead ancestors, and to unify Moravians with those of other faiths. Sessler writes that, as a symbol of such fellowship, the kiss of peace "was also interpreted as a greeting from the saints who had passed on, the ancient races, the Lutherans, the Reformed, the heathen in distant lands, the Ancient *Unitas Fratrum*" (134).

In such terms, Moravianism might seem an unproblematic source for H. D.'s conception of desire and vision in her prophecy, especially insofar as Moravian faith seems to include a homosocial ritual as a necessary component of the visionary expression of human desire: Christ is the central figure of Moravian representations of desire, and is married to the soul of each believer. Of the Moravian conception of the soul and desire, Sessler writes that "[s]ince Christ is the husband of all souls, they are of necessity all female, whether of man or woman. Physically men are male but spiritually female" (151). Such traces of homosocial signification—for men—in Moravian religious practices could suggest an easily traceable line from embodied Moravian sacraments to H. D.'s poetics. However, H. D.'s revisionary prophecy depends, here and elsewhere, on her effort to reconceive the relationship among power, desire, and divinity, even within Moravian discourse.

Moravianism inspired H. D. to posit fully embodied, human figures of divinity in *Trilogy*; however, Moravian faith specified that only heterosexual desire could be a legitimate expression of divinity. For H. D.'s attempt to transform religious and scientific verities into variance, Moravianism is the troubling religious analogue to psychoanalysis. H. D.'s integration of Moravianism and analysis broke her writer's block in the years preceding the war, helping her to compose the autobiographical account of her Moravian childhood, *The Gift*, during the same period in which she wrote *Trilogy*. Like psychoanalytic theory, Moravianism encouraged a dialogic relationship between subject and tradition; yet this relationship was not enough, either in analysis or in her Moravian reading of the Bible, to create a subjectivity fueled by the sense of agency necessary to realize H. D.'s "suppressed desire to be a Prophetess" or to create "Marys a-plenty." Simply to say that Moravian tradition offered a path of linguistic resistance is to miss the political elements of Moravian conceptions of desire, elements to which H. D. would have to respond.

Just as she transformed Freudian psychoanalysis, H. D. revised the authorizing influence of Moravianism in her poetic prophecy. Sessler himself reflects Moravian limits on desire when he says that the soul is female "of necessity" because Christ is considered the husband of all souls. The conjugal divinity of Christ could be seen only through heterosexual desire: "In this married relationship of souls to their God-husband," Sessler observes, "all aspirations and desires were fully realized" (151).[14]

In order to conceive a prophetic imagination based on the divinity of human desire in *Trilogy*, H. D. both continues and revises the "body politics" of psychoanalytic theory and Moravianism. This transformation is crucial to her attempt to remake scientific and religious conceptions of nature into prophetic vision in *Trilogy*. Such a transformation resembles significantly the rhetorical strategies of Blake's prophecies. In Blake, the prophetic potential of all humans is articulated through the representation of the imaginative mind's ability to embrace artistically the visionary material of the natural world. For Blake, Poetic Genius is a sacred capacity universal to all humans—"all deities reside in the human breast"—and the imagination's potential to perceive the "minute particulars" of visionary nature is an expression of the Human Form Divine. In *Notes on Thought and Vision*, H. D. describes an analogous process.[15] She writes that the imagination's ability to mediate material and metaphysical consciousness re-envisions the minute particulars of the world as visionary. H. D. represents this level of consciousness, where body, mind, and "over-mind" work as one, through the image of a "painter who concentrated on one tuft of pine branch with its brown cone until every needle was a separate entity to him" (*Notes*, 42–43). Blake represents a turn in the prophetic lineage where the consolidated religious vision of prophecy gives way to a profession of the individual divinity of "minute particulars," where "every thing that lives is holy." Reviving Blake's system for the twentieth century, H. D.'s *Notes on Thought and Vision* conceives of a relationship between imagination and nature where each minute particular is a divine "separate entity."

H. D.'s use of prophecy in *Trilogy* comes from the desire to redeem these minute particulars amid conscious and unconscious (and public and personal) experiences of wartime violence. This particular conception of divinity is significant in *Walls*, where H. D. asserts that the ruinous effects of an embodied nature, fragmented by the technological conflict of World War I, must be repaired by a visionary conception of nature where body, mind, and over-mind work in tandem:

> . . . [each mind] differs from every other
> in minute particulars,
>
> as the vein-paths on any leaf
> differ from those of every other leaf
>
> in the forest, as every snow-flake
> has its particular star, coral or prism shape.
>   (38.23–28)

H. D. imagines in *Notes on Thought and Vision* the sense of vision necessary to transform the body in nature into a visionary body in *Walls*. In *Trilogy*, the mediating force of what H. D. terms *mind*—later with Freud, of course, the unconscious—creates the conditions for the representation of unrestrained desire as "over-mind," or consciousness. As with Blake's Four Zoas, any of the states alone attains nothing: H. D. likens dominance of the brain alone to "disease"; of the body alone to "degeneracy"; and of over-mind alone to "madness." More specifically, given the Greek root of *prophecy*, H. D. describes anyone ruled only by over-mind as a "maniac" (*Notes*, 17). H. D. conjoins discourses of religion and medical pathology, creating a language that authorizes itself by casting nonsyncretizing models as pathological "others." H. D.'s rhetorical strategy embraces religious and medical discourses in order to revise the concept of "divine madness"; her language inhabits authorizing discourses in order to erode them from within. The mind, she writes, is capable of both divine madness and over-conscious visionary intimation; and because of the power of the imagination to perceive both bodily delirium and mystic consciousness, the mind is the mediating power necessary to re-create the natural world as vision.

H. D.'s image of what Blake terms Poetic Genius seeks wholly to represent a visionary natural world while embedded in what Foucault terms the modern episteme, where any sense of an inherent divinity that might be recuperated as Logos gives way to a belief in the inherent groundlessness of language. H. D.'s anagrammatic method in *Trilogy* takes past models of visionary language as the impetus to project forward a representation of an apocalyptic future created by the industrious labor of the poet-prophet. In *Flowering*, for instance, multiple representations of Mary are rewritten into an image of a Christ child whose identity is never stable. The "rule and rite" of both science and the Church become mediating structures between the poet-prophet's forward and backward movements.

H. D.'s imaginative encounter with nature produces a vision of divine interconnectedness circumscribed by re-envisioned scientific sight: the minute particulars of nature exist together in "a clear relationship like a drawing of a later mechanical twentieth century bridge-builder" (*Notes*, 43). H. D.'s conception of nature as vision depends on her revision of metaphors of scientific observation as metaphors of vision.[16] Indeed, from her earliest Imagist origins, H. D. seeks in poetry the minute precision of observation that her forebears sought; in *Trilogy* she seeks to transform reificatory observation into transferential vision.

This transformation of observation into vision reinvents the relationship of prophet and audience. For modern prophecy, the process of remaking the world proceeds in some part from a remaking of the sciences of the world: from science, the poet moves "backward or forward" and seeks "to find new words" to represent this movement. H. D. uses images of technology to represent the relationship of modern prophet to audience; in this relationship, the creation of prophetic language depends on recasting the frame of reference of the audience as prophetic also. Thus, H. D. represents the effects of prophecy on prophetic audiences as a telegraphing of vision. Prophets need prophetic audiences, she writes; prophetic art "needs an over-mind or a slight glimmering of over-mind intelligence to understand over-mind intelligence" (*Notes*, 24). Poised between modernist elitism and what Ihab Hassan terms postmodern communality, the vatic scribe of *Notes on Thought and Vision* anticipates the rhetoric of vision in *Trilogy*.[17] Prophet and audience together undertake the work of vision: "Two or three people, with healthy bodies and the right sort of receiving brains, could turn the whole tide of human thought" (*Notes*, 27). In order to communicate, however, the prophet and her audience together must interpret the dots and dashes. These dots and dashes are H. D.'s hieroglyphs of vision, combining the iconic sign of the hieroglyph with the modern groundlessness of the arbitrary—here, telegraphic—signifier.

H. D.'s 1920 vision at Corfu with Bryher demonstrates a significant instance of this blurring between prophet and audience. The addition of Bryher's frame of reference is crucial to H. D.'s extension of the seer-seen combination into a vision that remakes the boundary between prophet and audience, and which remakes language so that this blurred boundary is representable. H. D. eventually collapses under the strain of working to maintain the vision. Bryher continues the work of vision at the point where H. D. stops. This development is remarkable in the narrative precisely because Bryher has been with H. D. throughout the vision but heretofore has seen nothing on the wall. Significantly, H. D.'s representation of this collapse between seer-seen and prophet-audience calls to mind a use of contrariety that echoes Blake's method in *The Marriage of Heaven and Hell*. H. D. writes: "But though I admit to myself that now I have had enough, maybe just a little too much, Bryher, who has been waiting by me, carries on the reading where I left off" (*Tribute*, 56). Visionary rhetoric is conversational also in Blake's Proverbs of Hell, the gateway to visionary inspiration in *The Marriage of Heaven and Hell*. The Proverbs of Hell are read jointly by Blake and his once-adversarial angel, just as H. D. and Bryher "read" the vision at Corfu together. Of the joint reading of his characters, Blake writes, "You never know what is enough unless you know what is more than enough"; and he concludes in the Proverbs of Hell that the work of transferring vision into language is "Enough! or Too much." Like the role of language in Blake's later prophecies, H. D.'s "new words" are relational rather than absolutist. If the prophet in an industrial era requires a prophetic audience, she might be said to do so as part of a shift from High Modern authority to postmodern provisionality.

2. "THE WALLS DO NOT FALL": THE PROPHET "TAKES PRECEDENCE OF THE PRIEST"

Claire M. Tylee has shown that women's writing of World War I shares a narrative strategy in which representations of emotional death lead to representations of resurrection. These narratives often culminate in the "traditional 'new life' of motherhood" in which "[a] child was a new beginning, a commitment to the future" (229).[18] Tylee's observations might frame an understanding of the narrative of *Trilogy*, where from destruction, in *Walls*, comes the seemingly conventional promise of the manger scene in the final sections of *Flowering*. Donna Krolik Hollenberg argues, however, that H. D.'s tropes of motherhood and creativity revise paternal metaphors of birthing, and in so doing counter "an androcentric myth of language built upon women's subordination and silence."[19] Additionally, both the trauma of war and the resurrective potential of childbirth must be seen in light of how motifs of apocalypse—specifically, of apocalyptic rebirth—are registered in *Trilogy*. As with her vatic transformations of Moravianism and Freud, H. D.'s use of apocalypse continues a tradition (here the apocalypse of St. John), while also seeking to redeem it (here attempting to envision an alternative to the traditional violence of apocalypse).

Although Tylee is primarily interested in H. D.'s novel of World War I, *Bid Me to Live: A Madrigal*, the circumstances of the composition of this novel suggest that H. D.'s rhetorical strategies therein should not be neglected in a discussion of her World War II writing. The first draft of *Bid Me to Live* was completed in 1927. H. D.'s revisions in the 1930s coincided with her psychoanalysis with Freud; she revised the novel again in 1949, after completing *Trilogy*. *Bid Me to Live* was published in 1960.[20] Tylee's understanding of H. D.'s *Bid Me to Live: A Madrigal* sees H. D.'s concern with pacifism as more important than her critique of culture and science: "H. D.'s target was not so much scientism, or historicism, as militarism" (243). In *Bid Me to Live*, the actions of H. D.'s central character, Julia, are circumscribed by the ebb and flow of World War I. For Julia, isolated in her London apartment, writing and sexual experimentation are life-affirming substitutes for war and separation in the novel. Julia's stream-of-consciousness narration emphasizes her personal struggle against militarist enthusiasm; militarism is the greatest challenge to the poetic imagination in *Bid Me to Live*. Of her husband, Rafe, and his frequent shuttling between temporary leaves and the trenches, Julia observes: "Back and forth from France—now he is actually enjoying it. Now he likes it. But I can not serve God and Mammon, not serve poet and hearty over-sexed . . . young officer on leave" (46). The war "absorbed everything," and only a visionary imagination offered protection, much as the poet-prophet's work in *Trilogy* enables "protection for the scribe": for Julia, "the thing that bound body and soul together seemed threatened, so that she seemed to tune-in to another dimension" (68). However, Julia's turn to "another dimension" is not an escape from materialist representation into a private imagination; instead, Julia emphasizes the need for a material language of this "other" dimension. Rather than turn away from a culture rife with militarism, Julia imagines a language that is both other-dimensional and engaged in the immanent, sensory world: "Anyone can translate the meaning of the word. She [Julia] wanted the shape, the feel of it, as if it had been freshly minted" (163). As with H. D.'s conception of visionary language in *Trilogy*, Julia's vision of language carries both the authority of the past and the revisionary energy of translation; for Julia, the language that underwrites war enthusiasm can be revised and "freshly minted" as retranslated signs of pacifism.

Where *Bid Me to Live* engages pacifism more than scientism or historicism, *Walls* conjoins all three. There, H. D. stages the major tensions of the whole of *Trilogy*: first, a concern to remake the language of the "sciences of man" with a visionary language that reconceives representations of natural measurement—especially of time and space—as representations of the imagination; and second, a desire to shape a language that recuperates a visionary potential H. D. understands to be buried in patristic forms of orthodox, linear religious history. H. D. seeks to retrieve religious representation from the past in order to represent the futuristic resurrective potential of the apocalyptic sensibilities engendered by the war.

H. D.'s anagrammatic method in *Walls* begins to evoke the redemptive potential of such an approach to language. Anagrams are deployed in *Walls* as a means of asserting a visionary counter to Bell's history:

relying on displacements and deferrals of meaning, anagrams are the transferential alternative to the universality of Bell's conception of church orthodoxy. In *Walls*, H. D. conceives a language that blurs the boundary between the conflicts of Church history and the transhistorical nature of apocalyptic representation. In *Trilogy*, the Christian *Amen* is ancient Egyptian *Amen-Ra*. Egypt's Osiris becomes an affirmation of patristic kingship: *O-sire-is*.

The language of anagrams in *Walls* represents a "correction" of the religious pacifism publicly espoused during the war by Bell. Where Bell sees a redemptive universal cohesiveness in the Church, H. D. crafts a prophetic language grounded in a visionary history that reconceives this Church as an institution that has reified its war against "heresy" into natural law. Unlike Bell, H. D. asserts that the conflicts of history are not just between nations, but also occur within the institution of the Church itself, the site Bell identifies as outside of history and immune to argumentation. Bell asks "What is the function of the Church in war-time?" (23). His answer affirms Christianity to be "supernational." As H. D. demonstrates in *Trilogy*, such an answer proffers a conception of divinity bound to Church efforts to reify the historical battles of orthodoxy into naturally inarguable doctrine.[21] Bell argues that during war "it is the function of the Church at all costs to remain the Church" (23). For Bell, only the universal sign of institutional orthodoxy can mend the conflicts of history. He argues that the uneasy peace after World War I developed into the current war because "[i]n none of the victorious countries had the Church sounded the supernational note" (25). In *Walls*, the transcendent sign of orthodoxy—the "super-national note"—is wedged in the Church's historical battles between orthodoxy and heterodoxy, and represents "seven-times-seven / bitter, unending wars" (*Angels*, 3.11–12). Yet for Bell, the greatest threat to the Church during World War II is that the universal sign of orthodoxy is poised to collapse into the contingent particulars of history: "Will the Church in the warring countries strike the universal note, or will it say ditto to the State?" (25). Bell's emphasis on transcendence can help show how H. D.'s anagrammatic language for prophecy instead is poised on a border between the immanent and the transcendent.

Yet anagrams suggest a potential repetition dangerous for the apocalyptic aims of the poet-prophet. Although the rearrangement of letters creates new meanings, these rearrangements risk mere word-play, which might endlessly reproduce only decontextualized meaning— "words for words' sake" (*Walls*, 32.8)—thereby resulting only in a reaffirmation of transcendence at the expense of material language. Finding *Isis* or *Sirius* in *Osiris*, and critiquing phallic language in *O-sire-is*, may not offer a new language; instead it may point only to exhausted rearrangements of the old. In the first book of *Trilogy*, H. D. seeks to avert such danger through the use of an anagrammatic style that reconceives past forms of language in terms of visionary representations that decenter the institutional authority of the established church.

For H. D., anagrams stage the prophet's chronological move to the past for a language that might contain fragments of divine essence. Like the journey in Blake's *Milton*, the pilgrimage of *Trilogy* consists of a search for a language of prophetic origins, where the past can be remobilized for a present that keeps a resurrective future in the offing. The prophetic speaker of the poem must reconcile "resurrection myth / and resurrection reality" (*Walls*, 40.5–6). She represents herself as a "crude mason" whose task is to build a visionary history that "would cover deplorable gaps / in time" (*Walls*, 40.8, 10–11).

Yet the speaker admits that her language for this history—her masonry—is crude, and that she is "not too well equipped." As such, the speaker's "cover" of gaps in time might just as well represent a concealment as a recovering. Edmunds has shown that H. D.'s search to recover a "oneness" in Osiris-Isis-Sirius is linked to her attempt to recover the hermaphroditic qualities of the Hatshepshut figure in Egyptian tradition. By demonstrating a connection between those cartouches that house mummies and those that house bullets, Edmunds argues convincingly that H. D.'s anagrams constitute an ambivalent turn to violence in a prophetic poem otherwise committed to pacifism. According to Edmunds, the speaker's attempt to see Osiris as both male and female—as both Sirius and Isis— "reveals the persistent anxiety that a god who cannot transcend the divisions of sex and gender can be neither truly one nor truly eternal."[22] As a statement on sex and gender, section 40 of *Walls* is important to the speaker's ambivalent construction of identity and difference in her pilgrimage. Drawing on H. D.'s comment in a letter to Bryher that Hatshepshut only "pretended" to be double-sexed, Edmunds argues that, in section 40, H. D. "lays the ground for the poem's later inquiries into the nature and authenticity of divine being, inquiries that will themselves repeatedly return to the problem of sexual and gender division."[23] The speaker's ambivalence toward the role of identity and difference in her pilgrimage induces her desire to "equate" the values of the anagrams created from Osiris's name; later in the poem, this urge to equate becomes a less assured, even conditional, commitment simply to "relate" myth and reality.

Nevertheless, seen through the lens of H. D.'s prophetic strategies, this search for the metaphysical "One // in the beginning" (40.20–21) is an attempt to return to orthodox Christianity in order to plunder the absolute authority of the Logos. In section 40, the reiterations of her anagrammatic method reinforce the lack of referentiality that marks the "regrettable chasm" between language and vision that the speaker seeks to bridge (40.11). To craft this bridge—to cover deplorable gaps in time—the speaker invokes the conventional "before-and-after schism" between pre- and postlapsarian representation so that the separation between the two might be collapsed (40.12).

Of course, the recurrence of conventional biblical rhetoric in the precise section of *Trilogy* where the speaker declares herself a "crude mason" reinforces the ambivalence of the speaker's revisionary linguistic pilgrimage. The speaker's trust in the power of prophetic language in section 40 is haunted by the words of Christ in the Gospel of John. When questioned in John about the divine authority of his language, Christ says, "Before Abraham was, I am" (8:58). Questioned as a false prophet by the Pharisees, Christ affirms a separation between the language he speaks and the material language of the natural world: "Why do ye not understand my speech? even because ye cannot hear my word . . . He that is of God heareth God's words: ye therefore hear them not, because ye are not of God" (John 8:43, 47). Such a rhetoric of separation between the material and metaphysical pervades chapter 8 of John.[24] H. D.'s speaker invokes Christ's defense of his language for prophecy as a means of authorizing her own, yet Christ's words carry with them the traces of biblical authority that would doom her project from the start. The speaker aims to "relate" myth and reality, and thereby to close the schism of the mythological fall. However, Christ's rhetorical emphasis in the chapter from which H. D. quotes seems, on the contrary, to reinforce such a schism.

H. D.'s prophetic argument is more complex than that allowed by a simple dichotomous reading of separate Edenic and fallen realms of nature and representation. Throughout *Trilogy*, the authority of the Bible is invoked as a means of creating the initial conditions for prophetic utterance; once invoked, however, these initial conditions proceed eventually to the unraveling of such authority. In what the speaker of *Walls* suggestively terms the "jumble" of the medieval tradition, a strict separation was assumed between god and prophet, and between prophet and audience.[25] Such separation maintained the power of the church: to assume anything but a separation between metaphysical and material worlds was to commit the capital offense of heresy. In *Trilogy*, however, the industrious poet-prophet must spin her own shroud from this tradition.

The prophet stands in for the God in *Trilogy*. Thus, H. D.'s speaker revises the biblical tradition that authorizes her voice in the first place, a tradition in which the prophet receives the Word of God as separate, extra-natural articulation and must translate the Logos to a fallen world. The speaker argues in section 8 of *Walls* that if the trauma of war makes "protection for the scribe" an urgent leitmotif, then the prophet necessarily "takes precedence of the priest." Here, H. D. follows ancient Egyptian prophetic tradition in which Thoth, the inventor of writing, is a poet-prophet whose visionary work is not circumscribed by a separation of material and metaphysical modes of representation.

H. D.'s use of Thoth as a figure for the role of the modern prophet comes from the Egyptian narrative of Thoth's initiation as regent of the moon. Re's statements to Thoth in this narrative would have appealed to H. D. as a means of representing a prophet who, for the modern world, deploys the power of revision, here signified by his co-regency of the skies with Re, and represented in *Trilogy* by the revisionary power of anagrams. Re grants Thoth godly authority: "Thou shalt be in my place, a place-taker. Thus thou shalt be called: 'Thoth, the place-taker of Re.'"[26] Re later adds that Thoth's power is visionary, and will nurture vision in his followers. Re explains to Thoth that "the faces of all who see thee shall be opened through thee, so that the eye of every man praises god for thee."[27] H. D. may have been familiar with this inscription, given her 1923 journey to recent Egyptian excavations—including the tomb of Tutankhamen—and her great interest in the work of E. A. Wallis Budge and early twentieth-century British Egyptology.[28]

Section 4 of *Walls* stages H. D.'s representation of such place-taking. H. D. invokes an image of visionary identity that echoes that of Blake's in *Milton*, where the poet-pilgrim must embrace the "annihilation" of an identity based on unity in order to conceive a prophetic language of polysemousness. In *Milton*, the poet-pilgrim's self-annihilation is the precondition for a prophetic assault on the solitary representation of orthodox Judeo-Christian divinity: as the Urizenic Old Testament God, Satan sets himself up as sole ruler of the heavens in *Milton*. The prophet's task in the poem is to remake the monovocal Yahweh with alternative forms of language and identity that multiply differences in meaning rather than negate these differences.

The shell that speaks in section 4 of *Walls* undertakes a similar task. The shell represents a radical shift in perspective that decenters the self who speaks in sections 1–3, and that conceives of a language adequate to this displacement of absolutist identity. In the process of such displacement, the shell provides a staging ground for a strategy whereby H. D. borrows from the authority of biblical tradition in order to rupture this tradition.

The voice of the prophet in sections 1–3 of *Walls* becomes in section 4 the voice of the Christian pearl. The speaker of sections 1–3 introduces the historical context of the prophecy—the war and its effect on Londoners—specifically calling in section 3 for the healing Caduceus to "brin[g] life to the living." This same speaker begins section 4, although by the midpoint of the poem her voice becomes that of a prophetic sea shell. H. D. equates the power of the shell with what later becomes the "masonry" of the work of the poet-prophet:

> There is a spell, for instance,
> in every sea-shell,

continuous, the sea-thrust
is powerless against coral,

bone, stone, marble
hewn from within by that craftsman,

the shell-fish:
oyster, clam, mollusc

is master-mason planning
the stone marvel. . . .
                        (4.1–10)

In *Notes on Thought and Vision*, the pearl is H. D.'s visionary touchstone, and is the centrifugal point of her "jelly-fish" experience: "I am in my spiritual body a jelly-fish and a pearl" (50). The pearl is no solipsistic reminder of private experience, however; H. D. writes that "[w]e can probably use this pearl, as a crystal ball is used, for concentrating and directing pictures from the world of vision" (50). Whereas in 1919 the pearl represented a realm of vision separate from the natural world, and one that required the mediation of the crystal ball, by the time of the composition of *Trilogy*, the pearl is a seamless extension of the natural world.

The shell creates a boundary between immanence and transcendence. Despite an exterior impervious to the beating sea, the shell is paradoxically engulfed by its environment: the hard shell is a "shrine" interdependent upon "sea thrust" and the "tide-flow" of the moon. The speaker is both metaphysical Christian shell and immanent poet-prophet. The identities of speaker and shell commingle in a third voice as section 4 continues. Speaker and shell together draw from the immediacy of the sea and the mythopoeic qualities of the moon.

The rhetorical strategy of this interdependent identity—or, earlier, with Thoth, of collapsing the boundary between prophet and poet—requires a suitable language to represent a visionary natural world in section 4. The sea becomes a trope for the challenge of crafting a language for such vision, a language whose meaning is "nothing-too-much" (4.22). Thus, H. D.'s prophetic language, like Blake's, risks the nonsense of polysemousness, and this risk is both its sustenance and its limitation. Once having committed to a prophetic language saturated with meaning—after declaring that the pearl is the Blakean "nothing-too-much" word—the speaker commences a journey through Blakean self-annihilation; she now speaks from the vantage of the shell, and in so doing declares intersubjectivity (speaker, shell, sea, moon) to be the measure of a prophetic frame of reference:

I sense my own limit,
my jaw-shells snap shut

at invasion of the limitless,
ocean-weight; infinite water

cannot crack me, egg in egg-shell. . . .
(4.23–27)

Paradoxically, from inside the hard crust of the mollusc shell comes the porous egg of public prophetic language. What is borne from this "self-out-of-self" is the "pearl-of-great-price," Christ's representation of the king-dom of heaven in the Gospel of Matthew.

The pearl is also crucial to Gnostic tradition. In section 2 of Walls, sev-eral female images of divinity represent a "harlot"; for each, the instrument of prophecy is a "stylus," "dipped in corrosive sublimate," which scratches a "devil's hymn." As in *The Marriage of Heaven and Hell*, where heretical devils are the truest angels, and where the words of the prophet are corro-sive illumination, in the opening of *Walls* traditions of heresy are the corro-sive path to redemption. The "pearl-of-great-price" is H. D.'s heretical re-envisioning of Christian faith as the secret wisdom of gnosis.

According to G. R. S. Mead, whose work on Gnosticism was familiar to H. D., the pearl is an overdetermined image of visionary self-conscious-ness in Gnostic tradition, especially in Gnostic works such as "The Hymn of the Robe of Glory."[29] This pearl brings to the seeker significant "ves-tures" of the "higher self": the pilgrimage of "The Hymn of the Robe of Glory" culminates in a retrieval of the pearl and a reinscribing of earthly clothing with the "kingly sign" of Gnosis. As with Blake's use of language in *Milton*, H. D.'s source in the Gnostic "The Hymn of the Robe and the Glory" localizes prophetic redemption in woven earthly garments inscribed with revelatory language. "The Hymn of the Robe of Glory" locates this pearl in ancient Egypt, which would appeal to H. D.'s revisionary conjunc-tion of the orthodox Christ with the Egyptian Thoth, and with her use of bodily desire as the locus of prophetic vision.[30] H. D.'s "pearl-of-great- price," then, is both a statement on the revisionary power of the prophet (Thoth) and of the role of immanent human desire (Egypt) in the creation of a language adequate for the metaphysical task of prophecy.[31] H. D. asserts in *Notes on Thought and Vision* that everyone possesses the power to achieve such vision; the "over-conscious world . . . is there for everyone." Thus to render this vision in prophecy entails a revision of the orthodox prophetic tradition whereby the prophet is separate from both God and audience. The prophet takes precedence over the priest, and in so doing replaces the abso-lute authority of the institution with an authority mediated between poet-prophet and prophetic tradition—or, as H. D. writes in *Notes on Thought and Vision*, "The oyster makes the pearl in fact" (51). To make the pearl, rather than to accept it as part of a metaphysical visitation of a god whose identity is separate from the prophet, is to align oneself with traditions considered to be heretical. For H. D., as for Blake, such heresy is a crucial stage on the path toward conceiving of nature as a vision. Heresy is redemptive corrosion.

Such a frame of reference, where corrosiveness is an essential component of vision, is necessary for the speaker if she is to disentangle the representation of Christ from its orthodox moorings. The speaker realizes that "now it appears obvious / that *Amen* is our Christos" (18.11–12). Of course, what is "obvious" about *Amen* is not its role as the final articulation of conventional Christian prayer. Instead, it is obvious to the speaker that "Amen" is the anagrammatic product of Christian, Gnostic, and Egyptian mythos. The astrological ram who comes in section 21 as a figure of redemption, of Christian "Amen," conjoins these three religious systems. The Amen-Christos-image must be rewritten by the poet-prophet to conceive a vision of a redemptive natural world. In this way, the presumably fallen world that produces the closing "Amen" of conventional prayer is replaced by a corrosive world of visionary natural forms "where the grasshopper says / *Amen, Amen, Amen*" (23.9–10). The speaker seeks to evoke past images of prophecy to re-envision the landscape that opens *Walls*, a setting where technological progress has reduced the natural world to ruins. From the fires of the Blitz come the prophet's revelatory, corrosive stylus.

Yet anagrams seem to have "disentangled" Christianity from violence only to remake orthodoxy into an equally mythic—transcendent—astrological ram. The recursive rhetoric of *Walls*, that which seeks to retrieve past prophecy in order to authorize a prophecy that revises the authority of the past, also produces moments of ambivalence for the speaker. Book 1 of *Trilogy* eventually moves toward a closing that questions the anagrammatic method that has both emptied referentiality from representations of divinity and regretted the resultant loss.

The border between logic and contrariety was a crucial component in Blake's anticipatory language for a prophetic unconscious, staged in Beulah. For H. D., the unconscious is the site where a language on the border of material and metaphysical representation is crafted. At the end of *Walls*, however, the speaker of the poem is unconvinced that such a mode of representation can produce anything but nonsense. The anagrammatic language of the prophetic unconscious "spews forth / too many incongruent monsters" (32.1–2). From this "depth of the sub-conscious" the poet-prophet of *Trilogy* has produced resurrective pearls that now seem to her both "fixed" and "indigestible." The promise of a prophecy that rearranges the value of prophetic tradition by rearranging the letters of its discourse now seems to amount to nothing but "nonsense, / juxtaposition of words for words' sake, / without meaning, undefined" (32.7–9).

The work of vision is not confined to the prophet; prophets require "receiving centres for dots and dashes" (*Notes*, 26). Strangely, the speaker links prophet and audience with a muddle of seemingly "sterile invention." The speaker steps back and addresses the reader ironically: "you find all this?" (32.16). Prophet and audience conjoin in a statement that is both a caution and an invitation. The relationship of prophet to audience demands a blurring of the visionary boundary that would separate seer from seen. Her "you find all this?" initiates a challenge to the prophetic reader to "find" such a boundary condition between scientific observation of nature and prophetic vision. From the speaker's challenge to her reader comes the speaker's recasting of a frame of reference that would differentiate the particulars of the natural world, and that would assign hierarchical values to these particulars, to a frame of reference where the geometry of the natural world is visionary. Recasting sight in this way is painful, yet revelatory, because it decenters the authority of observation in favor of vision. Speaker and prophetic audience make meaning on the border between decentering doubt and metaphysical verity—here, between natural disaster and visionary science:

> we were caught up by the tornado
> and deposited on no pleasant ground,
>
> but we found the angle of incidence
> equals the angle of reflection. . . .
>   (32.21–24)

Recast in terms of Snell's Law, from classical physics, H. D.'s vision of nature must produce an audience response equal to the force of the initial prophetic utterance: the poet-prophet must produce a cultural angle of reflection equal to a cultural angle of incidence. For H. D., the visionary potential of Snell's Law lies in the concealed knowledge of "the meaning that words hide." To recover — to redeem — "deplorable gaps" in consciousness, gaps that naturalize linear time, H. D. conceives of a mode of rhetoric for prophecy wherein time and space are visionary. Vision becomes a law that naturalizes the relationship between modern prophet and audience.

Yet the walls in Book 1 that separate prophet from God, prophet from audience, and nature from vision do not fall. The walls in the poem that separate particular physical structures crumble from Luftwaffe armaments; one might conclude that such destruction is an inevitable apocalyptic effect of H. D.'s image in *Notes On Thought and Vision* of a sterile world of "dull houses" that stand between the human and the visionary. However, the conditional voice of the speaker at the end of *Walls* suggests that only "*possibly*" might "*haven*" become "*heaven*." After the nightly raids, "*the air / is independable, / thick where it should be fine*." The re-visionary

potential of the world has spiraled into an apocalypse that is *only* destructive. No conception of rebirth exists where the air is so *un*dependable that it
exists *in*dependent of the speaker's experience: as "*independable*," the air
reminds the speaker that her effort to recalibrate the measure of observation into a measure of vision has left her nevertheless in an "*unregistered
dimension*." Her anagrammatic rhetoric once transformed Amen to Amen-
Ra, and transformed Osiris into a critique of patrilineal kingship (O-sire-
is) and of religious gender politics (the ambisexual Osiris-Sirius-Isis). In
the closing section of *Walls*, however, redemptive Osiris is transformed
anagrammatically into the "*zrr-hiss*" of German bombs falling on London.

3. BETWEEN CLOCK-TIME AND REVELATION: THE LADY MAKES ALL THINGS NEW

The war transmutes Osiris to zrr-hiss; thus the pearl retains its indigestibil-
ity. The poet-prophet's apocalyptic vision fails to reconceive images of
destruction as representations of revelation. To stage the revision of apocalypse so that representations of destruction might suggest those of renewal,
H. D. condenses the dominant countertraditional images of prophecy from
Walls into the alchemical tradition of Hermes Trismegistus. H. D.'s revisionist alchemy confronts the failure of apocalyptic representation in Book
1 by rewriting the monologic voice of the Apocalypse of Saint John in
order to redeem images of women in divine discourse. In doing so, H. D.
rewrites a dominant Christian pacifism from World War II in which, to
recall Bell, the Church seeks "at all costs to remain the Church."

Angels opens with a declaration by Hermes that seeks to revivify the
failed vision of *Walls*: "Your walls do not fall, he said, / because your walls
are made of jasper . . ."(2.1–2). Hermes' words echo those of John in Revelation; John, upon seeing a vision of the New Jerusalem, proclaims that
the divine light of the city "was like unto a stone most precious, even like a
jasper stone, clear as crystal" (Revelation, 21:11). H. D.'s walls of differen-
tiation do not fall because, it seems, their crude masonry is of nonporous,
orthodox jasper.

H. D.'s speaker reconceives the walls between nature and vision as a
problem of measurement, and in doing so undertakes a revision of the Book
of Revelation. In chapter 21 of Revelation, John is taken to the New Jerusalem; there, where the border between nature and vision has collapsed, he
measures the boundaries of the city and finds its borders all of one length:
"And the city lieth foursquare, and the length is as large as the breadth: and
he measured the city with the reed, twelve thousand furlongs. The length
and the breadth and the height of it are equal" (21:16). The golden streets
of the city gleam like "transparent glass"; within these streets, the twelve

gates of the city are "twelve pearls" (21:21). The language of vision in Revelation needs no mediation, and its meaning is clear—absolute—to both prophet and audience: John sees in the city "no temple therein: for the Lord God Almighty and the Lamb are the temple of it" (21:22). Moreover, "the city had no need of the sun, neither of the moon, to shine in it: for the glory of God did lighten it, and the Lamb is the light thereof" (21:23).

In *Trilogy* the charred streets of London are recast as the golden, glassy streets of the New Jerusalem. Yet the divine muse of *Angels* is the heretical alchemist Hermes, not Christ; and whereas John's futurist vision imagines the eternal presence of unmediated Logos, H. D.'s vision is girded by the immanent, anagrammatic alchemy that proved problematic at the close of *Walls*. Although H. D.'s anagrammatic method in *Walls* fails to move beyond reiterations of dismantling, anagrams in Angels nevertheless begin to frame a rhetoric of modern prophetic biblical revision. H. D.'s speaker argues that if Hermes is patron to alchemists, he serves the same function for "orators, thieves and poets" (2.6). The poet-prophet is, then, more akin to a tradition of thieving than of divine madness; she plunders the tradition that has authorized her voice. The speaker of *Angels* conceives such thieving as the recuperation of Gnostic wisdom from the later orthodox church, the same church that authorizes John's words in Revelation as the monological truth of Yahweh:

> steal then, O orator,
> plunder, O poet,
>
> take what the old-church
> found in Mithra's tomb,
>
> candle and script and bell,
> take what the new-church spat upon
>
> and broke and shattered. . . .
>   (1.7–13)

The fragmented glass of traditions repressed by the orthodox church are reinvoked here as elements of the renewing alchemist's crucible. The charge of the poet-prophet is to "melt down and integrate" the fragmented glass of heretical tradition and to "re-invoke" and "re-create" in the prophetic unconscious those inspired "shards / men tread upon" (1.17–18, 20–21).

Despite (and because of) the influence of Revelation, H. D.'s speaker states that her walls, unlike those of the New Jerusalem in Revelation, are "not four-square." Section 2 stages a prophecy that both continues and diverges from Revelation, a rhetorical device that biblical authority anticipates and judges heretical.[32] Her prophecy—self-constructed, not received from above—replaces the measured walls of the New Jerusalem with a re-envisioned geometry of visionary nature, with "another shape" that

> slip[s] into the place
> reserved by rule and rite
>
> for the *twelve foundations*,
> for the *transparent glass*,
>
>
> for *no need of the sun*
> nor *moon to shine*. . . .
>   (2.5–10)

Although her role as prophet originates in the Bible, H. D.'s apocalyptic vision here disavows John's Celestial City: the twelve foundations of the walls of the New Jerusalem are "garnished" with precious stones, though with none of the stones invoked at the beginning of *Angels*; and the "transparent glass" to which John compares the streets of the City is, for H. D., an image of "rule and rite" that must be revised by her prophecy.

H. D.'s strategy is not simply to replace the figurative language of John, but to recast the ground of his metaphor—to revise his frame of reference from monologic (immutable) to transferential (mobile) language. For John, the actual light of God is the temple, a light so strong that "the city had no need of the sun, neither of the moon, to shine in it." However, H. D. revises the metaphoricity of a situation where divine light needs no "*sun* / nor *moon to shine*." John's language is based on a separation between God and prophet, where the light of God produces an extraordinary brilliance outside of the possibilities of humanity and nature. H. D.'s speaker instead combines representations of biblical revelation with those of immanent, linguistic revision, and reinscribes scientific observation of nature as prophetic vision.

The speaker of section 3 of *Angels* conjoins the voice of John and the voice of Christ. Although the authoritative voice of John from Revelation opens section 3 of *Angels*, his words in H. D.'s poem are fused with Christ's words from Revelation in such a way that the two voices are oppositional. John names what he has witnessed; H. D.'s Christ answers *naming* here with *making*:

> *I John Saw. I testify;*
> *if any man shall add*
>
> *God shall add unto him the plagues,*
> *but he that sat upon the throne* said,

I make all things new.
I John saw. I testify. . . .

(3.1–6)

H. D.'s commingled voices here more than simply oppose the prohibitive voice of John with the voice of a corrective image of Christ who makes things new. They also suggest rhetorical strategies of naming and making that are crucial to the movement in *Trilogy* away from the failure of prophecy in *Walls*.

The first lines of section 3 of Angels suggest that John both "sees" and "testifies." Indeed, John's sight is crucial in Revelation, as is his witnessing. John is the visual medium between God and the fallen world. John opens chapter 21 with the statement that he has seen the "new heaven" and "new earth." The controlling image of the chapter, his vision of the New Jerusalem, is inaugurated by the words H. D. excerpts for section 3 of *Angels*: "And I John saw the holy city . . ." (Revelation, 21:2). Nowhere in Revelation, however, does John specify that he "testifies," as H. D. has him doing in *Angels*. Instead, in Revelation 22:18, Christ proffers the testimony H. D. puts in the voice of John in section 3 of her poem: "*I John saw. I testify; / if any man shall add // God shall add unto him the plagues.*" Christ says in Revelation 22:18, "For I testify . . . If any man shall add unto these things, God shall add unto him the plagues that are written in this book." Through the sacred text of the Bible, the Logos becomes the protector of its own closure. H. D.'s Christ revises this vision of completeness and closure with a strategy that confers divinity on *making* rather than *naming*, *adding* rather than *witnessing*.

H. D.'s revisions of Revelation are consistent with her revision of popular conceptions of Christianity and pacifism during the war. Arguing that the Church is the natural, transhistoric complement to the materialist State, Bell asserts that the Church redeems because it is "witness to a Revelation in history. It speaks of the realities which outlast change."[33] If, however, "it is the function of the Church at all costs to remain the Church," then the witnessing of which Bell speaks is actually outside of an ahistorical Church itself: for Bell, only the orthodox have the power to redeem a world rent by war. H. D.'s focus on heretical countertradition foregrounds the history Bell ignores. Her speaker conceives of a Revelation in history: not a history only of commerce and war between nations, but also the history of interchurch transactions suppressed as part of the account of an external God's transhistorical victory over heresy. Like Moravianism, H. D.'s version of visionary history welcomes a conception of unfixed moral law, where the Church is based on the variance of individual particulars rather than the sealed protection of closure.

Indeed, as H. D.'s use of Thoth in *Walls* suggests, her representations of prophecy demand that the prophet take on the attributes of the god whose frame-of-reference s/he writes from. The prophet is the god, and speaks from an illuminated perspective that, H. D. suggests in *Notes on Thought and Vision*, is available to all. Although John speaks from the point of view of Christ at the beginning of section 3 of *Angels*, the perspective of the section eventually shifts. John's articulation of Christ's prohibition in Revelation is contrasted in *Angels* with the redemptive words of Christ—of *"he that sat upon the throne"*—in the same book. Whereas John warns in *Angels* against prophetic revisionism, Christ follows with a correction of John that emphasizes a revision of the orthodox belief that the Logos is the irreducible measure of divine representation: *"I make all things new."*

By drawing from biblical authority, H. D. risks the possibility that John's controlling metaphor for femininity, the Whore of Babylon, might remain as a residue in her own prophecy. H. D.'s strategy here might seem to negate her use of embodied female desire as a sign of redemption. The Whore of Babylon is saturated with prophetic signifiers H. D. takes from the Bible: she is "arrayed in purple and scarlet colour, and decked with gold and precious stones and pearls" (Revelation, 17:4). However, the function of female sexuality in John's image of her, as the begetter of false prophecy, stands in direct contrast to H. D.'s emphasis on immanent desire as a crucial component of prophetic representation. She holds "a golden cup in her hand full of abominations and filthiness of her fornication" (Revelation, 17:4).[34]

As the failure of vision in *Walls* suggests, even H. D.'s images of redemption must be revised under the apocalyptic pressure of the Blitz. Therefore, the distinction between true and false prophecy in Revelation serves a second purpose in H. D.'s revision: by putting the words of Christ into the mouth of John's debased representations of femininity, H. D. differentiates the Christ of monotheism from the Christ of *Notes on Thought and Vision*. In so doing, she distinguishes the patristic Christianity of Revelation from heretical Gnostic theodicy. Her privileging of heterodoxy over orthodoxy sharply contrasts the prohibitive elements of John's representation of Christ with those elements of Christ that signify redemption in the New Testament and in *Trilogy*. Whereas an anagrammatic representation of Osiris might hold forth the ambisexual promise of Sirius-Isis, it also might degenerate into the *"zrr-hiss"* of wartime violence circumscribed by religious orthodoxy. H. D.'s John violates the prohibitions of his own orthodoxy when he speaks the words of Christ; H. D.'s Christ renews the world, yet comes bearing the signs of "bitter, unending wars":

> *I John saw. I testify,*
>
> but *I make all things new,*
> said He of the seven stars,

> he of the seventy-times-seven
> passionate, bitter wrongs,
>
> He of the seventy-times-seven
> bitter, unending wars.
>   (3.6–12)

The speaker of section 3 has rendered the authoritative voices of both John and Christ indeterminate; in doing so, she has initiated a process whereby an alternative representation of Messianic redemption might be crafted.

H. D.'s delineation of false prophecy stages the drama of redemption that constitutes the remainder of *Angels*. The speaker will defy the prohibitions of Revelation, just as she has done with her conjunction of John and Christ; with such a method H. D. re-envisions the patristic violence of Revelation and, as she sees it, the world war it underwrites. Yet her rupture from Revelation does not erase the continuity of a prophetic authority that draws on the Bible as one of its religious sources. Thus in section 4, the speaker directly speaks back to Christ, and emphasizes the inability of traditional prophecy to adequately represent what H. D. sees as the redemptive needs of the current age. Images of biblical violence pervade this section, framed by the speaker's emphasis on the insufficiency of the prophetic lineage she rewrites: "Not in our time, O Lord, / the plowshare for the sword . . ." (4.1–2). The lack of signs of redemption during the war—the lack of pacifist voices (traditionalist or revisionary)—is linked to the lack of a prophetic voice adequate to the task of representing revelation in the modern world:

> no grape-leaf for the thorn,
>
> no vine-flower for the crown;
> not in our time, O King,
>
> the voice to quell the re-gathering,
> thundering storm.
>   (4.6–10)

H. D. wrote *Angels* during a temporary lull in the bombing, a period that nevertheless assured a "regathering" of the "thundering storm" of military force. To take on the task of regathering a prophetic voice for modern prophecy, H. D. first sets out to rename the Angels of Apocalypse, the angels in Revelation who themselves herald the "thundering storm" to which John's prophecy builds.

The basis for H. D.'s authoritative renaming lies in fragments of original Hebraic representation, as it did for Blake in *Milton*. What is at stake in this section of *Angels* is precisely who is authorized to voice—to offer tribute to—the Angels of Apocalypse. Reaching back to fragments of Hebrew and

Christian countertradition, H. D. creates an alternative to the coercive impulse of John's language in Revelation. In her re-envisioning of Revelation, H. D.'s speaker has shown that the figure who names the Angels of Apocalypse also marks out the "not four-square" boundaries of prophetic representation. In *Trilogy*, H. D.'s speaker names angels of apocalypse who authorize the alchemical "plunder[ing]" of established prophetic tradition, where John's Whore of Babylon and Christ's prohibition against prophetic revision construct the New Jerusalem of Revelation on the foundation of patristic, prohibitive monotheism. Here, in the figural crucible of "broke[n] and shattered" heretical tradition (1.13), the speaker combines *marah* and *mar*, the respective feminine and masculine Hebrew words for "bitter," to create a mode of prophetic representation that resists the patristic representation of apocalypse in John:

> Now polish the crucible
> and set the jet of flame
>
> under, till *marah-mar*
> are melted, fuse and join. . . .
>   (8.7–10)

Whereas in traditional Christianity, Adam names the earth and John names the New Jerusalem, H. D.'s speaker re-enacts the divine representation of Pistis Sophia, the female figure of resurrection in the Gnostic faith (36.1–2). *Marah-mar* becomes "mer, mere, mère, mater, Maia, Mary, / Star of the Sea, / Mother" (8.12–14). Representations of divine femininity and masculinity become heterodox figures of female divinity.

More important for modern prophecy, the speaker's focus on heretical renaming infuses representations of metaphysical transcendence—of the desire for the "Holy Ghost"—with immanent images of rebirth. The flowering apple tree of section 23 becomes in section 25 a re-envisioning of John's image of the visionary New Jerusalem: the ticking mechanism of the clock and the inspirational apple tree represent materialist manifestations of metaphysical revelation. In Revelation, John reports that the Celestial City was so bright from the light of God that it needed no sun or moon for illumination; H. D. borrows this image to offer an immanent frame for her prophetic vision of the Lady, whose presence transforms the phosphorous mechanism of the illuminated clock face into the "dim, luminous disc" of a clock-like moon (and moon-like clock) that has no need of the God of Revelation to shine in it. The measure of prophecy here is both mechanical and mythopoeic; it is "Phosphorous at sun-rise, / Hesperus at sun-set" (10.13–14).[35]

For H. D., the power to create such vision emerges, of course, from the revisionary potential of psychoanalysis to turn the contrarietous observations stored in the unconscious into visionary transformations of the conscious mind. As a figure of both materialist psychoanalysis and transcendent vision, H. D.'s Lady is as much a figure who "makes new" the metaphysics of modern prophecy as she is a coded figure of desire.[36] Freud, the speaker's "patron" in section 13 of *Angels*, encourages the speaker to rename the natural world as visionary. He asks her to name the color of the jewel she holds. She replies that its color cannot be represented by the immanence of the color spectrum; it emits "a vibration that we can not name" (13.10). She repeats that "there is no name" for the light of this jewel, a stone that prefigures the precious stones and illuminations of the Celestial City. The stone also represents the prophetic renaming, hence re-envisioning, of the Celestial City in *Angels*: the speaker renames the Angels of Apocalypse by re-envisioning the discourses of science and religion whose coercive representations elide representations of female divinity.

The Lady arrives in a moment between clock-time and the imaginative instant, part of H. D.'s modern prophetic revision of scientific measurement. Despite psychoanalytic explanation for the dream, in which the ticking becomes dream-knocking only so that the body might keep itself asleep, the speaker of *Angels* dramatizes a vision in which materialist psychoanalysis mediates immanent and transcendent measurements of vision. Even though her appearance can be explained by Freud's science, the Lady nevertheless is not explained away. The Lady "was there more than ever, / as if she had miraculously / related herself to time here" (27.2–4). Although such vision is "difficult / even for the experienced stranger," H. D. insists, in *Notes on Thought and Vision*, that gods are not the only creatures capable of a visionary fusion of immanent and transcendent representation: the Lady who remakes the world is both a product of the speaker's unconscious and a revelatory apparition (27.5–6). The central figure of prophecy for H. D. is a condensed form of she who has been the Lady, Mary, Pistis Sophia, and the Pythoness throughout.

4. "GEOMETRY ON THE WING": APOCALYPSE AND "THE FLOWERING OF THE ROD"

The task of the speaker in *Angels* is inspired by her patron's remarks on the stone in section 13. After the speaker reiterates that no name can represent the illumination of the stone, the patron articulates what will become both the speaker's call to action and a representation of her revision of this call to action: "he said, / 'invent it.'" Although prophecy in *Angels* is fueled by energetic renaming, H. D.'s strategies for reinvention are met with resistance in the opening sections of *Flowering*. The core of this resistance lies in

H. D.'s conception of language and nature in *Trilogy*, and her work to fashion a prophetic language adequate to the representation of nature as visionary.

The troubling insistence of her patron's urging to reinvent the prophetic line in *Angels* carries over into *Flowering*. The speaker asserts in the opening of *Flowering* that resurrection frames the entire book. Yet once asserted, the desire for resurrection immediately develops into ambivalence. Much like her response to the failed anagrams of *Walls*, the speaker is alternately "[s]atisfied, unsatisfied" by her prophecy in sections 4 and 5 of *Flowering*. Her words articulate a "double nostalgia" of dissatisfaction, represented by images of unfulfilling transformations of the natural world: winter produces "insatiable longing" for summer, whereas flecks of foam from summer tides recall images of winter she refuses to relinquish.

Double nostalgia becomes a trope, however, for the dichotomies H. D. negotiates in her rhetoric of vision:

> In resurrection, there is confusion
> if we start to argue; if we stand and stare,
> we do not know where to go. . . .
> *(Flowering, 3.1–3)*

The problem for the speaker of *Flowering* is to construct a language that will deploy ambivalence as a vital component of vision. In *Flowering*, figures of prophecy "argue" and "stare" as the speaker conceives of a mode of language that turns monovocal utterances into conversational multivocality, that transforms the stare of observation into visionary perception.

The speaker's confusion is cast as a failure of geometric vision: the speaker's "despair" at her patron's words in *Angels* results from a failed "desire to equilibrate / the eternal variant" (5.4–5). For the speaker, "the desire to equilibrate" must not negate metaphysical variance, but rather oscillate within the epistemological continuum suggested by such variance. Her prophetic assertion, finally, that "resurrection is a sense of direction" repositions the ambivalence of the earliest parts of this section on the border between the visionary and the observational: she states in section 7 that her prophecy makes a "bee-line" to the "plunder" of the ancient traditions that, paradoxically, authorize her as poet-prophet and also present the greatest challenge to her desire to equilibrate a resurrective "eternal variant."

Later in section 7, a possible resolution emerges, grounded in H. D.'s experience with Moravian "gift" economy. The speaker states that "resurrection is remuneration" (7.6). As *remuneration*, then, resurrection is the hidden "treasure" her syncretist method has sought to reveal all along in the poem. More importantly, the etymology of *remuneration* indicates that resurrection in *Trilogy* rewards with a treasure that has never truly been hidden, never truly in need of revelation because always present. Remuneration, "giving back," derives from the Latin for "gift." Considered in light of H. D.'s Moravian tradition, her use of *remuneration* here combines the resurrective potential of the present-day war with Moravian insistence on a spiritual "gift" economy. In her autobiographical novel, *The Gift*, H. D. represents Moravian gift economy in terms of a matrilineal prophetic tradition: her grandmother, Mamalie, initiates H. D. into a line of seekers, possessors of a spiritual gift of vision. If "resurrection is a beeline" to "the honeycomb" of matrilineal, remunerative prophecy, then the speaker argues in section 8 that she is "the first or the last / of a flock or a swarm." Although the speaker adopts the words of Christ in Revelation, the "Alpha and Omega, the beginning and the end, the first and the last," the voice of Christ she appropriates assures, of course, no revelation for revisionist prophets. However, as the Alpha and Omega of a "swarm"—an image of the modern prophet's bee-line away from an orthodox flock—the speaker revises the authoritative language of Revelation, a crucial mode of rhetoric in the previous two books of *Trilogy*. H. D.'s speaker voices the words of Christ in *Flowering*; as when John takes on the voice of Christ in *Angels*, this strategy is part of the speaker's revisionary method to empty the transcendent value of Revelation.

In *Flowering* the speaker portrays what seems like biblical precedence for such revisionary rhetoric. Yet her rhetorical strategy empties the transcendent, monotheistic Christ of Revelation by turning biblical irony against itself. In Acts 2:17, Yahweh articulates a mode of prophecy that seems closely allied to the apocalyptic rhetoric of both Blake and H. D.: "in the last days, saith God, I will pour out of my Spirit upon all flesh: and your sons and your daughters shall prophesy, and your young men shall see visions, and your old men shall dream dreams." H. D.'s speaker incorporates the ironic language of Acts that derides those who speak false prophecy. "I am *full of new wine*," H. D. writes, alluding to Christ's distinction between true revelation and false, drunken prophecy: some found the speaking in tongues to be revelatory, while true Christians "mocking said, These men are full of new wine" (Acts 2:13). In Acts, the inspired are mocked for vision; in *Flowering*, however, H. D. mocks all who would believe that only authorized biblical texts are visionary.

H. D. uses the double function of *tongues* here to remake her double nostalgia. Her embrace and revision of biblical prophetic tradition is "[n]o poetic fantasy / but a biological reality, / a fact" (9.1–3). Speaking in tongues is both a metaphor for an overlay of divine language and a representation of the localizing of prophecy in many bodies, many real tongues, and many directions of desire. These embodied tongues speak from an internally authorized divinity that, in the context of H. D.'s rhetoric of vision, violates the prohibitions against prophetic revision in Revelation.

Even though Yahweh decrees in Acts that as the apocalypse approaches,

many would speak in divine tongues and commit themselves to prophesying, such a statement must be seen in the context of literary-historical biblical exegesis in order for the full extent of H. D.'s countertraditional method
to be understood. Convention would demand a reading of Acts in which
Yahweh does not will individuals to respond with original prophecy. Instead, Yahweh's remarks in the passage to which H. D. alludes are interpreted to mean that the prophesying foretold in Acts is a future phenomenon
wherein the work of the biblical prophets will be retold by those speaking
in divine tongues. As Gershom Scholem explains, tradition demands that
"Truth must be laid bare in a text in which it already pre-exists."[37] To speak in
tongues, then, would be simply to reaffirm the words of the biblical prophets.

H. D. instead crafts a revisionary rhetoric that is, like Blakean Poetic
Genius, available to all, and is "infectious" (9.10). Her tropes nevertheless
veer dangerously close to self-dismissive divine madness, where the speaker
indeed might only be "full of new wine." Sections 8 and 9 of *Flowering*
nearly identify her voice as divinely mad. The speaker blithely acknowledges that she is "so happy" despite the violence of the war; her body becomes passive and is consumed by the Logos, "branded with a word"; as a
figure for dangerous prophetic mania she is "burnt with wood," the fate of
those who identified themselves in the medieval era as countertraditional
prophets (8.1, 5–6). Furthermore, the "biological reality" she describes as
"infectious" is "ecstasy," which identifies her with the liminal ancient Hebrew "ecstatic prophets" and with those who, like Plato's Ion, become
smitten with maniacal enthusiasm as a result of their own exegesis.

Yet *Trilogy* has emphasized that poetic prophecy is "remunerative." What
seems like divine madness actually is "a sense of direction." The speaker's
disavowal of discourses of mania reinforces the role of gender politics in
the construction of prophetic agency in *Angels*. Proof of the rightness—the
empirical or biological "reality"—of the female prophet's voice is found in
the wartime ruins of the natural world: "It is no madness to say / you will
fall, you great cities, / (now the cities lie broken)" (10.1–3). The words of
the female prophet, she argues here, are not traditional prophecy at all:
these words do not emerge from prophetic mania, nor are they the product
of a hysteric's "wandering womb." Double nostalgia and polysemous spoken tongues are crafted into a language whose purpose is to transform observation into prophetic vision. The "lonely Pythoness . . . who sings / in
broken hexameters" shatters the traditional metrics of biblical prophecy—
hexameters, according to Lowth, a reading later embraced by Blake—into
a moment of visionary measure. In a world where Osiris becomes the *zrr-
hiss* of the Blitz, prophecy "is simply reckoning, algebraic, / it is geometry
on the wing" (10.11–12).

The goal of *Flowering*, however, is not to make geometric the particulars of prophetic vision; instead, H. D. re-envisions prophecy in terms of

her effort to recast the body in time as the visionary body in nature. The book culminates in a sense of apocalypse that reclaims the tree flowering amid the ruins in the previous book as the resurrective product of matrilineal prophecy: the prophecy of the Pythoness "*is the greatest among herbs / and becometh a tree*" (10.31–32).

Much has been written about how H. D.'s fluctuating protagonists in the poem—H. D. herself, the third-person speaker of the poem, and the voices of John and Christ—culminate in *Flowering* as a figure for the modern female prophet.[38] H. D. herself sees the identities of her female prophet as overdetermined: "O, there shall be Marys a-plenty" (*Flowering*, 16.9). Of course, the condensed figure of Mary is crucial to the re-envisioning impulse of the whole of the poem. H. D.'s Mary is both female and male ("for Magdala is a tower"), both painful and resurrective ("[though I am Mara, bitter] I shall be Mary-myrrh"), and both the countertraditional Mary of Magdala ("unseemly") and the traditional mother of Christ ("I am that myrrh-tree of the gentiles").[39] In section 16, then, H. D. makes an important distinction, insofar as her "Marys a-plenty" represent female prophecy grounded in an oscillating identity: that is, a female prophecy that is a fluid plentitude measurable only by the transferential language of modern prophecy, and not representable by the reificatory language of the established Church.[40] H. D.'s "Marys a-plenty" are part of an attempt to resist coercive, phallic language; in this way, Mary might also resist the disciplinary sphere of religious discourse that would reify authorized prophetic language into justification for patristic religious institutions. What is at stake in *Flowering* is more than H. D.'s revision of prophecy to include a significant voice of female agency. H. D.'s feminist prophecy revises a linguistic tradition where "one God, Father Almighty" circumscribes a world predicated upon absolutist, univocal material representation.

The figure for H. D.'s resistance to the established Church emerges in H. D.'s turn from narration to conversation in *Flowering*: the point where, to echo Blake, Mary and Kaspar "converse in visionary forms dramatic." H. D.'s revisionary modern prophetic strategy, like Blake's, is predicated on a method that re-envisions biblical authority in terms of apocalyptic representation. Thus, in section 21 of *Flowering*, a direct echo of the scene in John where Mary anoints the feet of Christ, apocalyptic representation is staged in terms of an "un-weaving," an *un-writing* of the authority of the metaphysical Logos. Mary "deftly un-weav[es]" her long hair, which will wipe the feet of Christ, and in so doing forecasts the scene of her apocalyptic conversation later with Kaspar.

H. D. dramatizes a fetishistic aspect of the Magdalene's unweaving in her revision of Moravian sacraments of desire. Moravian enaction and repression of the homosocial component of same-gender foot-washing is recovered in H. D.'s revisionary portrayal of the Magdalene's "[e]xtravagent" and "extraordinary" hair (21.8, 18). The unweaving undertaken by the female prophet creates the conditions for her visionary exchange with Kaspar, whereby the "minute particulars" of a visionary nature can be conceived. Like the apple-leaf in *Notes on Thought and Vision*, or like the grains of sand in Blake's "Mock On Mock On" and "Auguries of Innocence," the gems that circle Mary's head become, collectively, for Kaspar "the speck, fleck, grain or seed" which is "the whole secret of the mystery" of visionary consciousness (30.8, 11).

The language of Mary and Kaspar, then, must be suffused with what H. D. describes in *Walls* as the "minute particulars" of the visionary, natural world:

> And he saw it all as if enlarged under a sun-
>   glass;
> he saw it all in minute detail,
> . . . .
>
> and through it, there was a sound as of many
>   waters,
> rivers flowing and fountains and sea-waves washing
>   the sea-rocks,
>
> and though it was all on a very grand scale,
> yet it was small and intimate,
>
> Paradise
> before Eve. . . .
>   (32.1–2; 9–14; H. D.'s ellipsis)

"[E]nlarged under a sun-glass," the particulars of Kaspar's vision point to an originary moment in Christian history. Kaspar's vision emerges from "minute detail," a "grand scale" that also is "small and intimate." As a moment of continuity and revision, this moment "before Eve" either threatens to extend the moment in Christian history when Eve is charged with the Fall, or it promises to renovate images of the feminine. As Susan Schweik notes, literature of World War II often divided its representation of maternity into two categories: first, where motherhood "prop[s]" the war with an "urging" that is "secretly and strangely jubilant"; and a second, where, by contrast, a gynocentric community emerges from "a maternity and a birth scenario before, beyond, and outside war."[41] Poised out of time at the birth of a Christian history of divided genders, Kaspar's vision is infused with material relevance. The solidarity of biblical redemption is revised by an attention to "minute particulars" on a "grand scale": maternity and birth "before, beyond, and outside" what H. D. terms "seventy-times-seven / bitter, unending wars."

H. D.'s incorporation of mechanisms of measurement in her prophecy revises the codes of masculinity and femininity that circulate within representations of maternity and wartime violence. The promise of the "sunglass" clarifies the opacity of "Paradise / before Eve," and represents the attempt in *Trilogy* to revise a world self-manacled by notions of the Fall. In *The Gift*, H. D. represents her desire to see the Blitz as apocalyptic by recalling childhood images of her father's professional work as an astronomer. The visionary gift of the Moravian community, H. D. argues, could be realized in science if observation were recast into vision. Her father is "a pathfinder, an explorer" who is guided to precise vision of the skies by "the new instruments" (*The Gift*, 41–42). Yet his work isolates him from the domestic sphere where cultural codes of womanhood circulate, and where these cultural codes are refashioned by Mamalie into a matrilineal line of prophecy. Her father is separated from the passing-on of "the gift" of prophecy from mother to daughter in *The Gift*. His gift of science takes him "out of doors," but H. D.'s gift is passed on in interior spaces—dreams and the domestic space of the home: "Papa did not tell us what he was doing. . . . What it was, was that he was separate . . ." (*The Gift*, 42–43). The remunerative gift, then, depends on sharply named lines of identity and work, even though the labor of vision in *Trilogy* produces a prophecy of unfixed nomination.

H. D.'s heretical prophecy blurs these lines of demarcation in the visionary conversation between Mary and Kaspar. What is transmitted in Mary and Kaspar's psychic dialogue is a visionary history presumably "out-of-time completely" to those whose frame of reference is circumscribed only by the Judeo-Christian theodicy. H. D. has made clear that her figures of prophecy here are outlaws in the traditional Western prophetic line. Mary is "unseemly"; she is so far from the law that her anointment of Christ's feet causes Simon to consider that the authority of Christ's prophecy might also be marginal: "*this man if he were a prophet, would have known / who and what manner of woman this is*" (*Flowering*, 23.13–14). Kaspar is a Hermetic who might even be "an old lover / of Mary Magdalene" (20.6, 19–20). Yet the demons cast from Mary Magdalene are figures Kaspar "might call / . . . *daemons*" (25.8–9). Indeed, both Mary and Kaspar undertake their visionary dialogue with the understanding that what is heretical or countertraditional about their conception of nature and vision is actually a source of inspiration. Kaspar invokes the revisionary power of the demons:

> he might re-name them,
> Ge-meter, De-meter, earth-mother
> or Venus
> in a star.
>
> (25.17–20)

The demonic is re-envisioned as the redemptive *daemonic* when seen from the frame of reference of H. D.'s prophecy, where scientific measure is transformed into vision: the demonic is renamed "Phosphorous at sun-rise, / Hesperus at sun-set." Kaspar can "whisper tenderly" the names of the demons "for technically / Kaspar was a heathen" (25.11–13).

The moment in *Flowering* when Kaspar gazes upon the precious stones in Mary's hair recalls the image and function of the inspirational shell in *Walls*, where the shell is the source for the speaker's construction of a prophetic language that represents nature as visionary:

> And Kaspar heard
> an echo of an echo in a shell,
> *in her were forgiven*
> *the sins of the seven*
> *daemons cast out of her*
>   (28.1–2)

The crux of the shell in *Walls* is its representation of the "nothing-too-much" word of modern prophecy. The speaker notes that the shell "opens to the tide-flow"; once she absorbs the identity of the shell, she claims to "sense [her] own limit." Together, the oscillation between flow and limit produces the resurrective prophetic word. The movement of selfhood occasioned by the shell "beget[s], self-out-of-self, / selfless, / that pearl-of-great-price." Kaspar experiences much of the same fluidity in *Flowering*.[42] He sees jewels both delimited and overflowing. Kaspar, the diamond merchant who "knew more about precious stones than any other," is struck by the power of the unorthodox stones to reflect this delimited and overflowing vision: at the sight of the stones, he is "filled with a more exalted ecstasy / than any valuer over a new tint of rose or smoke-grey / in an Indian opal or pearl" (28.15, 17–19).

Kaspar perceives in his visionary commerce with Mary the recasting of observation into vision that is crucial to H. D.'s rhetoric of prophecy:

> . . . the reflecting inner facets
> seemed to cast incalculable angles of light,
>
> this blue shot with violet;
> how convey what he felt?
>   (28.27–30)

What Kaspar sees in this moment is his own prophetic frame of reference reflecting back: "the echo / of an echo in a shell" becomes a "hieroglyph" seen "clearly / as in a mirror" (33.1–2; 39.23; 40.2–3).

As H. D. suggests throughout *Flowering*, the visionary dialogue of prophecy is not to be mistaken for divine madness. What the audience might see "mirror[ed]" is not necessarily a doubling back of repetitive, empty ana-grams—not necessarily a language of passions that bewitches prophet and audience because they are inspired by an extra-natural god. H. D. suggests in section 40 that Kaspar's "discipline and study / of old lore" contributed to his visionary dialogue with Mary (40.4–5). In this way, the labor of vision taken up by Kaspar and Mary is analogous to that of H. D. and Bryher on Corfu. Together, these visionary dyads form a metaphor for the relationship of prophet to audience in the modern world: as with Blake, in H. D. the prophetic poet needs an audience equal to the task of perceiving corrosive devils as inspirational *daemons*.

   She posits that the force that blurs the distinction between prophet and audience can be framed as a geometry of prophetic vision—that the mea-sure of such vision might be mathematized:

> no one would ever know
> if it could be proved mathematically
>
> by demonstrated lines,
> as an angle of light
>
> reflected from a strand of a woman's hair,
> reflected again or refracted . . .
>   (40.17–22)

As in *Angels*, where incidence equals reflection in visionary conscious-ness, in *Flowering* vision is represented as the measure of the natural world:

> . . . perhaps it was a matter of vibration
>
> that matched or caught an allied
> or exactly opposite vibration
>
> and created a sort of vacuum,
> or rather a point in time . . .
>   (40.24–28)

These concerns never extend beyond the conditional mood in *Trilogy*. What is at stake, however, is how the conditional mood might represent resurrective consciousness at the end of the poem, where an ambiguous Christ child is held *as if* myrrh in the arms of the outlaw, female prophet. Just as Christ is sexualized in Moravian theodicy and in H. D.'s *Notes on Thought and Vision*, here H. D.'s Christ exists in that conditional moment when angles of incidence and reflection coincide in a moment — "a point" in time that is an immanent principle of visionary desire.

The winepress Blake borrows from Revelation in *Milton* becomes the blossoming desert H. D. borrows from Isaiah for *Trilogy*. The double tongues of Mary and Kaspar's discourse spoken at once in visionary conversation equilibrate the apocalyptic "eternal variant," producing in *Flowering* a fecund, re-envisioned nature:

> . . . over-night, a million-million tiny plants
> broke from the sand,
>
> and a million-million little grass-stalks
> each put out a tiny flower,
>
> they were so small you could hardly
> visualize them separately . . .
>
> (37.3–8)

The unifying vision of the blossoming desert is represented by a language not beholden to metaphysical Logos; instead, H. D.'s anagrammatic method has emptied transcendent referentiality from language, so that prophetic language is constructed from material traces simply left by previous words and letters. Nature performs the unnatural — "snow falls on the desert"— as a result of the revisionary word, from "the bundle of myrrh" produced by the visionary conversation of Mary and Kaspar (43.7).

This birth is a figure for the visionary product of the dialogue between Kaspar and Mary, where prehistory and apocalyptic history are respective—and equal—angles of incidence and of reflection. Referentiality reaches its eschatological limit in the act of speaking in tongues, both in *Trilogy* and in H. D.'s biblical sources; but in *Trilogy* referentiality shatters, so that visionary conversation among immanent prophets might produce an apocalyptic vision of nature. The bundle of myrrh, both product and producer of this vision, enacts the unconscious logic of condensation in such a way that its identity can never wholly be fixed; the meaning of H. D.'s substitution of myrrh for the Christ child oscillates "back and forth / between the poles of heaven and earth forever" (*Flowering*, 11.5–6).

As Schweik has shown, images of the Christ child were popular tropes in World War II literature, a means of strengthening the Christian church in the face of wartime violence. Schweik also observes that crucifixion was used at the time to proffer the soldier as an image of hegemonic masculinity.[43] H. D.'s final scene, however, does more than just substitute master narratives of patristic orthodoxy for the tension of the war. As Edmunds observes, H. D. rewrites the manger scene so that the myrrh comes to represent the visionary potential of lesbian desire: "bundled from view like the unconscious, the myrrh with its invisibly escaping scent sets multiple and contradictory definitions of god's sexual identity flashing and fading upon one another" (85).[44] Moreover, with the orthodox and heterodox traditions at work in the poem, the child-as-myrrh represents the interchangability of positions within modern prophetic language, an interchangability that creates the conditions for the prophet to take the place of the god. As with H. D.'s anagrams, the myrrh draws on fragments of authorizing, monovocal past tradition in order to subject this tradition to the revisionary practice of a transferential language in which meaning is borne across multiple subject positions.

Prophetic language is reconfigured as a birth that revises the authority of the Logos: the irreducible meaning of the word (the identity of the myrrh) is displaced. John's Revelation constructs prophecy as a rhetoric that adheres to rigid, absolutist forms of meaning and privileges images of masculine power while pathologizing female power. Yet H. D.'s bundle of myrrh collapses the dichotomies that undergird traditional prophetic discourse. Walls do fall at the end of *Flowering*: walls that separate "Prophetess" from prophecy, prophets from gods, prophets from audiences.

What Edmunds questions as the debilitating "privatizing vision" of Kaspar is an opportunity for H. D. to collapse the boundary that separates the traditionally private sphere of feminine discourse from the traditionally public sphere of masculinist prophecy.[45] The figurative walls that fall in *Flowering* herald a literal unveiling: the birth of a Christ child who literalizes the redemptive urgency of the poem. As Margaret Homans notes in *Bearing the Word: Language and Female Experience in Nineteenth-Century Women's Writing*, the language of modern patriarchy structures the dyad of subject and object so that the woman who seeks the role of subject in language "must continually guard against" the cultural conditions that would define her by returning her "to the position of the object."[46] Such an effect of modern patriarchal structures is especially acute, Homans argues, in portrayals of motherhood. Androcentric literary tradition shifts the mother from subject to object by shifting her from speaking subject to literal, "silent object of representation," the "place of the absent object" (Homans, 32). If, as H. D.'s Gnostic sources would teach, God is both father and mother, then her closing scene represents a public form of discourse— prophecy—that revises the way mothering is deployed in modern patriarchal forms of culture. Traditionally the *object* of discourse, the mother here becomes the *agent* of public prophecy. The Mary of *Flowering* inhabits the space of the silent object in order to transform herself into speaking subject, into a prophet whose child—a fragrance—is a Messianic alternative to the orthodox Man of "seventy-times-seven / bitter, unending wars."

H. D.'s "suppressed desire to be a Prophetess" manifests itself during World War II in prophetic poetry that remeasures religion and science to conceive a world where nature is visionary. H. D. revises transcendent mythos into a materialist poetics of prophecy. This transformation places her work squarely at odds with a wartime culture whose only prominent pacifist voice, Bishop Bell, framed pacifism as a transcendentalist answer to armed conflict. Transcendentalism inspired and endangered H. D.'s prophetic response to World War II. In *Trilogy*, H. D. characterizes the same biblical sources that authorized her prophecy as discourses that also would substitute "poetic fantasy" for "biological reality." Within the Church itself, H. D. also found sustenance and threat. Bishop Bell's pacifism allowed the Church to "analyze the issues" and "rebuke the aggressor." Yet he envisioned the Church as "disinterested and independent" within its historical moment; for Bell, the Church stands outside of both historical contingency and national politics.

Although it may seem artificial to place final emphasis on the comparison between H. D. and Bell, I highlight their differences partly to demonstrate the paucity of voices speaking for pacifism during the war. More importantly, the contrast between H. D. and Bell illuminates important distinctions within the limited pacifist discourses in circulation: Bell's propounding an orthodox prophecy both supernatural and disinterested, H. D.'s a syncretic model so immersed in the history of Christianity that transcendentalism would be self-defeating. My point, then, is not to vilify Bell, but to emphasize that in *Trilogy* the monovocal "note" of universalist religious discourse is presented as untenable for modern prophecy.

H. D. shows that in a world where necessary knowledge is measured by the productions of industry and technology, a transcendentalist conception of prophetic language is nearly impossible. As a woman and modern prophet, H. D. crafts a voice to disrupt the traditions of masculinist science and religion. To do so, her language must revise the very discourses that authorize it; thus, she borrows from science and religion in order to collapse the distinctions each makes between visible and invisible, natural and supernatural. Because for Bell the Church is outside of history, a prophecy that induces a call to pacifism "should speak only what the moral law compels it to speak" (27). The Church only "touches the invisible" (25). H. D.'s prophetic call to pacifism in *Trilogy*, however, empties claims to universality from moral law and classical physics. *Trilogy* uses biblical prophecy to demonstrate that the Universal Church cannot exist: particular subjects—here women and those of heretical faiths—are elided by such universality; a more comprehensive pacifist response squares the metaphysical authority of prophecy with the immanent measure of its voice in language, time, and space.

4

"Sanity a Trick of Agreement": Madness and Doubt in Ginsberg's Prophetic Poetry

1. INTRODUCTION: "WE SAY ANYTHING WE WANT TO SAY"

In 1943, the young Allen Ginsberg traveled by ferry from his home in Paterson, New Jersey, to Columbia University for his freshman entrance examination. On the way, he "[p]rayed on ferry to help mankind if admitted —vowed . . . inspired by Sacco Vanzetti, Norman Thomas, Debs, Altgeld, Sandburg, Poe" (*Kaddish*, 214). Ginsberg narrates this excursion in *Kaddish*, and the prayer/vow recalled and recorded there affirms his childhood desire to become an "honest revolutionary labor lawyer" (214). As Michael Schumacher notes, Ginsberg concluded by his late teens that "if he was going to make an impact on his world, it would be as a lawyer, not a writer."[1] Barry Miles argues that the ferry vow "gave direction to Ginsberg's activities over the years, and that he used it as a benchmark whenever he was confused by a choice of courses of action."[2] As both vow and prayer, Ginsberg's articulation on the ferry affirms the activist impulse that would sustain his later prophetic poetry; that "benchmark" moment forecasts his later project as a writer of prophetic poetry situated at an intersection of law, desire, and religion.

Ginsberg's prophetic vows begin with lawyering. They are modulated by his emphasis on the visionary (and revisionary) possibilities of three influential religious and juridico-medical discourses of his era: the emerging revisions of adaptive psychoanalysis suggested by the antipsychiatric movement, Blake's biblical revisionism, and the Beat synthesis of Western religion and Buddhism. Later, these three converge in Ginsberg's study with Chögyam Trungpa, a Tibetan lama and practitioner of the "Crazy

Wisdom" school of Buddhism. Through his study in Crazy Wisdom, Ginsberg sought to "reconcile" law, religion, and desire by divesting all three of their "legality."

Like Blake's and H. D.'s, Ginsberg's prophetic poetry is sustained by an ambivalent desire for a primal language, a language both elemental and visionary. Ginsberg's language in *Howl* combines transcendent and immanent modes of representation, creating what he calls in his 1986 *Howl* annotations a "mystical" and "commonsensical" language for prophecy (*Howl: Original Draft Facsimile*, 124). Blake seeks an apocalyptic language of "Litteral expression" in *Milton*; however, his Christ is a revision of Milton's, combining the metaphysical authority of biblical prophecy with the conversational rhetoric of Milton's Satan. Blake's version of the "specular mount" of *Paradise Regained* is a secular mount, and produces a "litteral" language on the littoral boundary between metaphysicality and materiality. In *Trilogy*, H. D. recovers lost linguistic traces of female divinity, but rewrites them in an immanent representation of resurrection. H. D.'s Christ child is reborn as a representation of ancient language—Hebrew, Egyptian, and early Christian—yet this child is actually portrayed as a fragrance, a material sign of a transcendent authority whose gender remains unfixed and mobile. Like H. D.'s final image in *Trilogy*, the key bequeathed by Naomi in the closing narrative sections of *Kaddish* represents a prophetic language sustained and threatened by nonsense and doubt.

Ginsberg deploys the psychiatric institution as a locus of both inspiration and decay in *Kaddish*. The revisionary religious discourse of *Kaddish* emerges from the background of the worldwide antipsychiatric movement, a postwar shift in mind science that investigated whether the demonized experiences of mental patients might actually model visionary states of consciousness. While the distinction between psychiatry and antipsychiatry is well known, it has not been explored as a cultural context in Ginsberg's poetry. For such pioneers in the field as R. D. Laing and the sociologist Erving Goffman, the shift away from demonization entailed a re-envisioning of disciplining institutions such as the industrial-age family and the asylum. In texts such as *Sanity, Madness, and the Family* (begun just a year before the composition of *Kaddish*), Laing examines the etiology of schizophrenia not only from the perspective of the patient's perceived biological maladaptation, but also from the locus of the patient's family and social structures.[3] Goffman equates the lives and developments of asylum patients with the careers of persons in the professions, a comparison of no small consequence in an era when postwar industrial conformity created a professional, careerist middle class that both encouraged and criticized such pressures to conform. In *Howl* and *Kaddish*, Ginsberg identifies the adaptive process of industrial family life as the matrix of both madness and vision. For Ginsberg, this matrix is mythologized; family relations spawn monolithic figures such as Moloch and Oedipus, both of whom police the normative boundaries of language and identity.

Goffman's research into the similar experiences of patients in diverse asylum situations led him to conclude that the institutional experiences of a mental patient are hardly different from those of any person who forms his/her subjectivity in relation to the institutional parameters of a career. The Oedipal family and the totalizing asylum conjoin in Ginsberg's poetry. Both inspire prophetic language, yet both aim to silence the prophetic language produced in such a context by policing flows of language and desire. John Tytell argues in *Naked Angels: The Lives and Literature of the Beat Generation* that Beat writers responded to Cold War social and linguistic policing with figural and literal nakedness.[4] Tytell's claim that Beat nakedness "signified rebirth" and a "recovery of identity" is valuable, yet Tytell's history narrates only part of the story (4). For Ginsberg, silencing and policing work in tandem to produce a language for prophecy. Ginsberg's revisionary strategies proceed both from a *recovery* and a *re-covering* of postwar identity.

Ginsberg's vow on the ferry to Columbia combines the languages of law, desire, and divinity in a vision of language that is both immanent and transcendent. Ginsberg's development of a voice for the metaphysical aims of prophecy is rooted in his physical desire for Columbia classmate Paul Roth. Ginsberg writes in *Kaddish* that his journey to Columbia "to help mankind" resulted from his desire to follow Roth, his "high school mind hero" and "first love," who also would be attending the university (214). Ginsberg's journey to the entrance exam is superimposed upon the prophetic pilgrimage of *Kaddish*. Both combine apocalyptic transcendence with the emotional and physical urgencies of human desire, a common strategy in the prophetic poetry of Blake and H. D. The apocalyptic void threatened by Cold War nuclear proliferation—and the apocalyptic rebirth promised by the rhetoric of vision in the poem—reflects Ginsberg's willingness to "la[y] down life" for Roth and follow him to Columbia. Ginsberg's project to conjoin poetry and prophecy began at Columbia. His vow "to help mankind" was framed by his desire to join Roth, his first love, there; this vow took shape first as a commitment to law, and later as a commitment to visionary poetry.

Although Ginsberg abandoned the law as a career, his early interests in law and culture influenced his work as a poet-prophet. Ginsberg's poetic prophecies incorporate discourses of twentieth-century juridico-medical establishments in order to rewrite those languages; legal and medical discourses of sexuality and madness are critical components of Ginsberg's response as a poet-prophet to postwar industrial culture. In an era when legal, psychiatric, and religious languages relegated homoerotic desire to crime, pathology and heresy, Ginsberg championed desire as crucial to the representation of a redeemed natural world in his prophetic poetry.

Even before his 1948 Blake vision, Ginsberg imagined he could create a language for redemption through revisionary strategies located at a juncture of law, religion, and science. In a 3 September 1947 letter to his father, two years before his institutionalization by state authorities to avoid a prison sentence for theft, Ginsberg combined psychoanalysis and religious redemption in a manner that resembles H. D.'s conjunction of the two in *Tribute to Freud*. In the letter, he tells his father that he is considering postponing his last year at Columbia in order to save money for psychoanalytic treatment: "Don't worry about me becoming a wastrel just because I'm trying to 'save my soul' as scientifically as possible."[5] *Soul* and *science* take shape in *Howl* and *Kaddish* as competing apocalyptic discourses that must be negotiated by the poet-prophet. Ginsberg crafts a language for prophecy between soul and science, in a boundary condition between the monologic "Jehovic" mind of Moloch and the communal Westering apocalypse of Rockland.

Howl and *Kaddish* emerge from these shifting psychiatric and social contexts. Both poems are products of an era when American culture shifted to a career-based military-industrial economy. For the Beats, as Tytell has argued, this shift created a mass culture built upon the suppression of individual emotion. Tytell demonstrates that the "self-exposure" that characterizes Beat literature was a counterstatement designed to remake self-contained Cold War language dominated by the "catchwords" of "coordination and adjustment."[6] For Tytell, the bared emotions of *Howl* and *Kaddish* represent the Beats' "recovery of identity" from Cold War censoriousness. Ginsberg's discussion of the effects of "mysterious capitalisms" on Naomi's proud communism emerges from this social and linguistic shift toward nakedness (*Kaddish*, 217). Ginsberg sought to revise the "conditioning influences of language" that were reified during the Cold War into an ideology of "coordination and adjustment" promoting national unity against communism (Tytell, 16). Tytell argues that, faced with the limitations of adaptive psychology, the Beats "danced to the music of the absurdity they saw around them" (9).

Of course, this dance was not in and of itself liberatory. Ginsberg's publisher, Lawrence Ferlinghetti, nearly went to jail on obscenity charges brought against *Howl*. Tytell sees Beat nakedness as a dance of linguistic freedom; however, Ginsberg's portrayal of hysteria and madness in *Howl* and *Kaddish* dances both to destruction and liberation, as does his re-creation of Kali in the 1962 *Indian Journals*, later revised as "Stotras to Kali Destroyer of Illusions" for the 1963 collection, *Planet News*:

> The skulls that hang on Kali's neck, Geo Washington with eyes rolled up & tongue hanging out of his mouth like a fish, N. Lenin upside down . . . an empty space for Truman, Mao Tze Tung & Chang Kai Shek shaking at the bottom of the chain, balls with eyes & noses jiggled in the Cosmic Dance. . . .[7]

Ginsberg's linguistic dance seems always poised between the Dionysian revel suggested by Tytell and the apocalyptic "shaking" of Kali. Ginsberg's Kali resembles the annihilating mother of *Kaddish* (Naomi "of the hospitals") and the maternal source of prophetic consciousness in *Kaddish* (Naomi "from whose pained head I first took vision").[8]

Desire was incorporated in Ginsberg's linguistic dance, yet desire was policed by Cold War discourses that equated normative sexual desire with national security. *Life* magazine's 1964 photo essay on male homosexuality in the United States begins with a question that reveals much about the space that non-normative desire occupied in popular media representations of Cold War domestic and international relations: "Do the homosexuals, like the Communists, intend to bury us?"[9] Ginsberg's poetry of homosocial love and desire ("laying down life" for Roth in a fantasy of "laying down"), and his poetry of communist avowal, dramatize a redemptive language that embraces transgression in order to transvalue it. Ginsberg's rhetorical strategy is a response to an era when Cold War anticommunism in the United States disciplined desire and language. Homosexuality is described by the *Life* photo-essay as a "social disorder" that "present[s] a problem"; the magazine intends to unveil it (76). The article states that "for every obvious homosexual, there are probably nine nearly impossible to detect. . . . The myth and misconception with which homosexuality has so long been clothed must be cleared away, not to condone it but to cope with it" (66).

As Lee Edelman observes, the magazine "undertakes to expose the gay male body as a social 'problem' by exposing the problem of seeing or recognizing the gay male body itself."[10] Edelman notes that in an era when homosexuality was considered a threat equivalent to communism, the language of unveiling in the *Life* article is infused with a nationalistic urge to make its audience "*better* readers of homosexuality and homosexual signs" (556). The urge to unveil, then, produces greater containment. Edelman writes that the text of the *Life* photo-essay "encourage[s]" readers to internalize "the repressive supervisory mechanisms of the State . . . by reproducing in its readers the magazine's interest in becoming aware of and learning to recognize those denizens of the gay world who are 'nearly impossible to detect'" (559).

Ginsberg's revision of Cold War representation articulates desire in a prophetic language the blurs the boundary between writer and reader. In his 1966 *Paris Review* interview—famous as the first explicit account of his Blake vision—Ginsberg describes what he terms the "problem" of creating literature with Cold War modes of representation. The problem, he writes, occurs when the writer separates "muse" from common experience and thereby, for Ginsberg, suppresses the production of speech. Ginsberg declares that the distinction between poetic decorum and common speech must be erased:

We all talk among ourselves and we have common understanding, and we say anything we want to say, and we talk about our assholes, and we talk about our cocks, and we talk about who we fucked last night, or who we're gonna fuck tomorrow, or what kind love affair we have, or when we get drunk, or when we stuck a broom in our ass in the Hotel Ambassador in Prague—anybody tells one's friends about that. So then—what happens if you make a distinction between what you tell your friends and what you tell your Muse? The problem is to break down that distinction: when you approach your Muse to talk as frankly as you would talk with yourself or with your friends.[11]

Yet in *Howl* and *Kaddish*, Ginsberg creates a language for prophecy that incorporates the *inability* to speak frankly in its rhetoric of vision. Talking "frankly"—the impulse to counter the language of "coordination" and "adjustment"—assumes that "we say anything we want to say" about desire. Yet given the experience of the *Howl* obscenity trial and the opposition to this "common understanding" by seemingly coercive Cold War discourses, such linguistic freedom must be understood figurally, not literally.

Talking "frankly" with one's Muse is as much a matter of undisciplining speech as of undisciplining mind for Ginsberg. As Tytell has argued, insistent "self-exposure" was a Beat counterstrategy to Cold War concerns with personal and public discipline. The Muse to which Ginsberg refers in the *Paris Review* interview is reconceived as internal rather than external. As he explained to Lewis MacAdams in a 1989 interview, poetic prophecy comes from an internalized conception of inspiration.[12] In *Howl* and *Kaddish*, hysteria and nakedness critically affect the creation of a prophetic language that registers the "elemental" and commonsensical outside of the coercive unity of "coordination and adjustment." Both poems operate on a boundary between the control of speech and the free flow of speech, a strategy Ginsberg developed in his years as a marketing researcher.

Ginsberg's *Paris Review* remarks share the strategy of *Howl* and *Kaddish*. Both poems reconceive the "dance" of divine madness as a simultaneously authorizing and coercive "elemental" language. Ginsberg's discussion of assholes, cocks, and broomsticks parodies an age where authorized, "common-sense" ways of thinking about language are defined by "coordination and adjustment." However, Ginsberg's own career as a writer was built by the same language of Cold War coercion he sought to counter with the "dance" of beatitude. Ginsberg's work as a market researcher in the early 1950s helped finance his move to San Francisco. As Schumacher argues, Ginsberg's marketing savvy galvanized the nascent San Francisco Renaissance of 1955; Ginsberg was the de facto literary agent of the Beats, marketing their work to publishers, sometimes editing and assembling the fragments of his colleagues' manuscripts (134–35). Spending the early 1950s in the language and culture of marketing afforded Ginsberg the opportunity to hone his rhetorical skills, "whether they involved selling book ideas to editors or hyping commercial products" (Schumacher, 134–35).

For Ginsberg, the coercive language of hype and market research both authorized and limited speech. Postwar marketing research was as much a discourse of the human sciences as were psychiatry and law; and for Ginsberg, psychiatry and law produced ambivalent effects in the construction of a language for poetic prophecy. As Lyndon O. Brown argued in his 1955 *Marketing and Distribution Research*, the "essence" of marketing research "is the use of scientific method in the solution of marketing problems."[13] For Brown, the "pioneers in marketing research" understood that the evidentiary milieu of science provided "the greatest advance" in "the special problems of marketing" (73). These problems of marketing, of course, are problems of persuasion and rhetoric, what market researcher Emory S. Bogardus termed in 1951 the "making" and "controlling" of public opinion.[14] Bogardus claimed that marketing research could solve marketing problems and contribute to the development of a pluralist democracy. In a fusion of postwar industry and capitalist governance worthy of Foucault's repressive hypothesis, Bogardus claims that "democracy depends for its life on the free formation and free expression of opinion" *and* that the "making" and "controlling" of public opinion are essential to the development of a "democratic society" (3).

As much as talking "frankly" is represented as liberatory in the *Paris Review* interview, Ginsberg's remarks are voiced within a poetry renaissance derived from the language of marketing. Schumacher reports that Ginsberg's experience included work in New York for Ipana toothpaste, researching whether consumers preferred the slogan "Ipana makes your teeth glamorous" or "Ipana makes your teeth sparkle" (Schumacher, 135). Later, these experiences with marketing research surface in his 1953 poem, "My Alba," where Ginsberg portrays the generic new dawn as an insignificant product of Cold War industry. The frank talk of the 1966 *Paris Review* interview is, in "My Alba," a form of speech alienated from the bittersweet eroticism of the alba poem by the problems of marketing.

Ginsberg's language, like that of Blake and H. D., risks absurdity in its privileging of sense and nonsense as constitutive components of equal value. In *Howl* and *Kaddish*, his protagonists are mad: Carl Solomon and Naomi are institutionalized, as the poet himself briefly was during his undergraduate years at Columbia. Yet Ginsberg creates a language for modern prophecy that embraces and revises prophetic self-identification with divine madness. Ginsberg's refusal to subsume desire to law is itself a gesture of madness in the frame of reference of Cold War psychiatric discourse: in an era when homosexuality was deemed a perversion by judicial and medical authorities, a "social problem" and a threat to national security, Ginsberg's insistence on non-normative desire as a principle of redemption risked the charge of madness.

Ginsberg has described *Kaddish* as an attempt to explore how the post-war family induces madness. Indeed, in a 1984 interview with R. D. Laing, Ginsberg credits Laing as an influence on his development in *Howl* and *Kaddish* of a language that could represent a redemptive madness.[15] Laing and Goffman contributed to a transvaluation of mental illness in postwar sciences of the mind. Where the psychiatric establishment saw mental illness as a pathology inherent in the individual human subject, Laing and Goffman argued that mental illness resulted also from coercive conditions inherent in an industrial culture in which the family was considered a private, autonomous unit separated from a collective social order. Where Laing's *Sanity, Madness, and the Family* relocated the etiology of schizophrenia in the patient's family and social world, Goffman's "On the Characteristics of Total Institutions" (1957) and "The Moral Career of the Mental Patient" (1959) argue that twentieth-century social structures enforce and reproduce madness through the policing apparatuses of schools, jails, and, especially, psychiatric institutions themselves.

Both *Howl* and *Kaddish* use institutional experience as a map for the construction of prophetic language. In his 1984 interview, Laing expresses "gratitude" to Ginsberg for the influence of *Howl*. Laing explains that the poem afforded him "consolation" during his early intellectual development, encouraging him that others shared his attitude toward what he saw as the damaging role played by postwar institutional culture on the psyche. Ginsberg, in turn, declares that the two share a "common-sense awareness" of an element of "sacred intelligence" in humanity. For both Laing and Ginsberg, madness is an institutional name for alienated states of consciousness that are non-narratable in the modern world.

Laing writes that his attempt to make schizophrenia "intelligible in the light of the praxis and process . . . of family nexus" represents a shift in psychiatric research "*no less radical than the shift from a demonological to a clinical viewpoint three hundred years ago*" [emphasis Laing's].[16] This shift includes for Laing a re-envisioning of the industrial family: the postwar institution of the family must be emptied of its cultural primacy—its naturalness—so that its role in the reproduction of madness may be examined. Arguing that the "total" nature of control in an asylum alienates the patient from traditional modes of identity formation, Goffman claims that "the craziness or 'sick behavior' claimed for the mental patient . . . is not primarily a product of mental illness" but is instead the product of the total institutional control to which the patient is subjected ("Moral Career,"130). Goffman concludes that the development of social relations is so similar among asylum inmates, no matter what disorder brings them to the institution, that these similarities in individual identity and social interaction "occur in spite of" mental illness ("Moral Career," 129). Indeed, Goffman argues, once mental patients are institutionalized, they "are confronted by some importantly similar circumstances" of total control "and respond to these in some importantly similar ways" ("Moral Career," 129).

More recent than Laing's and Goffman's work, Gilles Deleuze and Félix Guattari's *Anti-Oedipus: Capitalism and Schizophrenia* may provide a theoretical language for understanding how antipsychiatric responses to schizophrenia inform Ginsberg's language for prophecy in *Kaddish*. Deleuze and Guattari theorize that when the Oedipal model is synthesized into lived experience, violence and fascism follow as a means of disciplining identities to fit this model. They argue that the psychic component of the productive forces of capitalism—the "theater" of representation that substitutes for the accumulated productions of the unconscious in the late twentieth century—produces its own liminal spaces in order to redefine normative desire as a bounded "territoriality." The productive force of the capitalist psyche "continually seeks to avoid reaching its limit while simultaneously tending toward that limit."[17] This paradoxical move both to delimit and to expand is resolved by the repetitive domination of disciplining institutions, "ancillary apparatuses" whose functions are strengthened with each "reterritorialization" of desire: "Everything returns or recurs: States, nations, families" (Deleuze and Guattari, 34–35). Bounded by "Backroom Metaphysics," the policing authorities in Ginsberg's *Kaddish* reproduce zoned territorialities that recur in Naomi's "career" as a mental patient.

Although *Anti-Oedipus* appeared eleven years after *Kaddish*, the conceptual framework it shares with the poem contributes a vocabulary that is useful in two particular areas. As a text that emerges from the antipsychiatric movement, *Anti-Oedipus* fuses theories of a productive unconscious with a social critique of capitalist culture. The book also is informed by poststructuralist theories of language, a difference between Deleuze and Guattari's 1972 study and the work of Laing and Goffman roughly contemporary with the composition of *Kaddish*. Deleuze and Guattari share Laing's emphasis on decentering "demonological" approaches to mental illness, but the "center" that resonates through *Anti-Oedipus*—the walking schizoid figure—is informed by an antifoundationalist philosophy that, like *Kaddish*, privileges linguistic flow over linguistic fixity as a path to decentering the demonizing subject.

Presuming that "Oedipus is the ultimate territoriality," Deleuze and Guattari construct a model of subjectivity—the schizoid—who inhabits these parcelled spaces as a means of eroding them from within. In this way, the psychic processes of Deleuze and Guattari's schizoid, and of the combined Naomi-Allen protagonist walking over the "sunny pavement" in *Kaddish,* contain the potential for a revolutionary language of "deterritorialization." Deleuze and Guattari write that if capitalist territorialities are indeed artificial, ancillary structures of power, separated from the privileged deterritorialized flow of their schizoid, then it follows that the schizoid must be seen as one who takes these artificialities more seriously than anyone else, insofar as the schizoid treats these territories as nothing but artificialities. For Deleuze and Guattari, the important difference between the deterritorializing schizoid and the territorialized capitalist subject is that the schizoid attempts to denaturalize the process of territorialization rather than its products (State, nation, family). The schizoid "takes the artifice seriously and plays the game to the hilt: if you want them, you can have them—territorialities infinitely more artificial than the ones that society offers us, totally artificial new families, secret lunar societies" (Deleuze and Guattari, 35).

Of course, Deleuze and Guattari's own theoretical language also "plays the game to the hilt." In *Anti-Oedipus*, Deleuze and Guattari's efforts to avoid traps of territorialization with what seems like their own "secret lunar society"—attempts to out-artifice the artifice of referentiality—constitute a divine madness of anti-foundationalist philosophy.

As "outrageous" as Deleuze and Guattari represent themselves to be, their own language for prophecy, like Ginsberg's in *Howl* and *Kaddish*, is nowhere more serious than when it professes outrage at the disciplinary practices of modern psychiatry. Mocking Freud, they adopt the authority of the analyst in order to empty that authority: "You weren't born Oedipus, you caused it to grow in yourself; and you aim to get out of it through fantasy, through castration, but this in turn you have caused to grow in Oedipus—namely, in yourself: the horrible circle" (Deleuze and Guattari, 334).

Law and desire, "horrible circles" and "lunar societies," converge in Ginsberg's readings of Blake and the Bible, where he constructs an immanent principle for transcendent experience. Ginsberg's journals from the mid-1950s illustrate how *Howl* grew from his own careful reading of the Bible. Ginsberg's notes in the journals indicate that he reread the Old Testament over a period of several years in the mid-1950s, at the same time that he was reading some of the other material which would influence the composition of *Howl*.[18] Gordon Ball, editor of the journals, notes that Ginsberg integrated biblical verse into his poetics while at sea with the Merchant Marine in 1955–56.

In an August 1956 journal entry, Ginsberg began a revision of the sexual prohibitions of the Book of Leviticus, a project that would become "Many Loves," published in *Howl and Other Poems* (*Journals: Mid-Fifties*, 300–303). The journal draft appeared one month after an entry in which he noted that he had finished reading the Old Testament; and it appeared during the same month that he read Blake's "The Everlasting Gospel" and concluded that homoerotic desire does not by nature transgress biblical law: "the body's five senses are expression of the soul, the body does not exist soul does, my love for Peter [Orlovsky] therefore doesn't sin against my body" (*Journals: Mid-Fifties*, 294, 311). This draft version of "Many Loves" maintains the paratactic line of biblical verse, but revises Leviticus so that the "shame," "timidity," and "distrust" of the first lines of the poem eventually rename moral law: "and his come flowed into me for an hour; then lay with his eyes closed, and rested" (*Journals: Mid-Fifties*, 302).

What Ball terms Ginsberg's "reconciliation" of religion, desire, and literary production in the mid-fifties also involves Ginsberg's studious readings in Buddhism (*Journals: Mid-Fifties*, 173). Jack Kerouac was Ginsberg's earliest Buddhist teacher, right away emphasizing the connection between Buddhism, science, and the process of writing. In a didactic 1954 letter to Ginsberg, Kerouac writes: "For your beginning studies of Buddhism, you must listen to me carefully and implicitly as tho I was Einstein teaching you relativity or Eliot teaching the Formulas of Objective Correlation on a blackboard in Princeton."[19] Ginsberg later traveled to India and eventually formed a Guru-student relationship with Trungpa, with whom he started Naropa Institute, the first accredited Buddhist college in the United States.

Trungpa became one of the first Tibetan lamas to teach in the West. Trungpa promulgated the "Crazy Wisdom" school of Tibetan Buddhism, a school that, as its name suggests, practices a discipline quite different from the hushed Zen sitting traditions that first characterized Beat transmissions of Buddhism in the United States. Madness produces a counterdiscourse of redemption in Crazy Wisdom Buddhism akin to the revisionary role of divine madness in *Howl* and *Kaddish*. In a transcription of his 1972 seminars with his first American students, Trungpa claims that the enlightened mind of Crazy Wisdom exists on the boundary between altruism and "the legality of karma."[20] According to Trungpa, practitioners in the Crazy Wisdom school seek to achieve a state of mind both untamed and awakened. Taking as its starting point the "infantlike mind" of "playful aggression," Crazy Wisdom is a revisionist Buddhism;[21] it takes the law of Karma, the certainty of cause-and-effect relationships in Buddhism, and challenges its inherent authority as "law."

In what follows, I discuss how Ginsberg responds to discourses of law, religion, and desire to define the role of the modern prophet in *Howl* and *Kaddish*. Both *Howl* and *Kaddish* seek a new form for industrial poetic prophecy, predicated on a breath-unit line that revises biblical forms. The "exhausting" breath lines of *Howl* become the clipped breath units of *Kaddish*. The form and content of *Howl* produce a language for prophecy from contradictory religious images: the prophet is both Yahwist and Buddhist, both patristic and Gnostic. *Kaddish* revises orthodox religious tradition with a counterhistory based in madness and doubt. Inspired by the Kaddish, the Hebrew prayer of mourning, Ginsberg's poem revises the tradition that authorizes it. In Orthodox Judaism, the Kaddish must be recited in the presence of a *minyan* of at least ten male members of the faith. Ginsberg, a gay man who revises his Judaism with the non-theism of Buddhism, is least authorized by the orthodox institution to offer a Kaddish, yet would still offer it: "I am unmarried, I'm hymnless, I'm Heavenless, headless in blisshood I would still adore."[22]

2. COMMON-SENSE NONSENSE: "WHERE YOU BANG ON THE CATATONIC PIANO"

For Ginsberg, prophetic language is primordial but also situational, located in the body, speech, and mind of the individual speaker. Visionary language emerges from the boundary conditions of his protagonists:

> who dreamt and made incarnate gaps in Time & Space through images jux-
> taposed, and trapped the archangel of the soul between 2 visual images
> and joined the elemental verbs and set the noun and dash of conscious-
> ness together jumping with sensation of Pater Omnipotens Aeterne Deus[.]
> (*Howl: Original Draft Facsimile*, 74)

Ginsberg's language for prophecy is both relational and visionary. Following Cézanne, the protagonists of *Howl* "trapped the archangel of the soul between 2 visual images." The visionary representations of their pilgrimage form a common prophetic language shared between prophet and audience in *Howl* itself; on the boundary between nonsense and referentiality, this relational and visionary language reaches backward past Cold War language "to recreate the syntax and measure of poor human prose" (*Howl: Original Draft Facsimile*, 74).

Prophetic discourse in *Howl* de-emphasizes referentiality and seems to trust only absurdity as a mode of representation. The seemingly spontaneous style and absurdist theme of *Howl* mask a visionary form and content carefully revised. The first draft of *Howl* begins:

> I saw the best minds of my generation
> generation destroyed by madness
> starving, mystical, naked.[23]

As I discussed in chapter 1, Ginsberg recast his "mystical" protagonists in a later draft as "hysterical," the revision that stands in the final draft of the poem. In his 1986 annotations to the poem, Ginsberg deems his revision of *mystical* to *hysterical* "crucial" because it infuses the "initial idealistic impulse of the line" with material representation (*Howl: Original Draft Facsimile*, 124). The revision reflects a blurring of the boundary between the visionary and the material, describing a point of contact between these states of consciousness rather than a divide. The substitution replaces a term that describes seemingly transcendental, visionary consciousness with a term that describes a condition embedded in the material practice of psychoanalysis.

Ginsberg claims that "common sense dictated 'hysteria'" (*Howl: Original Draft Facsimile*, 124). Yet in his poetic prophecies, "common sense" is a "hysterical" sense, a category of understanding in which signs are saturated with meaning and commonly evade what he would see as the censoriousness of referentiality. In a 1956 letter to Richard Eberhart, Ginsberg explains that in *Howl* he seeks to localize representations of transcendental consciousness in material forms. He argues that the poem affirms those who seek "mystical mysteries in the forms in which they actually occur here in the U.S. in our environment."[24]

The nonstop articulations of Ginsberg's protagonists in *Howl* create a hysterical language for these "mystical mysteries":

> who talked continuously seventy hours from park to pad to bar to Bellevue
> to museum to the Brooklyn Bridge,
> a lost battalion of platonic conversationalists jumping down the stoops off
> fire escapes off windowsills off Empire State out of the moon,
> yacketayakking screaming vomiting whispering facts and memories and anec-
> dotes and eyeball kicks and shocks of hospitals and jails and wars. . . .
>
> (16–18)

The inhabitants of Ginsberg's unreal city seem to speak nonsense; indeed, "platonic" metaphysical authority is undermined by their antimetaphysical "yacketayakking" and "conversational[ism]." For Ginsberg, the divinity of their madness is as much commonsensical as it is mystical. Yet their discourse is not meaningless: they utter "facts and memories and anecdotes" of the horrors of modern institutions of psychiatry, criminal justice, and war. Their language may "yacketayakk," but the suffering is real. An "eli eli lamma lamma sabacthani saxophone cry" produces the attempts of these isolated "platonic conversationalists" to recreate an "elemental" language. Thus, their frame of reference is unrepresentable within a referential discourse that circumscribes "hospitals and jails and wars." As an element of prophetic language, their "yacketayakking" echoes the redemptive, primal voice of Blake's Ololon in *Milton*. For Ginsberg, prophecy is best understood at the level of the individual "eyeball kick," Ginsberg's term for Cézanne's "hysterical" visual representations. Together, Ginsberg's hysterical language and breath-unit lines transform the biblical verity of prophetic language and form into a variant mode of modern prophecy. Section 1 of *Howl* foregrounds the tension between *mystical* and *hysterical*, and thereby frames the tension between the monovocal Moloch and the polyvocal modern prophet in the second and third sections, respectively, of the poem.

The protagonists of *Howl* cannot articulate an absolute language that will redeem their suffering. They "howled on their knees in the subway and were dragged off the roof waving genitals and manuscripts" (35). In this moment of self-referentiality, when the poet acknowledges his quest to find both a language and an audience for prophecy, prophetic language is displaced by external forces. Indeed, hysterical language is there to be countered, insofar as prophetic language in the poem is deployed on a boundary between hysteria (saying "anything we want to say") and Cold War monovocality (howling "incomprehensible leaflets"). The self-referential turn of the poem here blurs the boundaries between prophet and audience, and between audience and text, as in the poetic prophecies of Blake and H. D. Yet Ginsberg infuses *Howl* with disciplinary forces that prevent this blurring from producing language. On their knees in a posture of prayer, the protagonists howl in vain. Their attempt to fuse desire ("genitals") and language ("manuscripts") is policed, and they are "dragged off the roof" (35).

In *Howl*, Western visionary traditions alone are insufficient to craft a language for redemptive prophetic cleansing. Ginsberg's readings in Buddhism provide the revisionary alternative to the authorizing Western prophetic lineage of the poem. For Ginsberg, Buddhism offers a sacred tradition that combines matter and spirit. Buddhism's claim to metaphysical authority is based not on a transcendental creator, but on the belief that human beings have the ability to realize—to "awaken" (the word *buddha* derives from *bodhi*, Sanskrit for "awakened")—principles of the sacred within themselves. The immanent Body, Speech, and Mind of each individual are holy vehicles of redemption in Buddhism; the individual and the holy are conjoined in Buddhist tradition, sustained by the Buddhist doctrine that both are empty of an essentialist identity.

Ginsberg transforms the Buddhist conception of emptiness into a principle for prophecy in *Howl*. Within the varied Buddhisms available to Ginsberg in the twentieth century, the principle common to all is the doctrine of *shunyata*, Sanskrit for "emptiness." In Buddhism, the identities of phenomena are based upon the varied frames of reference that construct them. Identity is a constructed performance, not an irreducible ontological category. Buddhist emptiness does not signify a void; on the contrary, for a Buddhist to say the phenomenal world is marked by emptiness is to say that the phenomenal world is *full* of infinite frames of reference upon which the world depends for the conferral of identity. Unlike Christian metaphysics, Buddhism posits no ultimate frame of reference; even the historical Buddha is a manifestation of emptiness. Thus, in Buddhism, phenomena are *empty* of an essentialist existence independent of immanent causes and conditions, and *full* of multiple subject positions composed from infinite frames of reference.

Asked in a 1989 interview if Buddhism possesses a tradition of prophecy correspondent to Judeo-Christian prophecy, Ginsberg argues that Buddhist emptiness represents a mode of prophetic consciousness.[25] He argues that "the *shunyata* aspect" of phenomena is what "gives almost everything its sacred quality," and that *shunyata* provides a matrix of "prophetical sharpness."[26] Ginsberg's model of modern prophecy, like Blake's and H. D.'s, conjoins metaphysical and material modes of inspiration; Ginsberg turns to the East for traditions that were not available to Blake, and that were not as useful for H. D. as Greek, Egyptian, and Gnostic sources were.

As Ginsberg says to Lewis MacAdams in this 1989 interview, appropriating the opening of Sidney's *Astrophel and Stella* as a context for understanding the immanent and transcendent voice of the modern poet-prophet: "I always saw prophecy not as divine inspiration, but as *'Fool,' said the muse, look in your heart and write.*" Like Sidney, Ginsberg relocates the external muse internally, part of Ginsberg's strategy to adapt poetic decorum to "frank" speech. Yet Ginsberg's expressivism is emptied of the self-certain, sovereign romantic subject. For Ginsberg, this strategy implies the construction of a language for prophecy—talking "frankly" to one's muse, to oneself—in which the body, speech, and mind are the locus of divinity. From an emphasis on the *shunyata* nature of phenomena, Ginsberg crafts a language for prophecy that, as he says in the 1989 interview, seeks "the right words that would penetrate through all consciousness and wake earth up to its terrific, non-transcendent living possibility." For Ginsberg, then, prophecy is a conjunction of biblical vision and the Bodhisattva ideal of altruism crucial to all Buddhisms. Of the conjunction of Buddhism and poetic prophecy, Ginsberg tells MacAdams, "I want to save the world. . . . You know, 'Save the world, Bodhisattva,' or *penetrate* through the world with some great song, cry, mantra, or poem."

Of course, the significant role of Buddhism in Ginsberg's prophetic poetry has been noted by many critics. For some, such as Gordon Ball, a resident with Ginsberg in his Cherry Valley commune in the early 1970s, Buddhism and Blake are critical elements in Ginsberg's creation of a language for prophecy that "reconciles" God, sexuality, and imagination (*Journals-Mid-Fifties*, 173). The earliest critics of Ginsberg and the Beats dismissed their Buddhism as Bohemian dabbling. For Norman Podhoretz, Ginsberg's Columbia classmate who characterized the Beats as "know-nothing Bohemians," the turn from West to East by the Beats is part of a vacuous "conviction that any form of rebellion against American culture . . . is admirable." Writing in the *Black Mountain Review*, Michael Rumaker traces the "failure" of *Howl*, as he sees it, to the way in which a "hollow talk of eternity" and Buddhism "corrupts" the genuine "anger" in the poem. Others, most recently Helen Vendler, see Ginsberg's Buddhism as a force of "quietism that would turn every phenomenon into illusion" and that thereby diminishes the energy of the poems.[27]

Paul Portugés has written most extensively on Ginsberg's use of Buddhism in his poetry. According to Portugés, Buddhism is an essential part of Ginsberg's "theory of composition," especially in his use of spontaneous composition and his reliance on the visual techniques of Cézanne. Yet for Portugés, *shunyata* only signifies Ginsberg's attempt to evade Cold War censoriousness; Portugés writes that *shunyata* "is the Buddhist formula for the absence of rational, controlled mind."[28] Portugés is partly correct—*shunyata* empties rationality (as it does irrationality) of inherent existence—but his interpretation of Buddhism in this context considerably underestimates the rhetorical strategies of *Howl*. For Portugés, *shunyata* is "the Buddhist equivalent of Cézanne's Pater Omnipotens Aeterna [*sic*] Deus."[29] Later, in a 1978 interview with Ginsberg published in *The Visionary Poetics of Allen Ginsberg*, Portugés pushes Ginsberg to admit that the poet's study of Buddhism was the *necessary* catalyst in the evolution of his verse. Ginsberg evades Portugés's emphasis, often tracing meditative practices such as *samatha* (what Ginsberg translates as "mindfulness") and *vipasyana* (translated by Ginsberg as "wakefulness leading to minute observation of detail") to his own experiments with form and content in the 1950s.[30] While Portugés encourages Ginsberg to separate Western from Eastern influences, Ginsberg maintains that *samatha* and *vipasyana* are linked with his extension and revision of Western inspirations: "[M]y poetry was always pretty mindful anyway. I always had based it on elements of William Carlos Williams' elemental observations."[31]

Shunyata is more than just a strategy against rational containment; it contributes to Ginsberg's ambivalent language for suffering and redemption in the prophetic pilgrimage of *Howl*. At the time he wrote *Howl*, Ginsberg's knowledge of Buddhist traditions derived primarily from his reading of Dwight Goddard's *A Buddhist Bible*, also among Kerouac's first Buddhist sources.[32] The entire theory and praxis of Buddhism was available to Ginsberg in Goddard's translation of "The Four Noble Truths," the first selection from the original Pali sources in Goddard's book. According to this first discourse, suffering comes from a belief in the essentialist existence of sensory experience; and suffering is extinguished through a belief in "dependent origination," in a belief that the sense-based world is empty of inherent existence, interdependent and not reducible to a transhistoric cause (Goddard, 22). This principle for the origin and cessation of suffering suggests a rhetoric of vision for *Howl*, where redemption comes through an annihilation of suffering dependent on a blurred boundary between immanence and transcendence. As the Buddha in Goddard's translation states, the Path of the Cessation of Suffering begins with the "extinction of consciousness," with consciousness here defined as an illusory belief in an independent, essential subjectivity (Goddard, 41). For Ginsberg, writing in the shadow of the military-industrial complex and the arms race, the Buddha's remarks on cessation may have resonated with, as Ginsberg termed it, the Blakean "spectre" of Cold War consciousness. In Goddard's translation, the Buddha proclaims that "one may rightly say of me, that I teach annihilation, that I propound my doctrine for the purpose of annihilation . . . the annihilation namely of greed, anger, and delusion" (Goddard, 41–42).

Ginsberg did not read his source material as a Buddhist scholar would. Indeed, Ginsberg's identification of desire as a path to redemption in *Howl* seems antithetical—an attachment to the body rather than a redemptive surrender to emptiness. Ginsberg's particular appropriation of Buddhism is part of a response to Western policing of desire during the Cold War. Therefore, the *production* of desire is a major component of the path to the cessation of suffering in *Howl*. The madness of his protagonists derives from the strict boundaries of lawful desire during the Cold War, when homosexuals were classified as deviants and regularly arrested in police sweeps.

Desire is explored in detail in *Howl* so that the communal experience of desire is equated with the communality of suffering in the poem; and from this interdependent relationship comes the poem's "mercy," what Ginsberg calls, in the 1956 letter to Eberhart quoted earlier, its "sympathy" and communal "identification."[33] Disciplinary institutions would empty the redemptive howl of the poem, but the communal experience of suffering empties these institutions of their absolutist authority. "Weeping and undressing," the protagonists of *Howl* "bit detectives in the neck" and "shrieked with delight" when arrested for "no crime other than their own wild cooking pederasty and intoxication" (32, 34). They "broke down crying," but their howls alone are not redemptive (33). Instead, their articulations of protest are drowned out by the ululation of political and religious orthodoxy: "the sirens of Los Alamos wailed them down, and wailed down Wall, and the Staten Island ferry also wailed" (32).

Yet the "hysterical" protagonists create mystical ecstasy: they "let themselves be fucked in the ass by saintly motorcyclists, and screamed with joy" (36). In his 1986 annotations to the poem, Ginsberg states that this line attempts to transform representations of desire through a revisionary poetics that would "reverse vulgar stereotype with a statement of fact" (*Howl: Original Draft Facsimile*, 126). Noting that "[p]opular superstition had it that one screamed with pain in such a circumstance," Ginsberg writes that even his own revision is marked with *shunyata* and thus is not beyond change: "'screamed' is hyperbole — 'moaned' more common" (*Howl: Original Draft Facsimile*, 126).

Screams and howls serve a double function in the poem, both as reminders of the authority of ecstatic visionary precursors, and as attempts to rewrite dominant discourses of desire in the postwar era. As Ginsberg draws section 1 to a close, the self-referential linking of prophet and audience is

sealed by howling nonsense: here, the protagonists "scribbled all night rock-
ing and rolling over lofty incantations which in the yellow morning were
stanzas of gibberish" (51). Prophetic language is reduced to "scribble";
and the incantatory rhythms of the poem itself lead to a new day dominated
by mawkish light and "gibberish."

Ginsberg's expansive aims in *Howl*—saying "anything we want to say"—
always must contend with a Cold War consolidation of the same discursive
boundaries Ginsberg seeks to blur. In an era when the lived experience of
asylum patients might be explained by the theoretical framework of a "career," to recall Goffman, it should come as no surprise that the protagonists
of *Howl* create a language for prophecy but are "burned alive in their inno-
cent flannel suits on Madison Avenue" (56). As Herbert Marcuse argued in
his famous 1964 study of postwar culture, *One-Dimensional Man: Studies
in the Ideology of Advanced Industrial Society*, advanced industrial civilization produces a "voluntary compliance" by subjects in the "de-erotiza-
tion" of lived experience. As to the disciplinary boundaries imposed on the
body by industrial culture, Marcuse argues that sex is "integrated into work
and public relations and is thus made more susceptible to (controlled) sat-
isfaction."[34] In Ginsberg's poem, the howling, hysterical language of prophecy in section 1 is reduced to "waking nightmares" made into "stanzas of
gibberish" and "incomprehensible leaflets" by the Cold War policing of
desire. After a century of military-industrial development, Whitman's "fan-
cied readers" (*Howl: Original Draft Facsimile*, 126) are in the same
wretched situation as Ginsberg's Carl Solomon, the asylum inmate to whom
the poem is dedicated: "ah, Carl, while you are not safe I am not safe"
(*Howl: Original Draft Facsimile*, 72). The protagonists and their audience
are complicit in a downtrodden, beaten existence: with "the absolute heart
of the poem of life butchered out of their own bodies," their suffering criti-
cizes Cold War culture and encourages the development of alternative ec-
stasies (*Howl: Original Draft Facsimile*, 78).

The role of divine madness in *Howl* resembles that of H. D.'s double
trope of nostalgia in *The Flowering of the Rod*. H. D. is both nostalgic for
traditional natural representation and engaged in a project to revise nature
as visionary. Ginsberg, too, is fueled by a double nostalgia—here, for a
redemptive madness. He seeks to create a prophetic imagination from divine madness, and is determined to empty divine madness of its traditional
significances. The madness of Ginsberg's revisionary prophetic poetry
emerges not from a transcendental hand, but from the historical conditions
of postwar institutional discursive practices. Ginsberg deploys his influences from Cézanne and Buddhism, as well as material from his own psychiatric institutionalization, to create a prophetic language mindful of his
quest for both an elemental language and an antimetaphysical language
saturated with desire.

In *Howl*, Ginsberg's *one speech-breath-thought* poetics fuses language, body, and consciousness—or Buddhist Body, Speech, and Mind—in an effort to yoke "elemental verbs" of prophetic discourse with "the noun and dash of consciousness." The *one speech-breath-thought*, the nonreferential "howl" of the poem, indeed is "elemental" for Ginsberg, but cannot be irreducible because, as an articulation of *shunyata*, it is empty of an inherent identity. By locating a transcendental idea in the individual body, Ginsberg locates elemental language in a sensory foundation. He renders a visionary history from the *historical essence* of the individual body, speech, and mind of the poet-prophet—a paradoxical fusion of the elemental and contextual.

Prophetic language in *Howl* is an immanent principle in human consciousness "jumped" with the transcendental "sensation" of "Pater Omnipotens Aeterne Deus." This language creates an embodied link between prophet and audience. In his 1966 *Paris Review* interview, Ginsberg describes the visceral sensation he sought to produce in his audience in terms that acknowledge the influences of Blake, Cézanne, and Buddhism. For Ginsberg, Cézanne's visionary method was a "form of yoga"; indeed, he describes Cézanne's *petite sensations* of visionary experience as Western equivalents of Buddhist moments of sudden enlightenment, forms of "the *satori* . . . that the Zen haikuists would speak of."[35] Through juxtapositions of language and imagery similar to Cézanne's experiments with color, he sought to create in his readers the *petite sensations* of Cézanne's attempt to reconstruct the natural world as eternal. This process, Ginsberg says, "has something to do with Blake," insofar as both Cézanne and Blake seek to transform natural perception into visionary perception by seeing *through*, not *with*, the eye (Clark, 204–5).

Ginsberg argues that Cézanne's visionary "patience" of eye allowed him to "see *through* his canvas to God." He claims that Cézanne, like Blake, is "seeing through his eye" (Clark, 204). Ginsberg's source is Blake's "A Vision of the Last Judgment," from his 1810 catalogue: "I question not my Corporeal or Vegetative Eye any more than I would Question a Window concerning a Sight I look thro it & not with it" (*Complete Poetry and Prose*, 566). Blake's remarks here confirm his concern as a poet with, as Ginsberg says of Cézanne, seeing "*through* his canvas to God." Blake argues that the artist who sees *through* the eye and not *with* it thereby reconstructs the natural world as visionary: "When the sun rises do you not see a round Disk of fire somewhat like a Guinea O no no I see an Innumerable company of the Heavenly host crying Holy Holy Holy is the Lord God Almighty" (565–66). For Blake, divine language lies in the individual articulations of Poetic Genius; the Bible, as discussed in chapters 1 and 2, is the "<Peculiar> Word of God" which must be transformed by Poetic Genius so that "every man may converse with God & be a King & Priest in his own house."[36] For Ginsberg, Blake's peculiar divine word becomes the "elemental," nonessentializing vision of interdependence that Buddhists would call *shunyata*.

Anchored in chant-like repetition and hyperventilating lines, Ginsberg's rhetoric of vision in *Howl* links prophet and audience in an investigation of whether "certain combinations of words and rhythms actually had an electrochemical reaction on the body, which could catalyze specific states of consciousness."[37] As with Blake's and H. D.'s strategies for rewriting the unit of time as visionary, Ginsberg seeks to craft a language for prophecy that would re-envision time measurement as "incarnate gaps in Time & Space" that lead to representations of nature as visionary. Based on his reception of the Bible, of Cézanne, and of Buddhism, Ginsberg designed *Howl* to produce the moments of heightened consciousness it represents.

Whether such a relationship of production and representation can be measured in the poem is another question. Nevertheless, it is important to examine how the structure of the lines affect reading, and to consider the role of this formal experimentation in Ginsberg's development of a poetics of prophecy. The text begins with 72 breath-controlled strophes broken by a dash and a breath in line 73 — "ah, Carl" — whereupon the poem resumes a breath-chant catalogue in five lines that portray the "speechless" and "intelligent" protagonists experiencing continual cycles of death and resurrection (73–78). The first 78 lines of the poem are arranged in such a way that the fall and rise of each breath between lines is both hyperventilative and controlled. In "Mind Breaths" (1973), Ginsberg returns to such an iconic structure, where the organization of breath and line, in the act of reading, mirrors the content of the poem.[38] The travel of the reader's breath in the strophes of "Mind Breaths" parallels the travel of the poet's breath, beginning at Trungpa's meditation center in Wyoming and circling the world, returning back to the individual poet's opening breath-unit. The fall and rise of the reader's breath mirrors the dynamics of breath in the meditating poet.

With the one-speech-mind-breath unit of *Howl*, Ginsberg seeks to produce in the reader "an electro-chemical effect caused by art."[39] The heightened consciousness produced by the poem, Ginsberg says, would be the equivalent of that produced by Cézanne and the "Zen haikuists." Ginsberg speculates that his 1948 Blake vision might be a result of such an "electrochemical reaction."[40] If so, the Blake vision would be an example of transcendental consciousness produced at the immanent level of texts and audiences rather than created mystically by an external voice.

However potentially visionary these juxtaposed gaps in consciousness may be in the poem, the poet also describes himself as a product of the Cold War era using the same Urizenic terms that represent Moloch: "Moloch who entered my soul early! Moloch in whom I am a consciousness without a body" (86–87). Moloch is Urizen, the coercive manifestation of Pater Omnipotens Deus who blocks vision and answers prophetic pilgrimage with stasis: he is the Satan of Blake's *Milton*, the monovocal God of natural representation. Ginsberg declares in the second section of *Howl* that Moloch is the "sphinx of cement and aluminum" that blocked the pilgrimage of his protagonists and "bashed open their skulls and ate up their brains and imagination" (79). To solve the riddle of Moloch would be to reconceive the urban apocalypse of the poem as redemptive. Moloch consumes the prophetic imagination, casting it as unnatural and deviant; like Blake's Urizenic God, he reigns over a world cast in the image of his own singularity, and he is "alone in Heavn & Earth" (*Milton*, 38:56). Moloch represents an industrial barrier that blocks the productions of the imagination. He is an adaptive mechanism of physical survival in an industrial civilization, casting New York in the image of dying Thebes in *Howl*'s urban apocalypse. Yet Moloch signifies a maladaptive symptom that must be rewritten by the prophetic poet for whom transcendent escape is not an option. Moloch sustains the prison, the school, and the productions of industry. The "mind" of Moloch is pure machinery, and produces "skyscrapers stand[ing] in the long streets like endless Jehovahs" (*Howl*, 84). Ginsberg's howling protagonists create "dreams" of "incarnate gaps" in consciousness, but Moloch counters with his own articulation, in which his "factories dream and croak in the fog" (84).

Having faced the Moloch-Sphinx who limits the imagination, Ginsberg portrays the degradation of the world as an emanation of the degradation of the psyche: "Moloch whose poverty is the specter of genius! Moloch whose fate is a cloud of sexless hydrogen! Moloch whose name is the Mind!" (85). In his annotations, Ginsberg describes these lines as adumbrating "a recognition uncovered in the act of composition, a crux of the poem" (*Howl: Original Draft Facsimile*, 142). His practice of *one speech-breath-thought*, the awareness of spontaneous flows of breath and thought developed in concentrated Buddhist meditation, produces a turning point toward the end of the second section. This turn depends on his recognition of his own implication in sustaining Moloch—on the recognition that he, too, has become what he beheld, and that his own redemption depends on self-annihilation: "Moloch who frightened me out of my natural ecstasy! Moloch whom I abandon!" (87). The tension between Ginsberg's recognition and disavowal of Moloch produces a series of provisional "breakthroughs" in section 2: where once visionary consciousness was flushed "down the American river" by Moloch, a new hope emerges for "[r]eal holy laughter in the river" (93).

As laughter both "real" and "holy," this "breakthrough" is consistent with the desire in the poem for a combined immanent and transcendent language for prophecy. A language both real and holy substitutes "holy yells" for the howls that were policed in section 1, and the "laughter in the river" for the "loveless" and "soulless" urban Moloch of section 2. This revisionary, redemptive language at the end of section 2 carries the risk of self-destruction: the protagonists "bade farewell! They jumped off the roof! to solitude! waving! carrying flowers! Down to the river! into the street!" (93). The protagonists simultaneously leap into the redemptive "real holy laughter" of the American river and plunge apocalyptically to the street. Redemption and apocalypse work together in ambivalent tension; this ambivalence is crucial to the final section of the poem, set in Rockland State Hospital and based on Ginsberg's stay in the Columbia Presbyterian Psychiatric Institute in 1949.

Ginsberg's identification with Carl Solomon depends on a reconciliation of antipsychiatry with Ginsberg's Western and Eastern religious sources. Presuming that institutional life needed to be demystified in order to authorize the voices of patients, Laing sought a "more socially intelligible" explanation for madness than traditionally found in biochemistry and psychoanalysis.[41] By rendering mental illness "empty" of an essential etiology within the human being—by applying *shunyata* to the etiology of mental illness—Laing and Ginsberg infuse mental illness with full visionary potential. The term *shunyata* is not carelessly applied to Laing's motivations. In their 1984 interview, Ginsberg and Laing discussed the intersections of their individual meditation practices, and led the audience in a brief session of single-pointed breath meditation.

For Foucault, the continuum between poles of normative and insane behavior is created from social relations, and the classifications and definitions that occupy this spectrum change according to the exigencies of power in any particular historical period. Foucault's research into the social signification of madness and reason in *Madness and Civilization* and *Discipline and Punish* reveals coercive legal and medical paradigms similar to those that generated the counterdiscourse of antipsychiatry. Of course, Foucault describes the social function of the psychiatric institution as the disciplining of transgressive subjectivities. Psychiatric institutions classify as "mad" those who do not construct for themselves a docile subjectivity, and they render those subjects liminal within the disciplinary hierarchy and regimentation of juridico-medical institutional practices. Laing and Goffman also argue that the etiology of psychosis is not confined to biological causes in the human organism but is the result of both biological factors and oppressive environmental forces that emerge from such cultural structures as the state, the family, the school, and the workplace.

Not surprisingly, although Solomon is portrayed in *Howl* as "madder" than Ginsberg, neither is mad in the context of the narrative. If Solomon's experiences are indeed visionary, then this section would seem to conclude the poem with a traditional affirmation of the inspired madness of all prophetic articulation. Yet Ginsberg's emphasis on the absurd power inequities in Solomon's incarceration indicate that *Howl* satirizes, and therein revises, the trope of divine madness by which it is authorized: "I'm with you in Rockland where you must feel very strange" (95). Indeed, Solomon is self-aware enough to "laugh at this invisible humor," to mock with the poet the notion that the two of them "are great writers on the same dreadful typewriter" (98–99). In his annotations to these lines, Ginsberg includes two typescript drafts of unsent letters he and Solomon composed to Malcolm de Chazal and T. S. Eliot. The letter to Chazal is signed "Shirley Temple and Dagwood Bumpstead," and closes with the affirmation that "beyond a certain point there can be no spoken communication and all speech is useless" (*Howl: Original Draft Facsimile*, 143). In the letter to Eliot, written when supposedly Eliot-inspired New Critical control of language and irony dominated North American English departments, they declare that they "know exactly where you stand on the question of the existence of your great mind," and close with a royal "we" that plays Eliot's authority for the fool: "We take our leave by asking us to kiss you goodbye" (143–44). Madness is a Dadaist trope of "common sense" here; nonsense is reconceived in the poem as a strategy to reveal the constructedness of referentiality.

Incarcerated in an asylum, Solomon is Ginsberg's prophetic inspiration. Ginsberg tells him, "you imitate the shade of my mother" (*Howl*, 96). Ginsberg describes Solomon as a divinely mad prophet, yet eventually undercuts this description:

> I'm with you in Rockland
>> where your condition has become serious and is reported on the radio[.]
>
> (100)

Solomon may be touched by divinely inspired madness, but his "serious" condition is representable, it is observed and "reported," and is empirically verified on the radio. Solomon's condition is crucial to the construction of a prophetic language that represents both embodied and transcendent experience, one where "the faculties of the skull no longer admit the worms of the senses," where corporeality is a vision that neither *admits* nor *admits of* decay (101).

As satire, the third section of *Howl* is deadly serious. Solomon's divine madness is disciplined by electroshock therapy, an almost quotidian experience in what Goffman has called the "career" of the postwar mental patient:

> I'm with you in Rockland
>> where you bang on the catatonic piano the soul is innocent and immortal it should never die ungodly in an armed madhouse

I'm with you in Rockland
    where fifty more shocks will never return your soul to its body again
    from its pilgrimage to a cross in the void[.]

                                                        (106–7)

Desire and the body are immanent principles of redemption. In contrast, divine madness—a state of consciousness inspired and authorized by an external, metaphysical hand—produces a "pilgrimage to a cross in the void." Prophetic mania is powerless in an "armed madhouse," where only the artistic imagination—a "catatonic piano"—might speak a redeeming language.

Ginsberg's visionary conversation with Solomon situates divinity within material lived experience. Solomon and Ginsberg are in liminal positions outside of referential speech. Yet from this shared non-language in the poem emerges a visionary natural world:

I'm with you in Rockland
    where you split the heavens of Long Island and resurrect your living
    human Jesus from the superhuman tomb[.]

                                                        (108)

As the poem closes, Ginsberg imagines the entire population of Pilgrim State Hospital joined in a chorus of "mad comrade[ship]," singing "the final stanzas of the Internationale" (109).

Ginsberg responds to the compulsory capitalism of the postwar era with a conjunction of redemptive homoerotic desire and communal political consciousness: Solomon and Ginsberg "hug and kiss the United States under [their] bedsheets" (110). Representations of communality counter conceptions of independent individualism. Under the sheets—concealed but visible through the movement of the sheets—the competitive individual subject is eroded from within by his refusal to acknowledge communal experience. The discourse of capitalist individualism produced by Cold War language is "annihilated," as Ginsberg's source in the Four Noble Truths terms it, by a mode of consciousness that revises the language of "coordination" and "adjustment." Suffering is eroded from within; representations of communality represent a nullification of competing, independent figures of consciousness.

Ginsberg's affirmation of shared, visionary dialogue is apocalyptic. As institutions that consolidate normative identities are assaulted by apocalyptic "angelic bombs" — with the radical image of "mother finally ****** " — the visionary conversation of section 3 culminates in a "starry-spangled shock of mercy," where invasive institutional "cures" are transformed into a conscious "beat" pilgrimage:

I'm with you in Rockland
    in my dreams you walk dripping from a sea-journey on the highway
    across America in tears to the door of my cottage in the Western night[.]
                                      (112)

The sea-change of the prophetic pilgrimage in *Howl* produces a Westering vision of redemption inflected by the sacred materiality of *shunyata*. The madness of the protagonists of *Howl* is a divine language of "mercy" and "affirmation" that represents eternal "gaps" in consciousness through an attention to border conditions: boundaries between West and East, representation and nonreferentiality, immanence and transcendence, psychiatry and antipsychiatry, and individual authority and communality. The lives of these "best minds" seem non-narratable in *Howl* because dominant juridico-medical discourses of the era rely on language incapable of exploring gaps in the blurred boundaries inhabited by these protagonists. The divinity Ginsberg seeks to represent in the pilgrimage of the poem is narratable, and therefore for him *commonsensical*, because it is recovered by the prophetic imagination. As he later claims in *Kaddish*, "sanity" is a "trick of agreement," articulated and made visible by the revisionary labor of the poet-prophet (212).

3. "THE KEY IN THE WINDOW": ZONES OF REVISION IN "KADDISH"

In a 6 April 1959 letter, composed roughly during the time *Kaddish* was taking shape, Gary Snyder told Ginsberg that "[a]ll this contemporary vision, drug & hallucination bit is dualistic." Snyder took Ginsberg to task for creating a language for prophecy in which the "ordinary world of mind isn't enough" and in which a seeker "has to be high to dig the universe." At the close of the 6 April letter, Snyder stated (in ink, as if an afterthought to the typed letter) "I take it back about you being Dualist—will explain later." Yet Snyder's next letter, dated 12 April 1959, did not so much "take back" the charge of dualism as it qualified and extended Snyder's definition of the term. Referring to *Howl* and to the counterculture forming around the poem, he wrote, "I feel the drug & high kick of many Americans is basically a rejection of matter."[42]

Snyder claims that despite Ginsberg's attempts to fuse matter and spirit in *Howl*, he fails to reconcile the distance between the two in the poem. For Snyder, the rhetoric of vision in *Howl* fails to sustain ambivalence and collapses into dualism. Despite an attempt to revivify matter as "divine," *Howl* remains, for Snyder, an exercise in escapism. Noting the rhetorical strategy of "Footnote to *Howl*," Snyder argues that "[c]alling matter etc. 'Holy' doesn't necessarily change this [rejection of matter], because it may simply mean that one cannot accept things as they are, i.e. not particularly holy." However, as with his ink addition the earlier letter, Snyder's criticism culminates in a statement of ambivalence: "Again, one may be saying, the unholy & ordinary condition of things as they are is holy."

Snyder's ambivalence offers an insight into the contested politics of matter and spirit in *Howl*. The poem earned Ginsberg immediate fame; but, as Snyder suggests, the poem risks the repetition of familiar dualisms. Snyder's letters were written during the composition of *Kaddish*, and suggest a context for Ginsberg's revisions there of issues of authority and doubt inscribed in *Howl*. Ginsberg portrays his childhood as "unholy & ordinary" in *Kaddish*; and part of his strategy of representing the "holy" in *Kaddish* is to dramatize in his family the presumed "ordinary" conditions of industrial-age family life. As Ginsberg often has said in interviews, *Howl* was written as a personal statement, one not meant to be seen beyond the poet's circle of fellow writers and audiences. *Kaddish*, however, was composed as Ginsberg's public visibility as a writer was expanding substantially due to of the success of *Howl* and the publicity from the 1957 obscenity trial. As a poem tracing the "career" of his mother's madness and composed during a highly visible, public period in Ginsberg's writing career, *Kaddish* contains little of the tension between public and private utterance that frames *Howl*.

Too often critics conflate *Howl* and *Kaddish*, and in the process understate important differences between them. The premises for this conflation are clear enough, but ultimately limit the discussion of each poem. Both *Howl* and *Kaddish* are interventions in Western prophecy, and both conjoin religion and politics to decenter Cold War orthodoxy and highlight the "beatitude" of downtrodden, even oppressed, protagonists. For James Breslin, the two taken together are the "most powerful" poems of Ginsberg's early career, because they succeeded in "establishing an alternative to the well-made symbolist poem that was fashionable in the fifties." Incorporating biographical detail and interpretation, Ekbert Faas argues that *Howl* and *Kaddish* frame Ginsberg's early career through their search for a "hidden divinity" that "becomes ever more frantic and self-destructive." In *The Visionary Poetics of Allen Ginsberg*, Portugés combines the poems in his discussion of the liberating and constraining effects of Ginsberg's 1948 Blake vision. According to Portugés, *Howl* and *Kaddish* together represent Ginsberg's accomplishment in turning his external Blake vision inward, and both are "dedicated to the presentation of raw material and written in a natural voice." As prophetic poems that take apocalyptic themes for their raw material, the two are, for Portugés, Ginsberg's "ultimate poems of doom."[43]

Michael Schumacher's discussion in *Dharma Lion* of the period between *Howl* and *Kaddish* can begin to show the nature of the differences between the two.[44] Writing of Ginsberg's trip to Tangiers in 1957, roughly during the period when *Howl and Other Poems* was confiscated in San Francisco, Schumacher notes that Ginsberg began to feel that *Howl* was an inadequate statement of public prophecy. Ginsberg was "shaken" by his first-hand experience with police brutality and the inequities of colonialism during his trip (253). Schumacher reports that Ginsberg "admitted to Kerouac that 'Howl' seemed to be an inadequate statement in comparison to the worldwide plight of the masses, and he vowed to write an epic poem to address that issue" (253). Schumacher implies that *Kaddish* is the epic poem produced from this vow. The private feelings that produced *Howl*, then, become the public voice of *Kaddish*, as Ginsberg directs the movement of his career from private statement to epic with a long poem of his mother's "career" as an asylum patient.

Feeling that the poem was not "publishable," and that he did not want the biographical material of the poem to "reach the eyes" of his family, Ginsberg conceived *Howl* as a personal exercise in biblical litany that afforded him the opportunity to experiment with the politics of the prophetic voice. *Kaddish*, however, conjoins family matters and public politics. Like any confessional work, *Kaddish* is more than an exercise in personal purging; Ginsberg writes in "How *Kaddish* Happened," that his exploration of his family "in all its eccentric detail" was part of a larger process of exploring the political dimensions of family representations in the pre- and postwar United States.[45] Morris Dickstein argues that Ginsberg's work during this period hardly resembles confessional poetry, even though *Howl* and *Kaddish* often are seen as part of the confessional vanguard. For Dickstein, Ginsberg's "intense, vatic" imagery instead resembles "the same dialectic of fantasy and fact, politics and vision, that marked the new novel" in the 1960s.[46] Ginsberg acknowledged that the charged subject matter of *Kaddish*—whether confessional or not—could make readers uncomfortable. However, he believed that this discomfort would alert readers to the complex web of roles and representations that madness and institutionalization play in modern, industrial families: "I realized it would seem odd to others, but *family* odd, that is to say, familiar—everybody has crazy cousins and aunts and brothers" ("How *Kaddish* Happened," 345).

Like *Howl*, *Kaddish* is fueled by an attempt to create a language that would fuse matter and spirit, and would revise the representational boundaries of law and desire. *Howl* is organized around a dualistic split, as Snyder suggested; yet this dualism is more particular than that between matter and spirit. *Howl* represses signs of women in order to forge a pilgrimage of male prophetic comradeship. In *Kaddish*, by contrast, Ginsberg constructs maternity as a fount of vision, an influence that precedes and sustains prophetic language. In *Kaddish*, Ginsberg attempts to recover the voice of Naomi, muted in *Howl*. Naomi appears in *Howl* only within controlled contexts created by Ginsberg himself. Although she is catalogued as one of the "best minds" of the pilgrimage, her identity is masked by the other characters in the poem. In the closing visionary dialogue with Solomon, she appears within Solomon—who "imitate[s] the shade of [Ginsberg's] mother"—but is no more than an ancillary voice of prophecy, comparable to a Blakean emanation (96).

In *Kaddish*, Ginsberg seeks to mend the dualistic split in *Howl* between male and female figures of prophecy. For Ginsberg, familial and prophetic lineages are debts that must be both sustained and revised in the poem. This paradoxical strategy of continuity and rupture takes four forms in *Kaddish*: Ginsberg's superimposition of himself and Naomi in order to revise pastoralism as urban apocalypticism; his continuity and revision of the orthodox Kaddish prayer; his use of desire as a vehicle of redemption in modern prophecy; and his attempt to resurrect a principle of divinity from his mother's debilitating madness.

The language of the poem's pilgrimage revises the artificial landscape of the city into a visionary natural world. As *Kaddish* opens, the poet is wandering Manhattan sleepless, his focus scattered by a cacophony of cultural voices ranging from 2,500-year-old Buddhist texts to recent incarnations of the blues. His urban path is bathed in the pastoral sunlight of a "clear winter noon," yet he is surrounded by an urban landscape that foretells apocalypse. This contrast between the natural and the urban is a crucial component of the rhetoric of vision in *Kaddish*: the poem combines elegiac pastoralism with an urban, apocalyptic futurism, what Bruce Comens has described in another context as the postmodern tactic of using the presence of the Bomb as a signifier of "apocalypse and after."[47] In *Kaddish*, the romantic underpinning of the pastoral exists in tension with an urban landscape whose inhabitants are both cowed by and hopeful about the destructive and resurrective future signified by the Bomb. Discussing the actual predawn walk that occasioned the opening of *Kaddish*—when Ginsberg traversed the "sunny pavement" of Manhattan ruminating on "prophesy as in the Hebrew Anthem" and "the Buddhist Book of Answers" (*Kaddish*, 209)—Ginsberg describes the city as both apocalyptic and futuristic: "In the country, getting up with the cows and birds hath Blakean charm, in the megalopolis the same nature's hour is a science-fiction hell vision, even if you're a milkman" ("How *Kaddish* Happened," 345). Ginsberg's language disturbs any easy dichotomy between nature and artifice. The milkman displaces the cows ascribed to Blake, but the archaic "hath" suggests that the poet does not wholly rue this displacement, and indeed takes such displacement as an invitation to revise his own authorizing influences.

Past, present, and future combine during the poet's initial walk in *Kaddish*. This collapse of past memory and future desire into present lived experience is represented by Ginsberg's superimposition of his walk onto a memory recalled from stories of his mother's walks through the city as a child. Ginsberg's pilgrimage in the poem combines with his mother's in an exploration of the meaning and value of apocalyptic consciousness "and what comes after" (209). The city is the redemptive location of Allen-Naomi's pilgrimage; and in its "final moment," the city is "a flower burning in the Day" (209).

Using rhetorical strategies similar to those of Blake and H. D., Ginsberg re-envisions the authorizing power of naming. Ginsberg closes section 1 of *Kaddish*, "Proem," the overture for the poem as a whole, with a revision of the Aramaic Kaddish for the dead. According to Maurice Lamm, the Kaddish itself represents a "declaration of faith" and, of course, does not invite revision.[48] The prayer is a profession of belief, worshipping the name of God in the face of tragedy. The Kaddish "is a call to God from the depths of catastrophe, exalting His name and praising Him, despite the realization that He has just wrenched a human being from life" (Lamm, 150). The Kaddish professes that final, redemptive authority emanates only from the name of God.

Ginsberg's poem distrusts the monovocal certainty of the Kaddish. This revisionism prompted early reviewers such as Mortimer J. Cohen to denounce the poem as an "illegitimate use of Jewish tradition." Cohen, writing in the 10 November 1961 *Jewish Exponent*, accuses Ginsberg of "pouring into Tradition values that are not there and that are not genuine and legitimate." For Cohen, Ginsberg's revisionary response to the Kaddish is unlawful precisely because it decenters the authority of Hebrew monotheism and of the monovocal, "definite meaning" of the liturgy.[49] Cohen's remarks imply that the absolute primacy of the name of God circumscribes the legitimacy of the Kaddish.

To examine Ginsberg's continuity and revision of the Kaddish, I quote Lamm's translation of the prayer here:

> Magnified and sanctified Be his great name.
> In the world which He will renew,
> Reviving the dead, and raising them to life eternal
> Rebuilding the city of Jerusalem, and establishing therein His sanctuary;
> Uprooting idol worship from the land and
> Replacing it with Divine worship—
> May the Holy One, blessed be He, reign in His majestic glory.[50]

Following the tradition of the prayer, Ginsberg begins his Kaddish with a focus on the "magnified" intensity of faith. The opening lines of his revisionary prayer shift from dashed breath-units to the parallel structure of biblical verse. Ginsberg closes the section 1 narrative describing Naomi's death in a voice clipped by dashes:

> Cut down by an idiot Snowman's icy—even in the Spring—strange ghost
> thought—some Death—Sharp icicle in his hand—crowned with old
> roses—a dog for his eyes—cock of a sweatshop—heart of electric irons.
> (211)

In contrast, he opens the revisionary prayer of section 1 by honoring Naomi in lines that evoke the parallel structure of biblical verse: "Magnificent, mourned no more, marred of heart, mind behind, married dreamed, mortal changed—Ass and face done with murder" (212). As Robert Alter says of biblical parallelism, such verse suggests that the parallel elements represent "an emphatic, balanced, and elevated kind of discourse, perhaps ultimately rooted in a magical conception of language as a potent performance."[51] This shift from "dashed" verse to parallelism implies a shift from the subjective structure of the modern prophet to the authoritative form of biblical verse, a shift that is crucial in Ginsberg's search for an "elemental" language for prophecy begun in *Howl* and continued in *Kaddish*.

Ginsberg trusts an incantatory, "magical" language that is more performative than ontological. He places faith in his "mystic" mother, destroyed by Moloch, rather than in an orthodox God whose authority resides outside of history. Where God is "magnified," Naomi is "magnificent." He professes peace upon her body, ravaged by electroshock—her "Ass and face done with murder"—and her "mind behind" paranoid with hallucinations of murder plots and fallen to "mysterious capitalisms": "In the world, given, flower maddened, made no Utopia, shut under pine, almed in Earth, balmed in Lone, Jehovah, accept" (212). It would seem that, as Cohen claims, Ginsberg's poem is an "illegitimate" use of the Kaddish; but Ginsberg implores Jehovah to "accept" his mother, thereby affirming the power of orthodox monotheism. Naomi's communism "made no Utopia," and so with her "shut under pine" Ginsberg's cry of "accept" echoes the call of the Kaddish to implore Jehovah to "Uproo[t] idol worship from the land and, / Replac[e] it with Divine worship."

As a strategy of continuity and revision, Ginsberg's response to tradition could seem to resemble similar strategies emphasized in the twentieth century, most notably by T. S. Eliot and Harold Bloom. Ginsberg's response is unusual, however. The primary authorizing source from which he draws is neither a strong poet nor a tradition of individual talents. Ginsberg's revisions are perhaps more startling because they break a commitment to an essentialist authorizing source—not a routine gesture in Western prophetic poetry. As discussed in chapter 1, the *poet* traditionally becomes the *poet-prophet* precisely when touched by an authenticating metaphysical vision that positions the poet-prophet in a scriptural lineage.[52] Ginsberg's commitment, in contrast, is to revise a tradition whose authority as a lineage derives from an essential, un-revisable, Logocentric purity.

In Hebraic tradition, the Kaddish "without the [authorized] person is bare."[53] The Kaddish, Lamm writes, represents a "clearly-defined obligation" traditionally conferred upon the son of the deceased parent (165). The Kaddish is an honorific prayer that may, under most circumstances, be articulated only by the son. Ginsberg's act of composing and reciting a Kaddish prayer, then, is a profession of faith in tradition.

However, as Lamm notes, the Kaddish is also meant to "bind" the son "to the synagogue for the remainder of his life" (165). Too much doubt persists in Ginsberg's revisionary Kaddish for the poem to be seen as a "binding" of poet to monotheistic tradition. Indeed, this lack of a binding force is precisely what stages the construction of a revisionary prophetic language in the poem. Ginsberg's revision does not entrust Naomi to the "magnified" and "sanctified" name of Jehovah, who is in Ginsberg's revision as detached from the mourning son as He is redemptive. Jehovah, for Ginsberg, is "Nameless, One faced, Forever beyond me, beginningless, endless, Father in death" (*Kaddish*, 212); nonetheless, Ginsberg "would still adore Thee, Heaven, after Death" (212). He shifts the noun of direct address in the orthodox prayer from *God* to *Heaven*, and in doing so marks identity in *Kaddish* with the emptiness of *shunyata*. This is a prophecy of both the "Hebrew Anthem" and the "Buddhist Book of Answers." Ginsberg *would* worship Heaven, yet the Heaven of *Kaddish* is a conditional state qualified by the *nibbana* (nirvana) of the experience of *shunyata*. His Heaven is "One blessed in Nothingness, not light or darkness, Dayless Eternity—" (212). The "endless" telos of Judeo-Christian prophecy, circumscribed by the Logos, is conjoined with the beginningless, nontheistic epistemology of Buddhism. *Kaddish*, then, binds East and West and unbinds desire from religious law; and the son who speaks the poem locates artistic production between these poles.

Ginsberg's "illegitimate use of Jewish tradition" is a rhetorical strategy of necessity as much as of choice. In their biographies, Miles and Schumacher demonstrate that Ginsberg, at first, was committed to saying a traditional Kaddish for Naomi. Ginsberg's father, Louis, requested only a small service for his wife; Ginsberg himself was unable to travel from the west coast to attend, and only seven men were present, three short of the required *minyan* for a Kaddish. Both Louis and his son Eugene published elegies in the *New York Times*, but no official Kaddish was said at the service. Ginsberg's initial desire for a Kaddish *was* based on the authority of tradition, the "definitive meaning" of Jewish law from which Cohen draws in his attack on the poem. As Lamm describes it, the Kaddish is communal, and is meant to affirm faith in Hebraic law as a social, rather than individual, enterprise. The liturgical meaning of the Kaddish, he writes, "can be achieved only in concert with society, and proclaimed amidst friends and neighbors of the same faith" (164). According to Schumacher, Ginsberg was concerned that no traditional Kaddish had been said during the gathering at Naomi's grave; he explains that Ginsberg asked his father in a letter to send a copy of the prayer (233). Schumacher concludes that Ginsberg immediately intended to revise the traditional Kaddish; if "it was impossible to have the Kaddish read, Allen thought, he would have to write one for her himself" (233). Miles, however, concludes that Ginsberg's first intention was to request a burial Kaddish for Naomi, not to compose his own revision of the traditional prayer: "Knowing that Naomi had been denied the Kaddish at her graveside, Allen attempted to get one said for her" (207).

According to Miles, Ginsberg composed his own Kaddish only after attempting to organize a *minyan* for a traditional reading of the prayer. Miles reports that soon after Naomi's death, Ginsberg entered a synagogue with Kerouac and Peter Orlovsky to organize a *minyan*. Holding Eugene's letter describing the funeral as proof that no Kaddish had been recited at Naomi's grave, Ginsberg requested a Kaddish from the synagogue staff. Kerouac and Orlovsky were not Jewish; the synagogue was unable to organize a *minyan*. Miles explains that after this failure at the synagogue, Ginsberg wrote the letter to his father asking for a copy of the prayer. Louis sent the prayer, and in his response to his son affirmed the visionary history that frames the language of the original prayer and authorizes Ginsberg's use of language in *Kaddish*: "Those chants therein have a rhythm and sonorousness of immemorial years marching with reverberations through the corridors of history" (qtd. in Miles, 207).

The historical context of Ginsberg's composition of *Kaddish* points up a dual purpose in the poem: to eulogize Naomi and to offer a prophetic corrective to the institutional practices of Orthodox Judaism. Such a context also highlights the material urgency of Ginsberg's language for prophecy. As much as it claims the mystical, the poem is occasioned by a tangible failure to organize a *minyan* and is not, as Snyder says of *Howl*, a "rejection of matter." *Kaddish*, like *Howl*, represents mystical consciousness as a fusion of matter and spirit. Where Cohen and Lamm would speak for a Hebraic tradition of "definitive meaning" and an ontological certainty affirmed "amidst friends and neighbors of the same faith," Ginsberg intervenes in these continuities of visionary history to offer a counterdiscourse based in doubt. Like Blake and H. D., Ginsberg is estranged from the very tradition that grants his poetic prophecy whatever authority it has; thus, he affirms the power of the individual prophetic voice over the law of orthodoxy. As he addresses Jehovah in his revision of the burial prayer, Ginsberg affirms the authority of the individual to revise orthodox, and presumably timeless, language: "Tho I am not there for this Prophecy, I am unmarried, I'm hymnless, I'm Heavenless, headless in blisshood I would still adore" (212).

As M. L. Rosenthal has noted, Ginsberg maintains a tenuous balance in

Kaddish between Naomi's madness and her "mad idealism" (*Kaddish*, 219). Rosenthal argues that the political force of the poem lies in Ginsberg's "mock[ing]" of the historical forces that would deem as mad Naomi's "slightly exotic and generally despised Communist background."[54] In an era when Naomi's Communism was a sign of official madness—and in some quarters, treason—Ginsberg refused to separate Naomi's political discourse from her schizophrenic ravings. He instead uses Naomi's language to parody discourses of law and order that would equate communism with madness or criminality. Rosenthal terms Ginsberg's method in *Kaddish* a "refusal to repress."[55] This refusal produces Naomi's unchecked flow of language in the poem, and thereby privileges a desire otherwise confined by lawlike representation.

Ginsberg's revision of the Kaddish prayer in section 1 stages the narrative in section 2 of Naomi's counterhistorical biography of madness and religious doubt, her "refrain—of the Hospitals" (*Kaddish*, 212). His childhood bus ride with Naomi to a rest home in Lakewood, New Jersey, which ends with her "demand[ing] a blood transfusion," is described as a pilgrimage over a "Madness highway" (213). The material journey takes Ginsberg and his mother from Paterson to Lakewood. For Ginsberg, the highway is surrounded by representations of coercive histories of technological development in the twentieth-century United States. The "Madness highway" is located on a border between the devastation caused by Naomi's madness and the devastation that engendered it.

During his ride with Naomi from Paterson to Times Square, the 12-year-old Ginsberg first describes himself as only "tagging along" (213). As Naomi covers herself against the "breeze poisoned by Roosevelt"—a *one speech-breath thought* of real toxicity and paranoid delusion—Ginsberg simply wishes their ordeal "would end in a quiet room in a victorian house by a lake" (213). Yet the ride from Times Square to Lakewood is also a lesson in vision and history for the young Ginsberg:

> Ride 3 hours thru tunnels past all American industry, Bayonne preparing for World War II, tanks, gas fields, soda factories, diners, locomotive round-house fortress—into piney woods New Jersey Indians—calm towns—long roads thru sandy tree fields[.]
>
> (213)

The ride conjoins specialized war technologies with quotidian twentieth-century industry. Their journey "past all American industry" is equally a journey past *all-American* industry, insofar as "soda factories" and "diners" exist interdependently with the "tanks" and "gas fields" of war preparation. With a mother wrapped against the "invisible bugs" of Roosevelt, the young Ginsberg begins to understand a theme that would saturate his later poetry, namely that twentieth-century capitalism depends on interconnected economies of war and leisure.[56]

Moreover, *Kaddish* suggests that the interconnections of these economies exist as a result of the suppression of difference. The "calm towns"
that dot the landscape owe their tranquility to the Indian Wars of the previous centuries:

> Bridges by deerless creeks, old wampum loading the streambed—down
> there a tomahawk or Pocahontas bone—and a million old ladies voting for
> Roosevelt in brown small houses, roads off the Madness highway[.]
>
> (213)

Echoing themes of an earlier poem, "America," Ginsberg represents the
United States as a nation of isolated citizens living carelessly off the "deerless
creeks" of a natural world emptied of visionary potential by a twentieth-
century military-industrial economy. Surrounding the Madness highway is
a culture that represses its native heritage, submerging that culture entirely
and forging its reappearance in colonizing images of "tomahawk" and
"Pocahontas bone." This submersion is a sign of sanity, a "trick of agreement" brokered in "roads off the Madness highway."

Those who are sane vote for progress; the mad escape to Lakewood. In
Kaddish, the rest home has no place for Naomi in her condition, and she is
sent back out into the suburban streets. Ginsberg notes that from the frame
of reference of "millions of old ladies voting for Roosevelt," Lakewood's
suburban plots are untroubled, even thriving. Yet from the young Ginsberg's
perspective, Lakewood is a place of "shady lawn houses," whose streets
are "filled with crickets and poison ivy" (213). If sanity is an historically
produced "trick of agreement," then divine madness, too, might be as much
a constructed historical variant as a metaphysical verity.

For Blake and H. D., the poet-prophet's pilgrimage traverses the boundaries of natural and extra-natural worlds in order to redeem the natural
world as visionary. The pilgrimages of *Milton* and *Trilogy* revise the languages of classical science and religious orthodoxy incorporated within
their representational schemas. Similarly, representations of technology and
vision are the ground for Ginsberg's prophetic pilgrimage in *Kaddish*.
Ginsberg deploys images of scientific and technological progress to assert
and revise divine madness.

Moreover, just as he revises divine madness as a "trick of agreement,"
Ginsberg rewrites sexual pathology in a context both historical and mystical—a revision that, as discussed earlier in this chapter, represents for
Ginsberg "mystical mysteries in the forms in which they actually occur
here in the U.S. in our environment." After Ginsberg returns from the "Madness highway" excursion, his father scolds him for leaving Naomi alone at
the rest home. Ginsberg falls to bed that night "wanting to leave the world"
(*Kaddish*, 214). However, in a parenthetical aside several lines long, his
wish to escape is countered by images of immanent desire, by memories of

his love for Paul Roth. Ginsberg recalls that he was "probably that year newly in love with R—my high school mind hero, Jewish boy who came a doctor later" (214). Dropping *be* from *became*, Ginsberg reconceives coercive juridico-medical representations that would relegate homosexual desire to the realm of pathology; erotic thoughts of Roth *coming* reinforce rather than negate the institutionally sanctified role of the doctor that Roth eventually becomes. Roth is described only as a "first love" and a "crush," yet Ginsberg's unrequited desire for Roth was the impetus for his earliest significant impulses toward prophecy, those that emerged on the ferry ride to his Columbia entrance examination. Ginsberg "followed him [Roth] to college"; and "[l]aying down [his] life, for him [Roth]" represents his laying out a life of poetic prophecy. Ginsberg's articulations of desire represent a "release of particulars" that seek to redeem homoeroticism as a legitimate avenue of prophetic redemption. In *Kaddish*, a "mortal avalanche" of "whole mountains of homosexuality, Matterhorns of cock, Grand Canyons of asshole" is crucial to "imagining Infinity" arising from the disciplined desire of Ginsberg's childhood (214).

In *Kaddish*, acts of naming collapse the poles between the young Ginsberg's internal policing of homosexuality and his emphasis on material desire as a force of prophetic redemption. Ginsberg's "ignorant woe"— the "weight" of discipline on his "melancholy head"—is so strong that he cannot even name the object of his desire, although this "mortal avalanche" of desire is the key to "Infinity" in the poem (214). Ginsberg designates Roth as the source of his earliest impulses toward prophecy, but historical conditions prevent him from bestowing an identity on Roth in the poem. Therefore, the "Matterhorns of cock" that overwhelm the young Ginsberg in dreams actually conceal desire as they name it; Ginsberg's metaphors for homoerotic desire at this point in *Kaddish* re-cover desire under the guise of its recovery. The process of naming territorializes the young Ginsberg's desire as pathological. Citing material from an unpublished journal, Miles reports that less than a year after the vow on the ferry, Ginsberg used his job at the Paterson Public Library to seek out an explanatory name for his desires. Ginsberg "sneaked into the office of the librarian and looked up 'homosexuality' in Krafft-Ebing. 'Am I a homosexual?' he asked himself, seeking an explanation for the crushes he was always getting on other boys."[57] Ginsberg's account of the vow on the ferry is framed by the tendency of scientific discourse—here, of sexology—to constrain homoerotic desire with a pathological designation. The "crushes" he researches and names as "homosexual" in his clandestine trolling through Krafft-Ebing only reinforce desire as a "weight" on Ginsberg's "melancholy head."

For Ginsberg, this process of naming is located at the convergence of law and desire. Ginsberg dramatizes what Foucault later would term the "erasing" of the human from science, the end of the institutional practices that name human subjects by dint of studying them. Later in *Kaddish*, Ginsberg sneaks back to Paterson, an event designed to shatter the coercive limitations of normative desire. Confessing he "felt mysterious toward Paterson City Hall," Ginsberg narrates an attempt to disentangle law and desire from phallic representation:

> I sneaked inside it once—local Moloch tower with phallus spire & cap o' ornament, strange gothic Poetry that stood on Market Street—replica Lyons' Hotel de Ville—
> wings, balcony & scrollwork portals, gateway to the giant city clock. . . .
>
> (216)

Ginsberg's clandestine journey reveals the mysteries of Paterson City Hall: the "local Moloch tower" is the "gateway" to the boundaries of time measurement, and is crowned by "phallus spire & cap o' ornament." Phallic representation underwrites the naturalization of time measurement, an overdependence on reason that produces corrupt "madmen struggling over Zone, Fire, cops & Backroom Metaphysics" (216). Inside the Great Phallus, the young Ginsberg uncovers the origin of the "trick of agreement" he rewrites in the poem: a shadowy "Backroom" that parcels identity into zones, legislating lawlike and transgressive identities. Ginsberg's "Backroom" desire—his fantasy of "Grand Canyons of asshole"—is policed by authorities who would squelch ("zone") such fire within the territorialities of their own repressed "Backrooms."

Deleuze and Guattari's work in antipsychiatry, especially their *Anti-Oedipus: Capitalism and Schizophrenia*, contributes a vocabulary for understanding Ginsberg's journey to Paterson City Hall as a pilgrimage in which desire multiplies, rather than fixes, meaning. For Deleuze and Guattari, the language of the "schizophrenic taking a walk" (their model figure of psychic and social deterritorialization) seeks to empty the values imposed by absolutist naming and to shatter the conceptual spaces circumscribed by such naming. Ginsberg's narrative of City Hall deterritorializes representations of law, desire, and madness from the disciplinary practices of the human sciences. As the name *Anti-Oedipus* suggests, Deleuze and Guattari assault the primacy of the singularist nature of Freud's Oedipal model of identity. In their work, Oedipus is a transhistorical figure of absolutist identity in the West. Whether national, familial, or individual, all identity is circumscribed as normative or pathological according to its relation to the Oedipal model, a series of relations that zone identity in the West according to lawful (Oedipal) and transgressive (schizophrenic, anti-Oedipal) modes.

Ginsberg's relationship with his mother parodies the historical context of this "oedipalization," where postwar American discourses of homosexuality were framed by what Edelman terms a Cold War discourse of "momism," the equation of homosexuality with communism whereby the exposure of communists was linked to the exposure of homosexuals. According to Edelman, the urge to identify communists was portrayed in terms of protecting the domestic sphere of the country from a de-masculinizing invasion from within; the urge to identify homosexuals was portrayed in terms of protecting the family from a de-masculinizing invasion from within. "Momism" signified motherhood as an institution that must be protected and, as the medical discourse of the day would have it, as an institution producing the same threat from which it must be protected. Edelman writes that the popularized belief that the over-indulgent mother could produce homosexual identification in her son constituted a discourse "that implicated mothers in narratives of subversion through the weakening of masculine resolve against Communism."[58] Ginsberg engages "momism" in order to produce a revelatory fusion of Naomi's communism and her madness, even superimposing his pilgrimage with her "career." Inhabiting the discourse of "momism," Ginsberg's strategy does not portray internal collapse, as the *Life* article would suggest, but instead produces a "Blessed" poet who "builds Heaven in Darkness" (*Kaddish*, 225).

As a Jewish immigrant and a communist, Naomi experiences America as a land of "poisonous tomatoes" and "mysterious capitalisms." Naomi's "career" as a mental patient portrays the brutal consequences of the Oedipal "horrible circle," what Deleuze and Guattari would call a punishment for her inability to conform to "territorialization." She claims Roosevelt and Hitler plot against her, and believes her family sprays germs on her at night from the fire escape. She endures electroshock treatments; as part of this therapy, Metrasol injections cause her to gain weight, and she thereby loses control of the flows of her body. As a result of her psychiatric treatment, her body begins its own deterritorialization in the poem:

> One night, sudden attack—her noise in the bathroom—like croaking up her soul—convulsions and red vomit coming out of her mouth—diarrhea water exploding from her behind—on all fours in front of the toilet—urine running between her legs—left retching on the tile floor smeared with her black feces—unfainted[.]
>
> (218)

Naomi is "unfainted," denied the mercy of fainting as the result of constant shock treatments. Her identity subsumed by her illness, "Naomi of the hospitals" is "doomed" to what Goffman would call her "career" as a mental patient, subjected to what Deleuze and Guattari would term "Oedipal state control." Within the narrative of *Kaddish*, Ginsberg portrays her body caught in deterritorializing responses to "mysterious capitalisms." She is "unfainted," unable to respond to territorialization in any way except *to flow*.

Yet the "Backroom Metaphysics" of her historical moment is poised to reterritorialize her. As the poem emphasizes a primal language of flow—of "yacketayakk" and babble—Naomi responds to her treatment by investing the signs of her immanent familial and social world with a transcendent, unassailable power. Naomi's words grow more crazed with each trip to the hospital, an effect Deleuze and Guattari would describe as a defensive flow of desire against the omnipotent Oedipal "holy family" (51). For Deleuze and Guattari, the psychoanalytic Oedipal myth "make[s] the unconscious speak according to the transcendent uses of synthesis imposed on it by other forces: Global Persons, the Complete Object, the Great Phallus, the Terrible Undifferentiated of the Imaginary" (121). Naomi answers the "complete object" of Oedipal repression with the immanent flow of schizoid deterritorialization; for Ginsberg, this flow promises both unbounded mystic lyricism and the "unfainted" retching of diarrhea and vomit. At this time, 1943, after several trips in and out of mental hospitals, Naomi has resolved to "think nothing but beautiful thoughts" (*Kaddish*, 218). These "beautiful thoughts," however, are "zoned" by her asylum experiences.

Yet for Deleuze and Guattari, the schizoid is "the ultimate producer"— the ultimate destabilizer of zones. Against every instance of zoning, the schizoid "passes from one code to another" and "scrambles all the codes," whether these codes are linguistic, gestural, social, or psychic (15). Naomi shifts abruptly between "beautiful thoughts" and involuntary nerve shudders and uncontrolled flows caused by electroshock treatments. As Deleuze and Guattari argue, even when the schizoid internalizes "the banal Oedipal code," the code remains saturated with "all the disjunctions that this code was designed to eliminate" (15).

Ginsberg's search for a primal language is coded by the Logos, yet babbles "all the disjunctions" that the Logos would eliminate. Naomi eventually is reterritorialized. Her anti-Oedipal flows solidify into monotheistic vision, and she hallucinates that she hosts a dinner for God. Naomi's identification with an absolutist identity culminates in a vision of a God Whom she describes in singularist terms. Where God's singularity is transcendent in theology, Naomi revises this singularity as a principle of immanence: "he has a cheap cabin in the country. . . . He was a lonely old man with a white beard" (219). Seeing that God is absolutely alone, Naomi cooks him dinner and keeps him company: "he looked tired. He's a bachelor so long, and he likes lentil soup" (219). At the same time, she makes cold, rotting, "disconsolate" meals for her son. Continuing the vernacular of Naomi—speaking her language—Ginsberg remarks of the food, "I can't eat it for nausea sometimes" (219). Naomi's language must be deterritorialized in the prophetic pilgrimage of the poem; nevertheless, her language is the fount of vision in *Kaddish*. As Snyder suggests in his comments on *Howl*, "one may be saying, the unholy & ordinary condition of things as they are is holy."

For Ginsberg, Naomi's language is part of the process that produces the final, nonreferential sounds of the poem: "Lord Lord Lord caw caw caw" (227). Her words become the written signs of deterritorialization, a form of textuality Deleuze and Guattari characterize as a "writing that ceaselessly composes and decomposes the chains into signs that have nothing that impels them to become signifying" (39). Naomi's debased hospital experiences offer important linguistic and spatial representations in *Kaddish* that deterritorialize divine madness from its metaphysical boundaries.

Naomi's communism is silenced by the "cosmic financial murder plots" she discerns in the "mysterious capitalisms" of the United States and its allies:

'I am a great woman—am a truly beautiful soul—and because of that they (Hitler, Grandma, Hearst, the Capitalists, Franco, Daily News, the 20's, Mussolini, the living dead) want to shut me up—Buba's the head of a spider network'[.]

(221)

Naomi transforms "Buba"—grandma—and the rest of the family, along with major politicians and media figures of the first half-century, into one grand, paranoiac threat. In and out of hospitals, Naomi worsens: her "career" as an institutional patient is, as Deleuze and Guattari would term it, "legislated" by the institutional science of psychiatry. Naomi is "[t]ortured and beaten in the skull," and is made "lame" by electroshock and lobotomy (223).

Yet, as Deleuze and Guattari theorize, "Oedipus takes shape in the family, not in the analyst's office, which merely acts as the last territoriality" (121). From the vantage of antipsychiatry, the institution of the family is complicit in the territorialization of subjectivity. Writing within these debates in *Anti-Oedipus*, Deleuze and Guattari argue that the "loss of reality" in schizophrenia may not result entirely from schizophrenia itself, but from "its forced oedipalization[,] . . . its interruption" (123).

Ginsberg writes within and against a fear that prophecy is only divine madness, only a discourse inspired by external, absolutist figures such as God (Whom Naomi terms "the old bachelor") or the "Nobodaddy" of Blake. This fear emerges in Naomi's attempted seduction of Ginsberg, a scene that enacts his own "oedipalization," the truck with Moloch described in *Howl*. Immediately after Naomi claims to have seen God, a solitary male figure for Whom she cooks dinner, the narrative shifts to an overdetermined emphasis on the significatory value of the odors that trail Naomi. Ginsberg describes the meals she cooks for Yahweh as a "charity" that "stink[s] with Manhattan, madness" (219). The narrative displaces Naomi's smells onto the undercooked fish she offers her son. This fish, Ginsberg admits, constitutes a "desire to please me"; as a result, he displaces the odor of food onto representations of her body: "Her smells—and oft naked in the room, so that I stare ahead, or turn a book ignoring her" (219). Seeing Naomi consumed by Oedipalization, and revolted by the food she attempts to serve him, Ginsberg disincorporates the "stink" of the common sense language of territorialization.

What follows is a near-incestuous union with his mother, a passage crucial to the rhetoric of vision in *Kaddish*:

> One time I thought she was trying to make me come lay her—flirting to herself at sink—lay back on huge bed that filled most of the room, dress up round her hips, big slash of hair, scars of operations, pancreas, belly wounds, abortions, appendix, stitching of incisions pulling down in the fat like hideous thick zippers—ragged long lips between her legs. . . .
>
> (219)

Breslin, one of the few scholars to approach this section of the poem in detail, proffers an explanation of the unconscious effects of this scene. However, his commentary neglects the role of Naomi's institutionalization in the poem, and focuses solely on how this scene conforms to a classically Freudian explanation of homosexual object choice; thus, Breslin participates in the discourse of "momism" that *Kaddish* revises.

Breslin notes that Ginsberg's correlation of the female body and mutilation constitutes an "association frequent among male homosexuals who, perceiving the female's body as the castrated body of a man and frightened at the prospect of a similar fate for themselves, are more comfortable with sexual partners who also have penises."[59] Breslin argues that Ginsberg narrates a traditional Oedipal conflict, forming an identity for himself as a sexed subject by virtue of his ability "to deny both the powerful attraction he feels toward his mother—as well as the fears he experiences as soon as he imagines the possibility of acting on it."[60] Ginsberg's ambivalence toward the sexualized sight and smell of his mother *is* significant to this scene:

> . . . —What, even, smell of asshole? I was cold, later revolted a little, not much—seemed perhaps a good idea to try—know the Monster of the Beginning Womb—Perhaps—that way. Would she care? She needs a lover.
>
> (219)

As Breslin argues, Ginsberg's tone of "detached superiority"—when he claims, "She needs a lover"—threatens to negate the compassion of the narrative. If the poem, as Ginsberg writes, is a "saga" commemorating one whose "Ass and face" was "done with murder" in psychiatric hospitals, then Ginsberg's detachment seems to undermine the elegy.

However, Breslin fails to account for how Ginsberg uses his narrative of Naomi's treatment—her body scarred by invasive medical procedures—to rewrite the role of son and mother in the Oedipal drama. The Freudian Oedipal conflict is a representational schema that describes the male child's entry into desire: the sign of the mother is repressed and the father is installed as a sign of authority. As Deleuze and Guattari argue, Oedipus represents "a social investment of a paranoiac type"—a son who represses the mother for fear of castration (278). The prophetic impulse of *Kaddish* is to recover the mother, and rewrite her mental illness as redemptive through a discussion of the historical conditions of her inspired madness. The placement of this scene within the narrative is crucial to understanding Ginsberg's revision of divine madness: Ginsberg's idealization of incest as "know[ing] the Monster of the Beginning Womb" is part of a process in the narrative whereby he rejects idealization and the territorialization of identity by a mythic, Oedipal "Great Object." Freud's Oedipal drama depends on the repression of incestuous desire. The figure of Naomi in *Kaddish* seeks instead to break patterns of forced Oedipalization with her suggestion of seduction.

The incest scene is anticipated by an earlier scene that links metaphysical divine madness with "forced Oedipalization." First, as Naomi returns from one of her hospital visits, she lies on her bed in the same erotic postures that occasion the incest scene. Ginsberg frames this earlier narrative with the fear of madness, not with detachment or superiority:

> She went to the backroom to lay down in bed and ruminate, or nap, hide—
> I went in with her, not leave her by herself—lay in bed next to her . . .
> 'Don't be afraid of me because I'm just coming back home from the mental hospital—I'm your mother—'
> Poor love, lost—a fear—I lay there—Said, 'I love you Naomi,'—stiff, next to her arm. I would have cried, was this the comfortless lone union?— Nervous, and she got up soon.
>
> (217)

Ginsberg's language is fearful and ambivalent, eliding agency and intention from his representation of his young self's actions: "I went in with her, [in order] not [to] leave her by herself." As in the later incest scene, Ginsberg mythologizes his mother's body on the bed. The "comfortless lone union" anticipates "the Monster of the Beginning Womb." Ginsberg's visionary pilgrimage is conjoined with his mother's; he is the primary caretaker in the poem, and he claims to absorb vision from his mother's "pained head." Yet Ginsberg's attempts to take care of his mother often are troubled in *Kaddish* by her inability to recognize them as such, and by his own mythologizing of "the comfortless lone union." In this passage, she advises her "stiff" son not to fear her madness, but offers as reassurance only her familial authority — "I'm your mother"— a territorializing authority that already has been shattered by her breakdowns and hospitalizations. Instead of closing with superiority, Ginsberg affirms his fear: "Nervous, and she got up soon."

In *Kaddish*, if the human subject is to be un-zoned, and "Backroom Metaphysics" uncovered, then taboo must be emptied from within, just as Deleuze and Guattari's schizoid "plays the game to the hilt." As scenes on a prophetic pilgrimage, these two incest narratives demonstrate the impulse in *Kaddish* to empty the absolutist value of the Oedipal myth of psychoanalysis; the same impulse can be seen in *Howl*, where Oedipus is "finally" overturned as part of a process of deterritorialization. Ginsberg's idealizations in the second incest scene are circumscribed by absolutist religious signification more explicit than Naomi's visions of Yahweh. Immediately after musing that perhaps Naomi needed "a lover," Ginsberg follows with the original Aramaic of the first two lines of the Kaddish, then reaffirms his father's place in the family: "And Louis reestablishing himself in Paterson" (219). Indeed, as Breslin argues, this movement in the narrative from near-incest to the "reestablishing" of the father would suggest that the poem is framed precisely by a traditional Oedipal narrative, where the identity of the son is formed from the absolutist threat of castration—here, by the monovocal authority of original Aramaic signification. The repressed returns in the form of orthodoxy, what Deleuze and Guattari call the "horrible circle" of Oedipus.

Yet the identity of the protagonist within the prophetic narrative of the poem is not so consolidated as a traditional Oedipal framework would suggest. In Ginsberg's rhetoric of vision, language is a deterritorialized flow of "yacketayakking" gibberish, "Backroom Metaphysics," and "mad idealism." For Deleuze and Guattari, prophetic language is an immanent language of unconscious flow, with idealism kept in the offing. To be sure, Ginsberg's pilgrimage is commingled with Naomi's from the beginning. Ginsberg suggests, however, that the second incest scene represents a failure of forced Oedipalization. The "holy family" of Oedipal analysis breaks down. Louis indeed "reestablishes" himself, but not, as Breslin would argue, as the patriarch. Still supporting Naomi, he takes a "grimy apartment in negro district" and marries another woman (219). Louis establishes himself outside the territory of Oedipus, and thereby violates the white, patriarchal absolutism of the postwar, territorialized "Holy Family." Although paternal representation at first seems to be "reestablish[ed]" after the second incest scene, the father reappears outside the normative boundaries of Cold War social arrangements: divorced and remarried, he relocates outside of the communities of the white middle class.

Of course, Ginsberg's escape from incest is nevertheless a move toward

Oedipal repression. *Kaddish* shifts continually between babble and referentiality. Ginsberg calls the "final cops of madness" to "resc[ue]" him from taboo (222). Suggestions of incest in the poem produce anything but redemption in and of themselves; Deleuze and Guattari's "secret lunar" language does not substitute for the institutional praxis of the "career" of the mental patient.

Ginsberg's last visit to Naomi suggests that these incestuous scenes reproduce her Oedipalized experience as a mental patient. Near the end of her life, Ginsberg visits her in an institution that has become in itself the "Monster of the Beginning of the Womb." Again, the gateway to vision is incestuous: "Asylum spreads out giant wings above the path to a minute black hole—the door—entrance thru crotch—" (222). Naomi's sexuality again is identified by the odor of debasement, and Ginsberg implicates himself in the smell: "I went in—smelt funny—the halls again" (222). She is "lame now" and her body reads like a map of her institutionalization: "a scar on her head, the lobotomy—ruin, the hand dipping downwards to death" (223). If Ginsberg's portrayal of Naomi's scars only signals an identification with homosexual object choices, as Breslin suggests it does, then such identification neglects the historical conditions of her institutionalization. Indeed, such "scar[s]" and "ruin" are what produce antipsychiatric discourse in the first place.

Ginsberg once again counters images of Naomi's deterioration with attempts to escape into transcendent articulation. He closes the narrative section of the poem renaming his family as biblical: after describing the receipt of his brother's telegram informing him that Naomi has died, Ginsberg remembers her as "Naomi of Bible," an idealized image of "Ruth who wept in America" and "Rebecca aged in Newark" (224). He casts his brother as "David remembering his Harp, now lawyer at Yale," and himself again as "Svul Avrum."

However, Ginsberg's conversational rhetoric at the close of the narrative section ruptures the monovocal authority of this "holy family," otherwise absolutist in both biblical and Oedipal contexts. Naomi speaks back to Ginsberg in the final lines of narration in the poem, suggesting that the apocalypse of her death represents in language a materialist counterdiscourse to deterritorialize Ginsberg's own idealizations. Naomi's voice, described as prophetic, comes from a letter delivered after her death:

> Strange prophecies anew! She wrote— 'The key is in the window, the key is in the sunlight at the window—I have the key—Get married Allen don't take drugs—the key is in the bars, in the sunlight in the window. . . .'
>
> (224)

Of course this "new" prophecy is itself not absolutist. Neither is it strange: the key may be the immanent representation of divinity in nature—the "sunlight in the window" and the "sunny pavement" of the opening—but the "key" for Ginsberg's prophetic language is fixed neither as marriage nor straight sobriety.

The Kaddish binds the mourner to his faith in Yahweh; Ginsberg's *Kaddish* emphasizes ruptures of that bond. In Ginsberg's poem, the monotheistic God of Judaism is one of Naomi's hallucinations, an old man for whom she cooks lentil soup. God, this "old bachelor," inspires the prophecy only insofar as He is at the heart of the madness of Oedipalization. If such madness is "divine," this is so only through Ginsberg's revisionary language for prophecy. The poem operates as a redemptive biography, seeking to portray the madness of Naomi's life as a significant influence on the poet's own prophetic language, and as a representation of the poet's doubts about orthodox Western monotheism. The "key" to the lock of monovocality is a prophetic language dependent on ambivalence and an ironic containment of ambivalence. The poem recounts Naomi as both a source of vision and a figure against whom the young Ginsberg calls for the "final cops of madness." Like H. D.'s Christ child in *The Flowering of the Rod*—the fragrance that brings redemption through unfixed representation—this key in *Kaddish* infuses madness with divinity not through a standard metaphysical model but by moving continually between representations of the urban and the pastoral, immanence and transcendence, Oedipus and schizoid. Endless revision is the "key . . . in the window," a redemptive series of unfixed representations.

4. Conclusion: A Hymnless Heaven in the Darkness

In the final sections of *Kaddish*, "Hymmnn" and "Lament," Ginsberg reconceives religious laws that would relegate revisionary prophecy to a liminal, "hymnless" position. As he did in the revisionary final lines of section 1, Ginsberg opens "Hymmnn" with a response to the opening lines of the Kaddish:

> In the world which He has created according to his
>   will Blessed Praised
> Magnified Lauded Exalted the Name of the Holy One
>   Blessed is He!
>
>   (225)

Yet Ginsberg's prayer is a prophetic response to exclusionary orthodoxy. Ginsberg "lauds" a holy name that he emptied of absolute value in section 1; his project is to revise the regulation of the law strictly insisting that daughters cannot say the prayer, and that transgressive parents may not be worthy objects of it. The strict division of domestic and public spheres assigned to women and men, respectively, precludes daughters from reciting the Kaddish. According to Lamm, daughters are denied the bonding experience of the Kaddish because their "primary vocation is the home" (166). Moreover, Lamm emphasizes the Orthodox community's ambivalence toward parents who have transgressed religious law. He writes that those parents "who have sinned . . . and those who denied their faith or even who converted to other religions, are the subject of much scholarly controversy in regard to the requirement of saying the Kaddish" (170–71).

Ginsberg's revision of the Kaddish prayer seeks to "bless" those on the margins—those, like Naomi, who are denied the blessing of Judaic law or who "are the subject of much scholarly controversy." The domestic sphere, which distances women from the prayer, becomes Naomi's divine "madhouse"; that which is unlawful when framed by the marriage sacrament, Ginsberg's homosexuality, is as divine as her "paranoia":

> In the house in Newark Blessed is He! In the madhouse Blessed is
>   He! In the house of Death Blessed is He!
> Blessed be He in homosexuality! Blessed be He in Paranoia! Blessed be
>   He in the city! Blessed be He in the Book!
> Blessed be He who dwells in the shadow!
>
> (225)

"Hymmnn"—a fusion of hymn and *om*, a syllable that for Buddhists symbolizes a divine conjunction of body, speech, and mind—is Ginsberg's attempt to transform the "hymnless" speaker of the poem into a prophetic figure who redeems the margins: "Blessed be He who builds Heaven in Darkness!"

Ginsberg's revision, moreover, is designed to reinscribe the language of the original prayer with language circumscribed by apocalyptic representation. He closes "Hymmnn" with a blessing of cessation: "Blessed be He in the end! . . . Blessed be Death on us All!" (225). Ginsberg's emphasis on death seems at cross-purposes with a poem otherwise engaged in the life-affirming efforts of an elegy: elsewhere he re-invokes Naomi's life in order to "bless" the margins in which she existed.

Throughout the poem Ginsberg has sought a language for prophecy that could transform psychiatric science and Judeo-Christian orthodoxy into redemptive representations of visionary consciousness. As a modern prophetic poem, *Kaddish* is concerned with charting the boundary between referential and eschatological language, with the representation of "apocalypse and after," as Comens puts it in his description of postmodern poetic language in the nuclear age. Ginsberg re-envisions Naomi's final moments as an apocalyptic fusion of transcendent and immanent representation; the "key in the window," Ginsberg's image of a visionary urban and pastoral world, is deployed as the mediating force between these two categories of understanding.

Later, Naomi's final breaths defy material time measurement and suffuse the Kaddish with heretical Gnostic vision. Naomi takes her final breaths on a littoral boundary between materialism and transcendentalism: she comes "to that dark night on iron bed by stroke when the sun gone down on Long Island," where the "vast Atlantic roars outside the great call of Being to its own" (225). Between life and death, enduring the stroke that would kill her, she sees the immanent landscape of the poem as a Gnostic "nightmare" caused by "divided creation." Here, the Oedipalized God of lentil soup and bachelorhood in the poem becomes the monotheistic Ialdabaoth, the deranged twin of the Sophia of Gnostic cosmology who is the absolutist creator of the world in Gnosticism, and becomes the Jehovah of Blake's and H. D.'s poetic prophecies.[61]

Perhaps *Kaddish*, like *Howl*, risks what Snyder terms in his correspondence a Gnostic "dualism," positing matter as the deranged oppositional force to the inner spark of divinity Gnostics perceived in every human. Yet instead of "escaping matter," the tendency Snyder perceives in *Howl*, Naomi re-envisions time and matter as visionary. Naomi's final moments in the poem bequeath a vision that redeems the materialist primacy of this "divided creation," leaving a "key in the window" that bathes "all Earth" in "one everlasting light":

> But that the key should be left behind—at the window—the key in the
>   sunlight—to the living—that can take
> that slice of light in hand—and turn the door—and look back see
> Creation glistening backwards to the same grave, size of universe,
> size of the tick of the hospital's clock on the archway over the white
>   door—
>
> (226)

The *end* in apocalyptic representation is both a cessation and a purposeful beginning. Creation "glisten[s] backwards" to a grave as magnanimous as the universe, and as particular as the individual "tick of the hospital's clock."

Like each "pulsation of an artery" in Blake's *Milton* and each knock of the visionary Lady in the clock scene of *Tribute to the Angels*, each tick contains within it the apocalyptic promise of prophetic language—a key to a grave the "size of the universe"—while framed by "the hospital's clock on the archway over the white door." Naomi's death in the poem is more than a release from the hospitals that defined her life. In *Kaddish*, her death bequeaths a visionary language to rewrite as "holy" and "blessed" the measurement of time and matter that disciplines and polices these hospitals.

In his poetic prophecy, Blake transformed immutable selfhood into mobile representations of identity—Milton's redemptive self-annihilation in *Milton*. H. D. closed her prophecy with a Christ child reborn not as a human but as a fragrance. Just so, the closing moments of Ginsberg's "saga" of Naomi "of the hospitals" also affirm an end to the belief in fixed identity created and reified by the study of the human sciences. As the final section of *Kaddish* opens, crows "shriek in the white sun over grave stones," and invocations of "Lord Lord Lord" confirm the finality of death (227). Repetitions of "caw" and "Lord" commingle in images both materialist and metaphysical, eventually erasing attempts at referentiality. As this section continues, the repetitions suggest the revisionary possibilities of apocalyptic representation: "caw caw my eye be buried in the same Ground where I stand in Angel / Lord Lord great Eye that stares on All and moves in a black cloud" (227). Indeed, he is "in Angel": he is identified by a language both spatial and nominative, and never wholly fixed.[62] The visionary "eye" of the poet-prophet is both "buried" by death and made "Angel[ic]" by it. By contrast, the eye of the Lord is panoptic, static, and inaccessible; it is capable only of ineluctable movement and coercive "star[ing]."

Ginsberg eventually proclaims that the voice of the prophet redeems the eye of God. Ginsberg's "hymnless" heresy crafts a "voice in a boundless field in Sheol" to break the boundary between prophet and God. By re-envisioning time measurement as an imaginative instant, Ginsberg combines his voice with the name of God, fusing representations of a metaphysical God with those of a visionary natural world:

> Caw caw the call of Time rent out of foot and wing an instant in the
>   universe
> Lord Lord an echo in the sky the wind through ragged leaves the roar of
>   memory[.]
>
> (227)

Yet this "roar of memory" is not reified, does not construct a fixed self. Declaring the human propensity to reify selfhood as "a dream," Ginsberg seeks to portray prophetic language as the product of self-annihilation:

> caw caw all years my birth a dream caw caw New York the bus the broken
>   shoe the vast highschool caw caw all Visions of the Lord
> Lord Lord Lord caw caw caw Lord Lord Lord caw caw caw Lord[.]
>
> (227)

As in Blake and H. D., where time measurement is re-envisioned as an instant of the prophetic imagination, in *Kaddish* "the call" of imaginative time and "the roar of memory" can be equivocal. As components of a lan-

guage for modern prophecy, time measurement and mind science are emptied of the irreducibility that the "sciences of man" necessarily impose upon
them in order to create the belief in the intrinsic subjectivity of "man."

The final "words" of *Kaddish* are the nonreferential sounds of crows
and the ululations of the modern poet-prophet. Ginsberg anchors the line
with a final utterance of "Lord," an articulation made "hymnless" by the
unfixed representations of Ginsberg's representation of the modern poet-
prophet, but in a 1989 reading filmed by the Lannan foundation, Ginsberg
anchors the line instead with a final "caw," thus deeming the language of
God and nature equal.[63] Ginsberg's revisions suggest that the final articulation of the poem is not stable, and endlessly resonates between "caw" and
"Lord." Ginsberg's ultimate referent for prophecy is only the breath-unit,
what has become the anchoring articulation of "Ah" that marks his later
career. Ginsberg explains in his 1984 annotations to "Mind Breaths" that
"Ah" is a key to the "vocalization" of the "purification of speech." The
"Ah" vocalization represents a "one syllable summary of the Prajnaparamita
Sutra."[64] The Prajnaparamita Sutra, also translated as the Heart Sutra, discusses the Buddhist doctrine of the purification of speech; moreover, it is
known in all versions of Buddhism as the comprehensive sutra on *shunyata*.
As articulations of Buddhist emptiness, Ginsberg's alternating "caw" and
"Lord"—and, later, his emphasis on an "elemental" breath of "Ah"—suffuse a prophetic language empty of absolutist meaning with full, polyvalent linguistic referents.

As a foundation for prophecy, Ginsberg's principle of one speech-breath-
thought denies a transcendent referentiality; yet in its emphasis on embodied divinity it distrusts language that refuses to point beyond its own
immanent textuality. Ginsberg writes, with Carl Solomon, during his 1949
incarceration in the Columbia Psychiatric Institute: "[B]eyond a certain
point there can be no spoken communication and all speech is useless."[65] In
The Order of Things Foucault argues that in the modern era, madmen and
poets occupy opposing poles of discourse; the mad speak signs whose
meanings "never ceas[e] to proliferate," while the poet conversely "brings
similitude," and hence representability, to such signs (49–50). Ginsberg
constructs a language for prophecy that oscillates between these two poles.
"Caw" and "Lord" reverberate in Ginsberg's continuous revisions; thus, as
"useless" as speech might be, it is not to be replaced by silence in Ginsberg's
prophetic poetry. Instead, referentiality is suffused with *shunyata*, the annihilation of fixed designation, an idea that prophetic representation emerges
from an apocalyptic, "elemental" fusion of immanence ("caw") and transcendence ("Lord").

5

Conclusion: Apocalypse Without End

1. APOCALYPTIC REPRESENTATION AND A PROPHETIC IMAGINATION

For Blake, H. D., and Ginsberg, apocalypse overwrites ontological certainty with a revisionary language that combines immanent and transcendent categories of understanding. Each seeks a primal language adequate to the task of fusing material and metaphysical states of being. Blake is the apt opening figure for this study of the altering continuities of prophetic poetry precisely because his conception of language can be located between, in Foucault's terms, the Enlightenment belief in language as a mode of "mathesis" and the Modern view that language represents only itself, containing "no point of departure, no end, and no promise."[1] These poets crucially inscribe their language with biblical significance, looking back to authorizing Hebraic models to create a conversational language for redemption. The role of naming in the prophecies of Blake, H. D., and Ginsberg is suffused with the urge to recuperate lost biblical forms that, to borrow from Foucault's history of the human sciences, functioned during the Enlightenment as a series of "fragmentary monuments": "Hebrew therefore contains, as if in the form of fragments, the marks of . . . original name-giving."[2] Yet the initializing authority of the Bible for these poets is revised in light of their urge to rename history and language in terms of vision—to transform the authoritative, *received* language of the Bible into a language of endless *making* and *naming*. Hebrew marks "original name-giving," but in eras when naming is dominated by scientific observation, the originary precedence of Hebrew becomes for Blake, H. D., and Ginsberg a provisional site for continual transformations of observation into vision.

Derrida's 1968 lecture, "The Ends of Man," locates the "eschato-teleological situation" of apocalyptic language specifically within Foucault's archaeology of the study of "man."[3] Derrida addresses issues of politics,

173

language, and science that emerged from the Tet escalation of American involvement in Vietnam in January of 1968, and from the massive student and worker strikes that shook France that May. For Derrida, the events of 1968 demanded a new understanding of the relationship of nationalism and identity, an understanding that a revised Western apocalyptics might supply.

Derrida's conclusion confronts the paradoxical condition of apocalyptic representation that I argue is central to the conception of the modern prophet in *Milton, Trilogy, Howl*, and *Kaddish*. For Derrida, the ends of "man" are not a classically unified teleology, nor are they so far outside of representation that they are meaningless. Instead, the ends of "man" are conceived by Derrida as an articulation of both teleological and local modes of making knowledge. Derrida conceives of an "end" that is meaningful inasmuch as it represents "the basis of a 'formal' organization which in itself has no meaning, which does not mean that it is either the non-sense or the anguishing absurdity which haunt metaphysical humanism" (134). Derrida's restrictive clause here is crucial, as are his quotation marks around "formal"; they highlight the primary emphasis of his essay: the possible creation of new, mobile frames of reference, of indeterminate systems of thought that need not lapse into disorganized "non-sense."

"The Ends of Man" posits a mobility of reference frames to conceive, paradoxically, a language for nonapocalyptic apocalypse. I would argue that such mobility also describes the revisionary divine madness in Blake's, H. D.'s, and Ginsberg's poetic prophecies. Their resistances to reified modes of representation work to counter the charge of "non-sense" leveled against nonreferential language by transcendental humanism. Derrida's conclusion involves the use of deconstruction both within and without the original constructs—the "terrains"—that delimit knowledge according to the discourses of "man." He posits an initial strategy of exposing the constructedness of the terrain itself without venturing beyond this terrain; to "attempt an exit and a deconstruction without changing terrain, by repeating what is implicit in the founding concepts and the original problematic" (135). The historical urgency of the response by Blake, H. D., and Ginsberg to what they perceive as coercive language structures is worth recalling here. Each challenges the constructedness of science and history through traversal of spheres of representation specific to their respective historical moments. Each builds systems that, paradoxically, attempt to undo the dominant impulse toward system-building in their contemporary milieu.

Derrida appends to the urge to "deconstruc[t] without changing terrain" an equally urgent call to work from outside the terrain. One must also, he argues, "change terrain, in a discontinuous and irruptive fashion, by brutally placing oneself outside, and by affirming an absolute break" with and "difference" from the "original problematic"—from the presumably coercive authority of totalizing discourses of metaphysicality and materiality. Derrida argues that a "new"—but already old—"writing must weave and interlace these two motifs of deconstruction. Which amounts to saying that one must speak several languages and produce several texts at once" (135).

For Derrida, the late twentieth century is poised between two "eves of destruction": between an authoritarian quashing of difference—"the eve as the guard mounted around the house"—and a new mode of understanding language and consciousness —"the awakening to the day that is coming, at whose eve we are" (136). He writes, "Perhaps we are between these two eves, which are also the two ends of man. But who, we?" (136). For Derrida, "we" designates an identity comprised of—or emerging from—spaces on the boundary between these eves.

As in the prophetic poetry of Blake, H. D., and Ginsberg, Derrida's "we" suggests a sense of identity both spatial and nominative. Derrida collapses internal space with external time measurement to augment the idea of apocalypse as the end of history; here, apocalypse might also be the creation of continuously revisionary modes of consciousness and representation. Blake's idea of apocalypse is a redemptive fusion of Poetic Genius and nature that reconceives time measurement as an imaginative instant: "a Period / Within a Moment: a pulsation of the Artery" (*Milton*, 29.2–3). H. D. seeks to transform the "unregistered dimension" of apocalypse into a revisionary condition of redemption (*Walls*, 43.5); the prophetic Lady of *Tribute to the Angels* re-envisions clock-time as imaginative measurement, as a prophetic "moment" in time suffused with the revisionary power of the imagination. In *Kaddish*, Ginsberg portrays creation "glistening backwards" to an end that is both a cessation and a purposeful beginning, that conjoins the poet's imagination with the ticking of the clock in Naomi's final hospital room (226).

Poised between their own versions of oscillation and containment, *Milton*, *Trilogy*, *Howl*, and *Kaddish* also ask a self-annihilating, "Who, we?" Their answer: who can we *be* but we who *arise* from a language that combines internal and external, seer and seen, immanence and transcendence, prophet and audience, prophet and God? This "we" exists in boundless recombination in modern poetic prophecy: Milton-Los-Palamabron-Blake and the Starry Eight; H. D.'s interdependent shell, "Marys a-plenty," and the Christ child as bundle of myrrh; Ginsberg's combined Allen-Naomi pilgrimage, culminating in mobile representations of a revelatory key in the window and continually alternating ululations of "Lord" and "caw."

For Derrida, Foucault's claim that "[m]an had been a figure occurring between two modes of language" can only be stated within the referential boundaries Foucault would see erased.[4] Thus, Derrida writes, the articulation of the imminent end of "man" cannot claim the antihumanist liminality

Foucault advances in his work. Characterizing Foucault's project as a "trembling" of humanist security, Derrida writes that "this trembling—which can only come from a certain outside—was only requisite within the very structure that it solicits" (133). For Derrida, Foucault's sense of an ending is not "bothersome" enough (114). Derrida implies that Foucault has mistaken a *certainty* for a localized *particularity*: he argues for conceiving Foucault's "end" as more than just an oscillation of structure (a trembling "within the very structure it solicits"), and for conceiving it also as an effort to contain this oscillation, where the Latin *sollicitare* means both to disturb and to manage. Derrida implies that Foucault causes the terrain of metaphysical humanism to "tremble" but does not make a bothersome enough break from this terrain.

Within textuality and language, the sense of an ending in Foucault's archaeology of the human sciences is not, for Derrida, an erasure that leads to absence. This tension between ideas of the production and erasure of fixed language and identity mirrors the revisionary responses to vision and history in Blake, H. D., and Ginsberg. Derrida proposes that a revised apocalypse represents a new mode of consciousness, a new mode of thinking through language. Such an approach to understanding and language can begin to reconcile Blake, H. D., and Ginsberg's continuation of the Western search for a primal language with their desire to revise the absolutist nature of such a search.

As both a historical response to Foucault's *The Order of Things* and a speculation on the use of apocalyptic language, Derrida's "The Ends of Man" offers an important framework for clarifying the nature of apocalyptic representation in the poetic prophecies of Blake, H. D., and Ginsberg. Derrida stresses a sense of apocalypse that signifies both conclusion and awakening. He writes that the ends of "man" always represent both finitude and purpose; and, he argues, the linguistic representation of these two ends is best seen in the act of *naming*: "The name of man has always been inscribed in metaphysics between these two ends. It has meaning only in this eschato-teleological situation" (123). Like the immanent vision of transcendence in Blake, H. D., and Ginsberg, Derrida's critique of metaphysics breaks from transcendental humanism while maintaining the transcendental urgency of apocalypse. For these poets, if apocalyptic representation is to revise the authority of transcendental metaphysics, then it must do so through renaming. Specifically, as Derrida argues, apocalyptic representation would produce this break by revising those acts of naming that underwrite discourses of the human sciences. For Derrida, this break would be represented in material language, while also remaining paradoxically beholden to the metaphysical qualities suggested by apocalypse.

Calling for new ways of thinking about representation and action, Derrida posits a mode of language where meaning resides in the secular vision of conversationalism. His model in the essay is the philosophical colloquium as a form of discourse: as an opposition to absolutist law, the colloquium— what he calls a "form of democracy" that places "the accent on *form* no less than on *democracy*"—must revise its authorizing power to the extent that it is "bothersome" (114). For Blake, H. D., and Ginsberg, the Logos precludes a "colloquium" of religion and human science that might other-wise stage a visionary language. Yet as system-builders, they begin with the foundationalism of the Bible to authorize their poetic prophecies. Blake's, H. D.'s, and Ginsberg's revisionary counterhistories of individual truth exist in an uneasy relationship with the antihumanist projects of poststructuralism. If, as for Foucault, the end of "man" represents human-ity as a figure in the sand threatened by oceanic erasure, it would seem that the emphasis each of these poets places on modern prophecy as a matter of individual rather than metaphysical authority is undermined by the histori-cal shift to which Foucault points in *The Order of Things*. Apocalypse, then, would seem to unveil the erasure of a vibrant paradox—the imma-nent-transcendent figure of apocalyptic representation in these poets' proph-ecies—under the incoming swell of absolute groundlessness. Yet for all their emphasis on individual authority, these poets insist on a model of subjectivity that continually changes terrain, and maintains a bothersome relationship with its authorizing power and its historical moment.

The skepticism toward teleology in Blake's, H. D.'s, and Ginsberg's counterhistories might indeed point to an apocalypse that is after all noth-ing but an ending: a counterhistory overwhelmed by its own surge of era-sure. Given the Western propensity to certify meaning in the referential language of individual authors, such matters as literal/littoral expression, a Messiah as a bundle of myrrh, and the divine language of cawing crows all seem to point to meaninglessness. If so, then for all these poets' trust in apocalyptic representation, their prophetic poetry nevertheless debilitates itself within an apocalypse that produces nonsense—or the humanist "an-guish" of Bloomian silence.

What is at stake in the risky, shifting terrains of Blake, H. D., and Ginsberg are competing conceptions of sense and subjectivity. From the polar per-spectives of humanist metaphysics and postmodern materialism, the im-manent-transcendent representations of these poets' prophetic pilgrimages are absurd. However, from the perspective of a rhetoric of vision that lo-cates the metaphysical in the material and the material in the metaphysical, apocalyptic representation inhabits the terrain of referentiality in order to affirm a discontinuity that would offer redemptive possibility in "non-sense." Derrida's remarks can contribute a theoretical framework for the impulse in Blake, H. D., and Ginsberg to create a new language adequate to this polyvocal task. The apocalyptic language of modern, prophetic poetry is authorized by "several languages" at once—that is, by several traditions at once—and so creates a conversational, polyvocal "eschato-teleological situation" that in turn layers "several texts at once" on its pilgrimage toward an apocalyptic consciousness conceived without end.

2. Apocalyptic Consciousness: Future Prospects

What produces collocation rather than cacophony from this layering of languages and texts? I would argue that this is as much a question for the study of perception as it is for poetics and cultural studies. For Blake, H. D., and Ginsberg, prophetic poetry is a special use of the imagination, a use in which poetic language can reconfigure human experience as a mobility of encounters with eschatological and resurrective modes of consciousness. Recent work in cognitive science also has begun to bridge a gap between ideas of unified self-consciousness and of decentered selfhood. I will not, and could not, engage in a thoroughgoing examination of relations between cognitive science and poetic language here, but I will argue that poetry is a form of language and knowledge-making whose metaphoricity should be of vital concern to those researching how the mind constructs its world. I would like to close by making a connection between prophetic poetry and cognitive theory, a connection that comments on the forms of language and identity at work in the varying apocalyptic representations of Blake, H. D., and Ginsberg. This connection might well be pursued as an aspect of the interdisciplinary projects of poetics and cultural studies, and it could be of interest to those researching the role of language in our shifting conceptions of mind.

Suggestions of the end of "man," the end of the singularist, autonomous, independent subject of the human sciences, abound in contemporary human science, especially in cognitive science. Cognitive science is beginning to show that our conceptions of ourselves as autonomous and unique might always have been illusory. As Francisco J. Varela, Evan Thompson, and Eleanor Rosch argue in *The Embodied Mind: Cognitive Science and Human Experience*, our fields of perception may be *enactive* rather than positivist.[5] If perception enacts a world, then a language for perception must reflect how subject and object emerge conjoined in this enacted world. Such a language would resemble the transferential language of Blake, H. D., and Ginsberg; and in decentering the autonomy of the subject and the implacability of the object, this language would carry with it the urgency of apocalyptic consciousness I have discussed in Blake's, H. D.'s, and Ginsberg's work.

Varela, Thompson, and Rosch chart a shift in cognitive science that resembles the shifts in literary studies and critical theory that frame many of the readings in chapters 1–4. As I have noted, the revisionary language of modern prophecy nevertheless results from Blake's, H. D.'s, and Ginsberg's poetic pilgrimages in search of an essential, primal language for prophecy. Gesturing backward toward an unreachably perfect language, Blake, H. D., and Ginsberg create a material language for prophecy that keeps its transcendental authority in the offing.

While the empirical concerns of cognitive science are unlikely to propose transcendentalism, Varela, Thompson, and Rosch demonstrate that cognitive science is shifting toward a conception of mind in which perception defies referentiality, in which the essence of mind rests, paradoxically, on "groundlessness" (144). Instead of focusing only on indeterminacy as a conceptual framework "that can be disciplined by representational theories of the mind," cognitive science also is focusing on how representation is contextual and evades the boundaries of absolutism (145). According to this model, the mind is not an information processor, as a century of cognitive science had proposed, nor is language the code that makes such processing possible. Instead, "perception consists in perceptually guided action" in which "organism and environment cannot be separated," and in which the natural world is not a positivist a priori absolute, but is instead "enacted or brought forth by a history of coupling" between subjects and objects (200–202).

Borrowing from Marvin Minsky's work on the brain as a series of interconnected networks rather than a solitary central processor, Varela, Thompson, and Rosch propose a model of the relationship between mind and nature in which each gives rise to the other: rather than "*representing* an independent world," mind and nature together "*enact* a world as a domain of distinctions that is inseparable from the structure embodied by the cognitive system" (140). Their focus on the "continuous self-modifications" of the brain in response to stimuli suggests that recent cognitive science "requires that we move away from the idea of the world as independent and extrinsic to the idea of a world as inseparable from these processes of self-modification" (139). They argue for connectionism, a theory in which knowledge is enacted through interconnected relationships of brain and stimuli rather than through the efforts of a sovereign, perceiving subject separated from a static, perceived object.

Seer and seen collapse into each other in the model that emerges from the research in *The Embodied Mind*. With this collapse comes familiar skepticism about the ability of referential language to adequately represent the relationship between seer and seen. Thus, one-to-one representation, the dream of a perfect language in the postlapsarian tradition of prophecy, is inadequate to the task of cognition or prophecy. Varela, Thompson, and Rosch have little to say about the role language *could* play in this coupling relationship, and they dismiss without explanation the parallel move away from ontological certainty in the humanities. Varela, Thompson, and Rosch caution that their cognitive revisionism "is not an invitation to decenter the self and/or world into language as is so popular at present in the humanities" (227). Although their caution is well taken, their silencing of the (presumably failing) role of the humanities on this issue is remarkable, insofar as their work claims an authority from its interdisciplinary combination of cognitive science with the humanities (specifically, with Western phenomenology, Foucauldian cultural studies, and Madhyamika Buddhist philosophy). Mirroring, and at times borrowing from, the past three decades of voluminous work in the humanities on alternative approaches to language and identity, they find referentiality inadequate to the task of representing the world. However, they issue a cursory dismissal of the humanities on this same subject and offer no alternative conception of language.

Even so, I would argue that their description of the coupling of subject and object—or the collapse of object into subject—demands an attention to the language forms that arise from the connectionist relationships of mind and nature they describe. In the prophetic poetry of Blake, H. D., and Ginsberg, these relationships perform apocalyptic modes of representation, in which multiplicitous voices create a possibility for enactive modes of thought—for the representation of meaning as a literal/littoral boundary condition. Such representation suggests that what Hassan terms the "postmodern imagination" and what I term "prophetic imagination" are related. If so, the production and reception of both critical theory and apocalyptic literature also are interconnected: one cannot be subjugated to the other, just as (to recall chapter 1) neither the "asylum of un-reason" nor the "empire of reason" need subjugate the other. Rather, both enact critical fields of representation that are antifoundationalist and are concerned with how the layering of many languages at once can suggest new forms of representation, history, and agency.

Relations and transferences of meaning enact a language for redemption in the poetic prophecies of Blake, H. D., and Ginsberg: the literal is the littoral; angles of incidence and reflection work together to redeem "deplorable" gaps in linear time; "Lord," "caw," and "Ah" mark a boundlessness that, to echo Bloom and swerve from him, constitutes "[a]ll that is human."

In the wake of (re)visionary history, apocalyptic representation begins with the unruly conjunction of teleology and indeterminacy, decentering the Western sovereign subject without erasing subjectivity. What is erased at such an "end" is the belief in the unity of our language for perception. Apocalyptic representation *ends* the inability of material language to represent vision, and *unveils* a boundless language of continual attention to the otherness of polyvocality. Apocalyptic representation depends on a conversationalism that brackets the idea of an independent consciousness in favor of a collocation of multiplicitous voices.

The disestablished sites of the prophetic imagination conceive apocalyptic consciousness as a "historical essence." The possibility that the search
for a primal language could end in a performative coupling of language
and contextual experience might produce, to recall Bloom, a "sadness" at
the lack of control and order that comes from groundlessness. Yet if sadness is produced by the disestablishment of imagination in Blake's, H. D.'s,
and Ginsberg's prophetic poetry, perhaps that sadness only arises from, to
quote Kearney and bring the study full circle, the lack of a "cheerless"
universalism that would seek to lock the "prison-house of mirrors." For
Blake, H. D., and Ginsberg, apocalyptic language must combine multiple
voices to enact the experience of groundlessness, whether staged by the
contrariety of Beulah, by counterdiscursive anagrams, or by an elemental
"Ah." The "end of man" is the ending of the expectation that idealist language might adequately represent transcendental experience, an expectation perhaps doomed by its inability, as Derrida argues, to change "terrain."
Instead, the "end"—the purpose—of this ending points to an apocalyptic
language for visionary history located on a blurred boundary between immanent and transcendent modes of representation.

What I have termed *apocalyptic consciousness* recalls Hassan's idea of
a "New Gnosticism," a "complete gnosis or knowledge" that paradoxically
"insinuates itself" in the antifoundationalism of postmodernism.[6] I would
argue that revised apocalyptic representation affords an opportunity to explore religious language not as a transcendental system of signs—as if such
a system would admit the "empire of reason"—but instead as a mode of
conceiving a combined metaphysical and material mode of consciousness.
Such an approach to language and perception might best be examined within
modern prophetic poetry, where meaning oscillates on the boundary between religious master narratives and postmodern material distrust, between
metaphysical authority and polysemic unruliness. In a postmodern era when
visionary experience might be reduced to just another textual formation,
the prophetic imagination faces the language and forms of the phenomenal
world with a desire to simultaneously recall and revise. This site of continuity and revision affords the opportunity for an ongoing recombination of
vision in language, history, and deconstruction: Jerusalem in London, the
myrrh of "Marys a-plenty," and the "yacketayakk" of "Lord" and "caw"
made *Ah*.

Notes

CHAPTER 1

1. Richard Kearney, *Poetics of Imagining: From Husserl to Lyotard* (London: Routledge, 1991).

2. H. D., *Trilogy* (New York: New Directions, 1973). All subsequent references are to this edition. Throughout my text, I abbreviate the three books that comprise *Trilogy* as follows: *Walls* for *The Walls Do Not Fall*; *Angels* for *Tribute to the Angels*; and *Flowering* for *The Flowering of the Rod*. Lines from *Trilogy* are documented according to the section of each book in which they appear. Thus, this passage, from section 9, lines 1–2, of *The Flowering of the Rod*, would be documented: *Flowering*, 9.1–2.

3. *Milton*, 41:7, in William Blake, *The Complete Poetry and Prose of William Blake*, ed. David V. Erdman (New York: Doubleday, 1988), 615. Unless otherwise indicated, all references to Blake's poetry and prose are from *The Complete Poetry and Prose of William Blake*, abbreviated as *Complete Poetry and Prose* in parenthetical citations.

4. Robert Alter, *The Art of Biblical Poetry* (New York: Basic, 1985), 209.

5. Allen Ginsberg, *Kaddish*, 209. References to the text of *Kaddish* are indicated by page numbers from *Collected Poems, 1947–1980* (New York: Harper & Row, 1984). References to *Howl* are indicated by line numbers from *Howl: Original Draft Facsimile*, ed. Barry Miles (New York: HarperCollins, 1986). In *Howl: Original Draft Facsimile*, Ginsberg authorized each strophe of *Howl* to count as a line (the same lineation strategy that anthologized versions of *Howl* have followed).

6. Dwight Goddard, *A Buddhist Bible* (E. P. Dutton, 1938; rpt. Boston: Beacon, 1970), 41–42.

7. Ibid.

8. "Allen Ginsberg," Lannon Literary Videos, dir. Lewis MacAdams and John Dorr, 1989.

9. Richard Dellamora, *Apocalyptic Overtures: Sexual Politics and the Sense of an Ending* (New Brunswick, N. J.: Rutgers Univ. Press, 1994).

10. Harold Bloom, "On Ginsberg's *Kaddish*," in *The Ringers in the Tower: Studies in Romantic Tradition* (Chicago: Univ. of Chicago Press, 1971), 214.

11. Ginsberg, *Kaddish*, 227; Bloom, "On Ginsberg's *Kaddish*," 215.

12. Bloom, "On Ginsberg's *Kaddish*," 215.

13. Ihab Hassan, *The Postmodern Turn* (Columbus: Ohio State Univ. Press, 1987), 180.

14. Rosi Braidotti, "The Politics of Ontological Difference," in *Between Feminism and Psychoanalysis*, ed. Teresa Brennan (New York: Routledge, 1989), 103.

15. For a discussion of how church authority mediates tensions between divine scripture and human artifice, see especially Robert E. Lerner's "Medieval Prophecy as Religious

Dissent," *Past and Present* 72 (1976): 3–24, and Lawrence F. Rhu, "After the Middle Ages: Prophetic Authority and Human Fallibility in Renaissance Epic," in *Poetry and Prophecy: The Beginnings of a Literary Tradition*, ed. James L. Kugel (Ithaca: Cornell Univ. Press, 1990), 163–84.

16. Frank Kermode, *The Sense of an Ending: Studies in the Theory of Fiction* (New York: Oxford Univ. Press, 1967); Dellamora, *Apocalyptic Overtures*; Jacques Derrida, "The Ends of Man," in *Margins of Philosophy*, trans. Alan Bass (Chicago: Univ. of Chicago Press, 1982).

17. Jan Wojcik and Raymond-Jean Frontain, "Introduction: The Prophet in the Poem," in *Poetic Prophecy in Western Literature*, ed. Wojcik and Frontain (London: Associated Univ. Presses, 1984), 15.

18. Joseph Anthony Wittreich, Jr., preface to *Milton and the Line of Vision*, ed. Wittreich (Madison: Univ. of Wisconsin Press, 1975), xv.

19. Gershom Scholem, *The Messianic Idea in Judaism* (New York: Schocken, 1971), 289.

20. E. P. Thompson, *Witness Against the Beast: William Blake and the Moral Law* (New York: Norton, 1993), 33.

21. See annotations to Bishop Watson's *An Apology for the Bible* (*Complete Poetry and Prose*, 615). See also *The Marriage of Heaven and Hell*, plate 12. In Erdman's *Complete Poetry and Prose*, angle brackets around non-italic type indicate material written by Blake "to replace deletions, or as additions" (xxiv).

22. William Walwyn, *Just Defense* 8 (qtd. in Thompson, *Witness Against the Beast*, 23). See also A.L. Morton, *The World of the Ranters: Religious Radicalism in the English Revolution* (London: Lawrence & Wishart, 1970), 146–47.

23. Alexander Ross, *A View of All Religions* (1653), 252–57 (qtd. in Thompson, *Witness Against the Beast*, 32).

24. My account of the history and practices of Moravians in Bethlehem is indebted to Gillian Lindt Gollin, *Moravians in Two Worlds: A Study of Changing Communities* (New York: Columbia Univ. Press, 1967).

25. Gollin, *Moravians in Two Worlds*, 9.

26. Emphasis on Moravian universal grace through Christ is found in Thompson, *Witness Against the Beast* (16, 57), whereas Gollin stresses that the aristocratic background of Moravianism initially led instead to a belief in a Moravian elect (14–15). Gollin notes, however, that the prevalence of Moravian missionary works eventually "counteracted" the primacy of a belief in election (18).

27. Ginsberg, *Howl: Original Draft Facsimile*, line 6.

28. "Heaven in Darkness," *Kaddish*, 225; "caw" and "Lord," *Kaddish*, 227.

29. Ginsberg, *Your Reason and Blake's System* (New York: Hanumen, 1988), 29.

30. Barry Miles, *Ginsberg: A Biography* (New York: HarperCollins, 1989), 326.

31. Elaine Pagels, *The Gnostic Gospels* (New York: Random House, 1979), xxi. See especially chapters 3 and 4, "God the Father/God the Mother" and "The Passion of Christ and the Persecution of Christians."

32. Ginsberg, interview by Thomas Clark, in *Poets at Work: "The Paris Review" Interviews*, ed. George Plimpton (New York: Viking, 1989 [rpt. of 1966 interview]), 211–12.

33. As Geoffrey Keynes has noted, generations of critics have found evidence for Blake's purported madness directly in the poet's extravagant claims in the dining scene of plates 12 and 13. See Keynes's commentary on these plates in *The Marriage of Heaven and Hell* (Oxford: Oxford Univ. Press, 1975).

34. See also Paul Smith, "H. D.'s Identity," *Women's Studies* 10 (1984): 321–37.

35. See also the work of Susan Stanford Friedman, especially *Psyche Reborn: The Emergence of H. D.* (Bloomington: Indiana Univ. Press, 1981); Rachel Blau DuPlessis, *H.*

D.: The Career of That Struggle (Bloomington: Indiana Univ. Press, 1986); and Donna Hollenberg, *H. D.: The Poetics of Childbirth and Creativity* (Boston: Northeastern Univ. Press, 1991).

36. My study of H. D.'s continuation and revision of biblical authority is partly inspired by the commentaries of Alicia Ostriker, in her chapter on H. D. in *Writing Like a Woman* (Ann Arbor: Univ. of Michigan Press, 1983), and Robert Duncan, in his *H. D. Book* (unpublished as a complete manuscript). Most critics would agree with Ostriker's and Duncan's arguments that H. D.'s later poetry is best understood within and against the lineage of Western prophecy. Ostriker takes this issue further, however, arguing that H. D.'s *prophetic* and *feminist* poetics should not be separated, and that together they represent an apocalyptic urgency reminiscent most of all of Blake: "To read H. D., early and late work, is like reading early and late Blake . . . she also resembles Edmund Spenser, and the John Milton of the devil's party" (9). Duncan's scattered sections of the *H. D. Book* explicitly place H. D. in a line of poet-prophets that includes Blake as a foremost member, an image of H. D.'s intertextual echoes suited for Duncan's larger discussion of his own poetics. Yet a dismissal of Duncan's characterization of H. D. because of his concern with self-representation would be as unwise as dismissing Blake's *Milton* because of Blake's urgent self-representation in the poem.

37. H. D., *Tribute to Freud*, (New York: New Directions, 1973), 56.

38. Qtd. in Miles, *Ginsberg: A Biography*, 104.

39. Letter to Richard Eberhart, 18 May 1956. See *Howl: Original Draft Facsimile*, Appendix I, "Contemporaneous Correspondence & Poetic Reactions," 151–52.

40. For an important separation of Ginsberg's poetics from his self-fashioned "hipster" mythmaking, see also Marjorie Perloff, "A Lion in Our Living Room: Reading Allen Ginsberg in the Eighties," in *Poetic License: Essays on Modernist and Postmodernist Lyric* (Evanston, Ill.: Northwestern Univ. Press, 1990), 199–230.

41. Letter to Richard Eberhart, in *Howl: Original Draft Facsimile*, 154.

42. Ibid.

43. Ibid., 153.

44. Among others, Lionel Trilling, Ginsberg's former professor at Columbia, dismissed *Howl and Other Poems* as "all prose, all rhetoric, without any music" (*Howl: Original Draft Facsimile*, 156). From St. Elizabeth's Hospital, Ezra Pound admonished William Carlos Williams, Ginsberg's poetic mentor at the time, to "teach him [Ginsberg] the value of time to those who want to read something that wil tell 'em wot they dont know" (*Howl: Original Draft Facsimile*, 157).

45. Ginsberg, liner notes to *Holy Soul Jelly Roll: Poems and Songs (1949–1993)* (New York: Rhino Records, 1994), 26.

46. Isaac Newton, *Mathematical Principles of Natural Philosophy*, trans. Andrew Motte, rev. Florian Cajori (Berkeley and Los Angeles: Univ. of California Press, 1966), 545.

47. Jean-Joseph Goux, *Symbolic Economies After Marx and Freud*, trans. Jennifer Curtiss Gage (Ithaca: Cornell Univ. Press, 1990), 21.

48. Newton, *Mathematical Principles of Natural Philosophy*, 545.

49. Sigmund Freud, *Three Essays on the Theory of Sexuality*, trans. James Strachey (New York: Basic, 1962), 85.

50. Michael Lieb, *The Visionary Mode: Biblical Prophecy, Hermeneutics, and Cultural Change* (Ithaca: Cornell Univ. Press, 1991), 306.

51. Sigmund Freud, *The Interpretation of Dreams*, trans. James Strachey (London: Hogarth, 1953; New York: Avon, 1965); Michel Foucault, *The Order of Things: An Archaeology of the Human Sciences* (New York: Random House, 1970); Gilles Deleuze and Félix Guattari, *Anti-Oedipus: Capitalism and Schizophrenia*, trans. Robert Hurley et al. (Minneapolis: Univ. of Minnesota Press, 1983).

CHAPTER 2

1. Alter, *The Art of Biblical Poetry*, 209.

2. Andrew M. Cooper, *Doubt and Identity in Romantic Poetry* (New Haven: Yale Univ. Press, 1988), 59; Paul Youngquist, *Madness and Blake's Myth* (University Park: Penn State Univ. Press, 1989), 150, and "Criticism and the Experience of Blake's *Milton*," *Studies in English Literature, 1500–1900* 30 (1990): 555; and Northrop Frye, *Fearful Symmetry: A Study of William Blake* (Princeton: Princeton Univ. Press, 1947), 324, 355.

3. See Harold Bloom, *The Anxiety of Influence: A Theory of Poetry* (New York: Oxford University Press, 1973). Both H. D. and Ginsberg experienced psychoanalysis first-hand (H. D. with Freud); both were influenced by the inspirational effects of unconscious language, though both determined to rewrite the coercive effects of adaptive psychological models.

4. Diana Hume George, *Blake and Freud* (Ithaca: Cornell Univ. Press, 1980), 17.

5. Mark Bracher, *Being Form'd: Thinking Through Blake's "Milton"* (Barrytown, N.Y.: Station Hill, 1985), 3.

6. Nelson Hilton, *Literal Imagination: Blake's Vision of Words* (Berkeley: Univ. of California Press), 9.

7. For more on Blake's Gnostic sources, see Kathleen Raine, *Blake and Tradition* (Princeton: Princeton Univ. Press, 1968).

8. Stanley Fish, "Inaction and Silence: The Reader in *Paradise Regained*," in *Calm of Mind: Tercentenary Essays on "Paradise Regained" and "Samson Agonistes"*, ed. Joseph Anthony Wittreich, Jr. (Cleveland: Case Western Reserve Univ. Press, 1971), 25–48; Leonard Mustazza, "Language as Weapon in Milton's *Paradise Regained*," *Milton Studies* 18 (1983): 195–216; Steven Goldsmith, "The Muting of Satan: Language and Redemption in *Paradise Regained*," *Studies in English Literature, 1500–1900* 27 (1987): 125–40.

9. Stuart Peterfreund, "Blake and the Ideology of the Natural," *Eighteenth-Century Life* 18 (1994), 94.

10. Leslie Tannenbaum, *Biblical Tradition in Blake's Early Prophecies: The Great Code of Art* (Princeton: Princeton Univ. Press, 1982), 19–20.

11. Robert Lowth, *Lectures on the Sacred Poetry of the Hebrews*, trans. G. Gregory (1753; rpt. Boston: Crocker & Brewster; New York: J. Leavitt, 1829), 168.

12. I follow Foucault (*The Order of Things*) in using the term "classical" to designate the Enlightenment.

13. Another instance of Blake's continuation of and disengagement from Lowth revolves around the conjunction of prophetic form and prophetic prediction. For Lowth, prophecy eschews "minuter circumstances" in favor of "employing a vague and general style of description, expressive only of the nature and magnitude of the subject" (168). Later, though, he reserves a place for the prophet "rarely and cautiously descending to a circumstantial detail": namely, when prophecy addresses the ideal audience that "live[s] after the prediction is accomplished" (169). Blake represents, by contrast, the beginning of a strain of modern prophecy continued later by H. D. and Ginsberg, where visionary forms are best represented by "minute particulars" lest the magnitude of prophecy be lost. Lowth's emphasis on audience and apocalypse is important, however, to these continuities of prophetic modes of representation.

14. See Newton, *Mathematical Principles of Natural Philosophy*, 545.

15. Tannenbaum, *Biblical Tradition in Blake's Early Prophecies*, 21.

16. F. B. Curtis, "Blake and the 'Moment of Time': An Eighteenth-Century Controversy in Mathematics," *Philological Quarterly* 51 (1972): 462.

17. Ibid., 463.

18. In addition to Fish, Mustazza, and Goldsmith, all of whom foreground this issue in

terms of language, see also Edward Le Comte, "Satan's Heresies in *Paradise Regained*," in *Milton Re-Viewed: Ten Essays* (New York: Garland, 1991), 35–50; and Burton Jasper Weber, *Wedges and Wings: The Patterning of "Paradise Regained"* (Carbondale: Southern Illinois Univ. Press, 1975).

19. Compare the description of fallen, "Satanic" perception with which Blake opens *Europe*, where the five senses are "Five windows" which "light the cavern'd Man." The caverned man of *Europe* refuses the seemingly unnatural, extrasensory vision of the "small portions of the eternal world" available beyond those windows.

20. See also chap. 1, n. 21.

21. Wittreich, "William Blake: Illustrator-Interpreter of *Paradise Regained*," in *Calm of Mind*, 93–132. Wittreich observes that Blake's illustrations to *Paradise Regained* were the last he did for any Milton text, thus those illustrations presumably portray a "final crystallization" of his attitudes toward Milton's poetry (95).

22. Geoffrey Keynes, "Notes on Blake's Illustrations to Milton's Poems," *Milton's Miscellaneous Poems*, (London: Nonesuch, 1926; Grosse Point, Mich.: Scholarly Press, [1968]), 278.

23. Christopher Hill, *Milton and the English Revolution* (New York: Viking, 1978), 267.

24. Ibid.

25. Foucault, *The Order of Things*, 36.

26. See also David V. Erdman, *The Illuminated Blake* (New York: Dover, 1974). As Erdman notes on the opening plate to Book 2, the subtitles to the plate serve as reminders "that falling can reverse to rising, that lightning buried in ground . . . can rise as flames of life . . . that 'Nature is a vision of' Imagination" (249).

27. Freud, *The Interpretation of Dreams*, 135.

28. Ibid., 353.

29. Curtis, "Blake and the 'Moment of Time,'" 462.

30. Freud, *The Interpretation of Dreams*, 135.

31. Freud, "Negation," in *The Standard Edition of the Complete Psychological Works of Sigmund Freud*, trans. James Strachey, vol. 19 (London: Hogarth, 1961), 239. Linguistically, then, nothing is negated. The irony in Freud's title suggests that the unconscious always already is an alternative to the overdetermined censoriousness of the conscious mind. The Spectre of Negation in *Milton*, like the Freudian conscious mind, produces monovocal discourse by eliminating contraries.

32. Freud, "The Antithetical Meaning of Primal Words," in *Complete Psychological Works*, vol. 11, 156.

33. Abel, qtd. in Freud, "The Antithetical Meaning of Primal Words," 156.

34. Ibid., 157.

35. For Blake, "Every natural effect has a spiritual cause and Not / A Natural" (*Milton*, 26:44–45). Likewise, in Freud, the relationship between subjects and language in the natural world must reach beyond *matter* to *mind*—beyond conscious processes to unconscious ones—for the equivalent of redemption. Freud, in fact, concludes "The Antithetical Meaning of Primal Words" by observing that "we psychiatrists cannot escape the suspicion that we should be better at understanding and translating the language of dreams if we knew more about the development of language."

36. Tannenbaum, *Biblical Tradition in Blake's Early Prophecies*, 55.

37. Tannenbaum notes that "[f]rom the seventeenth through the nineteenth centuries, words such as 'emblems,' 'impresses,' and 'hieroglyphs' appeared in discussions of the nature and form of prophetic vision, each term emphasizing the particularly pictorial nature of prophetic utterance" (55). See, for instance, Charles Daubuz, *A Perpetual Commentary on the Revelation of St. John* (London, 1720); Simon Patrick et al., *A Commentary Upon the*

Old and New Testaments, with the Apocrypha, 7 vols. (1727–1760; rpt. London, 1809); and George Stanley Faber, *A Dissertation on the Prophecies that Have Been Fulfilled, Are Now Fulfilling, or Hereafter Will Be Fulfilled,* 3 vols. (London, 1818).

38. William Warburton, *The Divine Legation of Moses Demonstrated,* 6 vols. (1738–1765; rpt. New York: Garland, 1970).

39. See also Erdman, *"America*: New Expanses," in *Blake's Visionary Forms Dramatic,* ed. Erdman and John E. Grant (Princeton: Princeton Univ. Press, 1970), 92–114. Erdman observes that theatrical tropes for prophecy, common in seventeenth- and eighteenth-century biblical commentary, often are appropriated by Blake in his prophecies. Indeed, for Erdman, *America* is "an acting version of a mural Apocalypse" (*"America,"* 95).

40. That this movement from twofold to fourfold occurs in language can be confirmed by a peculiar inversion in plate 34 of the poem. If this diagram of the Four Zoas is turned upside down, so that the realm of Urizen were at the top pole of the plate, the flames of the "Mundane Shell" begin to resemble the flowing hair of Milton himself. "Miltons Track," then, begins in the upper-left corner of the inverted plate, and ends roughly where Milton's mouth would be framed. Seen in this way, Milton's movement from the "mazes" of heaven toward redemption is transformed once the unfettered Milton speaks.

41. In *Surprised by Sin: The Reader in "Paradise Lost"* (New York: St. Martin's, 1967), Fish notes that the seventeenth-century desire to "completely mathematize human knowledge" included an attempt to do the same with human language, and that such a desire can be seen in the poetry of the time (112).

42. See also G.E. Bentley, Jr., *Blake Records* (Oxford: Clarendon, 1969). Of Blake's reading in Socratic philosophy, Crabb Robinson asked him, "[W]hat affinity do you suppose was there between the *Genius* which inspired Socrates and your *Spirits*?" Blake's response: "I was Socrates. . . . Or a sort of brother—I must have had conversations with him. So I had with Jesus Christ. I have an obscure recollection of having been with both of them" (Bentley, 539).

43. Plato, *Cratylus,* trans. Benjamin Jowett in *The Collected Dialogues of Plato,* ed. Edith Hamilton and Huntington Cairns (Princeton: Princeton Univ. Press, 1982), 421–74.

44. Plato, *Symposium,* trans. Michael Joyce, *The Collected Dialogues of Plato,* 526–74.

45. Luce Irigaray, "Sorcerer Love: A Reading of Plato's Symposium, Diotima's Speech," in *Revaluing French Feminism: Critical Essays on Difference, Agency, and Culture,* ed. Nancy Fraser and Sandra Lee Bartky (Bloomington: Indiana Univ. Press, 1992), 72.

46. See Garry Hunt, ed., *Uranus and the Outer Planets* (Cambridge: Cambridge Univ. Press, 1982) and Mark Littman, *Planets Beyond: Discovering the Outer Solar System* (New York: John Wiley & Sons, 1990).

47. Hilton, *Literal Imagination,* 10–11; 83.

48. Daniel Stempel, "Blake, Foucault, and the Classical Episteme," *PMLA* 96 (1981): 388–407.

Chapter 3

1. G. K. A. Bell, "The Church's Function in War-Time," in *The Church and Humanity, 1939–1946* (London: Longmans, 1946), 27.

2. Solitary, that is, as poetic prophecy. Eliot's *The Four Quartets,* the most famous of World War II poems, resembles *Trilogy* in its attempt to craft a spiritual response to the war. Unlike *Trilogy,* however, Eliot's poem affirms the self-abnegating practices authorized by orthodox church tradition as a legitimate avenue of redemption.

3. H. D., *Tribute to Freud,* 57.

NOTES TO CHAPTER THREE

4. From a letter to Pearson dated 7 November 1943. See Donna Krolik Hollenberg, "'New Puritans' in a Civil War: Letters Between H. D. and Norman Holmes Pearson (1941–46)," *Sagetrieb* 14.1 and 2 (1995): 27–81.

5. For relevant references, see chap. 1, n. 35.

6. Claire Buck, *H. D. and Freud: Bisexuality and a Feminine Discourse* (New York: St. Martin's, 1991); Susan Edmunds, *Out of Line: History, Psychoanalysis, and Montage in H. D.'s Long Poems* (Stanford, Calif.: Stanford Univ. Press, 1994). See also "Gender Authority: 'Another Region of Cause and Effect, Another Region of Question and Answer,'" in DuPlessis's *H. D.: The Career of That Struggle*. Friedman explores H. D.'s complex constructions of female identity in light of H. D.'s analysis with Freud in "Against Discipleship: Collaboration and Intimacy in the Relationship of H. D. and Freud," *Literature and Psychology* 33 (1987): 89–108, and "The Writing Cure: Transference and Resistance in a Dialogic Analysis," *H. D. Newsletter* 2 (Winter 1988): 25–35. DuPlessis and Friedman consider specifically how H. D. writes and revises an unfixed conception of femininity in her later work.

7. For a notable exception, see Helen Sword's *Engendering Inspiration: Visionary Strategies in Rilke, Lawrence, and H. D.* (Ann Arbor: Univ. of Michigan Press, 1995). Sword explores how H. D.'s visionary poetry is predicated upon "transforming her own femaleness from a perceived liability into a source of creative power" (4). Sword provocatively examines gender, power, and visionary literature within the modernist era, a period generally hostile to the vatic speech of prophecy. Sword's readings emphasize H. D.'s transvaluation of conventional dichotomies that would assign active poetic composition to males and passive poetic inspiration to females; and Sword's arguments about H. D.'s transformative female prophecy draw considerable strength from H. D.'s revision of the hierarchies these active/passive, male/female dichotomies underwrite. My study shares much of Sword's concerns with the authorizing function of gender in modern prophecy. However, I would argue that H. D.'s distrust of the gender order itself—her focus on performative rather than ontological modes of gender identity in *Trilogy*—is of critical importance in mapping the central tensions between continuity and revision in H. D.'s poetics of prophecy.

8. Thompson, *Witness Against the Beast*, 33.

9. Gollin, *Moravians in Two Worlds*, 19.

10. Ronald E. Martin, *American Literature and the Destruction of Knowledge: Innovative Writing in the Age of Epistemology* (Durham, N.C.: Duke Univ. Press, 1991), 9.

11. Janice S. Robinson, *H. D.: The Life and Work of an American Poet* (Boston: Houghton, 1982), 83.

12. Jacob John Sessler, *Communal Pietism Among Early American Moravians* (New York: Henry Holt, 1933; rpt. New York: AMS, 1971).

13. Qtd. in Sessler, 133. The hymnal was first published in 1757, and then translated as *The Litany Book according to the manner of singing at present mostly in use among the Brethren* (London, 1759).

14. Sessler states that the kiss of peace was performed by those of the same gender only as a means of preventing heterosexual arousal: "The men and women being separated in their sittings, it was free from abuse" (133–34). As apt as Sessler's emphasis on abuse may be, his remark seems to negate the Moravian idea of divine human desire that Sessler himself emphasizes all along. If both foot-washing and the kiss of peace are accompanied by erotic hymns, and if the erotic hymns emphasize the human sensuality of divine experience, then it would follow that foot-washing and kissing among members of the same gender during Moravian worship would be a sacrament that multiplies rather than negates desire. The practice still lives up to the Moravian ideal of a transcendental marriage to a "God-husband" that incorporates "all aspirations and desires" of the faithful in its union. However, as the kiss of peace seeks to "realize" the entire scope of these desires, it realizes a

homosocial element that this concept of transcendental heterosexuality might otherwise regard as liminal.

15. H. D., *Notes on Thought and Vision, and the Wise Sappho* (San Francisco: City Lights, 1982). Hereafter abbreviated parenthetically in the text as *Notes*.

16. See Adalaide Morris, "Science and the Mythopoeic Mind: The Case of H. D.," in *Chaos and Order: Complex Dynamics in Literature and Science*, ed. N. Katherine Hayles (Chicago: Univ. of Chicago Press, 1991), 195–220. As Morris has written, H. D. portrayed science and poetry as "adjacent and complementary disciplines" in her work ("Science," 202). Morris argues that H. D. seeks in her poetry what her father and grandfather sought in their science: "to bring into focus regions hitherto invisible, to record what they see accurately and disinterestedly, and to turn their data into laws and equations" (202). H. D.'s re-envisioning of Snell's Law in *Trilogy* (discussed later in this chapter) is one instance of her strategy of remaking laws of scientific observation into visionary representations in her prophetic poetry.

17. See Ihab Hassan, *Paracriticisms: Seven Speculations of Our Time* (Urbana: Univ. of Illinois Press, 1975).

18. Claire M. Tylee, *The Great War and Women's Consciousness: Images of Militarism and Womanhood in Women's Writings, 1914–1964* (Iowa City : Univ. of Iowa Press, 1990). See especially Tylee's chapter 7, "'Old, Unhappy, Far-Off Things'—Women's Elegies, 1932–1960."

19. Hollenberg, *H. D.: The Poetics of Childbirth and Creativity*, 5.

20. H. D., *Bid Me to Live: A Madrigal* (New York: Grove, 1960).

21. For modern prophecy, the most important of these battles is between the Church of Paul—where the male creator-God exists apart from human consciousness—and Gnosticism's conception of an inner divinity in every human, sparked by the divinity of a God who is both masculine and feminine. See Pagels, *The Gnostic Gospels*, esp. chapters 3 and 4.

22. Edmunds, *Out of Line*, 51.

23. Ibid., 42.

24. See, e.g., John 8:14–15, 23, 45.

25. See Lerner, "Medieval Prophecy as Religious Dissent." Having organized the rhetoric of medieval prophecy into visionary, biblical, astrological, and pseudonymous modes, Lerner argues that each mode produced seemingly dissenting traditions that sought to reinterpret—rather than simply to explain—Revelation, in order to fit the apocalyptic predictions of each individual mode of prophecy. As a predictive discourse, medieval prophecy is grounded in contentious responses to the Christian Logos. Nevertheless, all predicted a future apocalypse where the direct revelation of God would be mediated by an orthodox institution, usually the Catholic Church.

26. James B. Pritchard, ed., *Ancient Near-Eastern Texts Relating to the Old Testament* (Princeton: Princeton Univ. Press, 1969), 8.

27. Ibid., 9.

28. See Louis H. Silverstein, "Planting the Seeds: Selections from the *H. D. Chronology*," *H. D. Newsletter* 2.2 (Winter 1988): 4–14. Working from Bryher's notes, Silverstein shows that H. D. and Bryher visited Tutankhamen's tomb more than once in February 1923. During their visit, materials from the tomb "were brought out almost hourly" (14).

29. G. R. S. Mead, *Fragments of a Faith Forgotten*, (New Hyde Park, N.Y.: University Books, 1960). See also Peter Crisp, "Pound as Gnostic? Creative Mythology and the Goddess," *Paideuma* 23 (1994): 173–93. Crisp explains that Mead's *Fragments of a Faith Forgotten* was a definitive Gnostic reference text for artists and scholars in the early twentieth century, a collection of "most of the then available texts on Gnosticism" (175). According to Crisp, Mead was connected to the London Theosophical Society (as was H. D.), and

Fragments of a Faith Forgotten was familiar to those in this circle.

30. See Mead, *Fragments of a Faith Forgotten*, 405–14. In "The Hymn of the Robe of Glory," the pilgrim is commanded by his parents to go "down into Egypt," and to bring the "one pearl" of Gnosis. Mead notes here that "Egypt" was a term for the body "common to many Gnostic schools" (407). The poem, then, is as much a self-pilgrimage into a visionary body as it is an external journey.

31. Edmunds explains that H. D.'s use of Egypt also is informed by her ambivalence toward that country's decolonization. H. D. projects sites of women's agency onto Egyptian landscapes, a "land whose current history is one of revolt," while at the same time H. D. "denies that there is any cause for unhappiness by restoring in that land all the lost pleasures of the pre-oedipal phase" (*Out of Line,* 147).

32. See Revelation, 22:18–19.

33. Bell, "The Church's Function in War-Time," 25.

34. See also Friedman, who notes in *Psyche Reborn* that "John's description of this woman . . . reveals her to be one of the protean forms of the Near Eastern Great Goddess whose religions so threatened the angry Jewish prophets" (246). Friedman notes that the biological signifiers of femininity localized in the Whore of Babylon become a force that must be thwarted in John's prophecy: "Woman's beauty (the gems), menstrual fluid ('scarlet colour'), sexuality ('fornication'), and womb ('golden cup') represent to John the essence of abomination and the source of defilement for men" (*Psyche Reborn*, 246; Revelation, 14:4).

35. "Phosphorous" [*sic*], the chemical element responsible for the glow of the clock face, comes from the Latin for Morning Star, another of the representations of Mary in *Trilogy*. "Hesperus" is H. D.'s Magdalene, or Venus as the Evening Star.

36. Edmunds explains how the psychoanalytic dream work of the speaker encodes the Lady as a figure of lesbian desire, as a figure who revises Freud's work on paranoia and homosexuality. Edmunds's discussions can help frame how H. D. uses coded representations of bodily desire to blur the boundary between materiality and metaphysicality. Edmunds argues that the vision of the Lady "provides a way out of the traps associated with earthly life in the first sequence of *Trilogy*" (*Out of Line*, 66); confined by "the constituitive divisions *within* the orders of gender, sex, and time," the speaker "springs the trap of the body by fusing the divisions *between* these orders" (66).

37. Scholem, *The Messianic Idea in Judaism*, 289–90.

38. See especially Friedman, *Psyche Reborn*; Robinson, *H. D.: The Life and Work of An American Poet*; Edmunds's discussion of *Trilogy* in *Out of Line*; Morris, "The Concept of Projection: H. D.'s Visionary Powers," in *Signets: Reading H. D.*, ed. Friedman and DuPlessis (Madison: Univ. of Wisconsin Press, 1990), 273–96; and Albert Gelpi, "Re-Membering the Mother: A Reading of H. D.'s *Trilogy*," *Poesis* 6.3–4 (1985): 40–55.

39. See *Flowering*, 16.3; 16.10; 18.5–8; 16.11.

40. See also Susan Schweik, *A Gulf So Deeply Cut: American Women Poets and the Second World War* (Madison: Univ. of Wisconsin Press, 1991). Schweik argues that H. D.'s collocation of Marys "emphasizes the inward variance and instability in any feminine identity, in an identity at all" (260).

41. Schweik, *A Gulf So Deeply Cut*, 262–63.

42. As Edmunds observes, Kaspar's gender identity also is subject to the fluidity of representation in this final dialogue: "with the mediation of Mary, Eve . . . also passes into Kaspar, whose laboring heart brings forth the return of the sea garden Eve lost" (*Out of Line*, 83). For a discussion of Kaspar as a coded feminine voice, see also Deborah Kelly Kloepfer, *The Unspeakable Mother: Forbidden Discourse in Jean Rhys and H. D.* (Ithaca: Cornell Univ. Press, 1989).

43. Schweik, *A Gulf So Deeply Cut*, 249.

44. Edmunds is careful to note that the revised significance of the myrrh is not a stable substitution for orthodoxy. She writes that H. D. "stage[s] neither the first nor the last but merely the newest manifestation of an eternal being who forgoes the masculine order of permanence to immortalize the feminine order of periodicity" (88).

45. On Kasper's "privatizing vision," see Edmunds, *Out of Line*, 92.

46. Margaret Homans, *Bearing the Word: Language and Female Experience in Nineteenth-Century Women's Writing* (Chicago: Univ. of Chicago Press, 1986), 5.

CHAPTER 4

1. Michael Schumacher, *Dharma Lion: A Critical Biography of Allen Ginsberg* (New York: St. Martin's, 1992), 22.

2. Miles, *Ginsberg: A Biography*, 35.

3. The antipsychiatric school of thought associated with Laing, especially, was an influence on Ginsberg at this time. R. D. Laing and Aaron Esterson, *Sanity, Madness, and the Family* (London: Tavistock, 1964; New York: Penguin, 1970); Erving Goffman, "The Moral Career of the Mental Patient" and "On the Characteristics of Total Institutions," in *Asylums: Essays on the Social Situation of Mental Patients and Other Inmates* (New York: Anchor, 1961), 1–124. My discussion of identity, madness, power, and discipline is indebted to the work of Foucault, especially *Discipline and Punish: The Birth of the Prison*, trans. Alan Sheridan (New York: Vintage, 1979), and *Madness and Civilization: A History of Insanity in the Age of Reason*, trans. Richard Howard (New York: Pantheon, 1965). Although the manner in which institutional practices tend to discipline subjectivity has been communicated in literary studies most frequently through Foucault's work, I prefer here to focus on material that was available to Ginsberg during his early career.

4. John Tytell, *Naked Angels: The Lives and Literature of the Beat Generation* (New York: McGraw-Hill, 1976).

5. Qtd. in James Breslin, "The Origins of *Howl* and *Kaddish*," in *On the Poetry of Allen Ginsberg*, ed. Lewis Hyde (Ann Arbor: Univ. of Michigan Press, 1984), 415.

6. Tytell, *Naked Angels*, 4–5.

7. Ginsberg, *Indian Journals: March 1962–May 1963* (San Francisco: Dave Haselwood and City Lights, 1970), 13.

8. Naomi "of the hospitals," *Kaddish*, 212; Naomi "from whose pained head . . .," *Kaddish*, 223.

9. "Homosexuality in America," *Life*, 26 June 1964, 66–80. See also Lee Edelman, "Tearooms and Sympathy, or, The Epistemology of the Water Closet," in *The Lesbian and Gay Studies Reader*, ed. Henry Abelove et al. (New York: Routledge, 1993), 553–74.

10. Edelman, "Tearooms and Sympathy," 556.

11. Ginsberg interview, 196.

12. "Allen Ginsberg," Lannan Literary Videos.

13. Lyndon O. Brown, *Marketing and Distribution Research* (New York: Ronald, 1955), 73.

14. Emory S. Bogardus, *The Making of Public Opinion* (New York: Association, 1951), 3.

15. "Allen Ginsberg with R. D. Laing," *Writers in Conversation* (London: ICA Video, 1984; The Anthony Roland Collection of Films on Arts, 1989).

16. Laing and Esterson, *Sanity, Madness, and the Family*, 27.

17. Deleuze and Guattari, *Anti-Oedipus*, 34.

18. Ginsberg's *Journals: Mid-Fifties, 1954–1958*, ed. Gordon Ball (New York: HarperCollins, 1995), 214, 294.

19. May 1954 letter to Ginsberg. Qtd. in Schumacher, *Dharma Lion*, 194.
20. Chögyam Trungpa, *Crazy Wisdom* (Boston: Shambhala, 1991), 30.
21. Ibid., 28–29.
22. *Kaddish*, 212. The important religious and political distinctions between Orthodox and Reform Judaism may seem blurred at times throughout this chapter. This blurring is a result of Ginsberg's own self-positioning in varied locations along an Orthodox-Reform continuum. The strict Orthodox practices that would be untenable from a Reform perspective are at times crucial to Ginsberg, and never more so than at the time of his mother's death; see Alicia Ostriker, "'Howl' Revisited: The Poet as Jew," *American Poetry Review* 26 (July/August 1997): 28–31. Ostriker argues that Ginsberg's complex relationship with Hebraic tradition is crucial to understanding him as a writer: "[A]mbivalence toward Jewishness . . . is a key ingredient of post-Enlightenment Jewish writing. . . . To believe in the host culture's own ideals about itself, and then to write as an indignant social critic when the host nation fails (of course) to embody those ideals: this is all normal for the Jewish writer" (31). Ginsberg's desire for both continuity and revision of Orthodox ritual—especially as this ritual relates to his desire for a traditional Kaddish for his mother—will be discussed in greater depth later in this chapter.
23. Ginsberg, *Howl: Original Draft Facsimile*, 13. The repetition of "generation" is part of the original draft.
24. Letter to Eberhart, 18 May 1956, in *Howl: Original Draft Facsimile*, Appendix I, "Contemporaneous Correspondence & Poetic Reactions," 152.
25. "Allen Ginsberg," Lannan Literary Videos.
26. Ibid.
27. Michael Rumaker, "Allen Ginsberg's 'Howl,'" in *On the Poetry of Allen Ginsberg*, ed. Hyde, 36 (first published in *Black Mountain Review*, fall 1957); Helen Vendler, "American X-Rays: Forty Years of Allen Ginsberg's Poetry," *New Yorker* 4 November 1996, 89; see also Norman Podhoretz, "A Howl of Protest in San Francisco," *New Republic* 16 September 1957, 20.
28. Paul Portugés, "Allen Ginsberg's Paul Cézanne and the Pater Omnipotens Aeterna Deus," *Contemporary Literature* 21 (1980): 444–45.
29. Ibid., 446.
30. Paul Portugés, *The Visionary Poetics of Allen Ginsberg* (Santa Barbara, Calif.: Ross-Erikson, 1978). See Portugés's interview with Ginsberg, 143–63.
31. Interview with Portugés in *The Visionary Poetics of Allen Ginsberg*, 148.
32. For more on Ginsberg's earliest Buddhist sources, see Schumacher, *Dharma Lion*, especially chapters 7 and 8, "Reality Sandwiches" and "In Back of the Real," 118–87.
33. Letter to Eberhart, 18 May 1956, 154.
34. Herbert Marcuse, *One-Dimensional Man: Studies in the Ideology of Advanced Industrial Society* (Boston: Beacon, 1964), 75.
35. Ginsberg, interview, 202, 205.
36. See also chap. 1, n. 21 on the use of angle brackets with Blake's text.
37. Ginsberg, interview, 205.
38. Ginsberg, "Mind Breaths," in *Collected Poems, 1947–1980*, 609–11.
39. Ginsberg, interview, 205.
40. Ibid.
41. Laing and Esterson, *Sanity, Madness, and the Family*, 12.
42. Unpublished letters of 6 April 1959, and 12 April 1959, are quoted with permission of the Stanford University Libraries and Gary Snyder; copyright © 1999, Gary Snyder.
43. Breslin, "The Origins of *Howl* and *Kaddish*," 402; Ekbert Faas, "Confronting the Horrific," in *On the Poetry of Allen Ginsberg*, ed. Hyde, 443; Portugés, *The Visionary Poetics of Allen Ginsberg*, 39, 45.

194 NOTES TO CHAPTER FIVE

44. See also Perloff, "A Lion in Our Living Room: Reading Allen Ginsberg in the Eighties." Perloff disentangles *Howl* and *Kaddish* to examine the tension between convention and experimentation in Ginsberg's career. Perloff's separation of the two poems usefully refutes common critical charges leveled against Ginsberg's work, most notably, she argues, the "charge of formlessness" and "of poetry as mere rant" (201). Though she focuses primarily on *Howl*, Perloff characterizes *Kaddish* as Ginsberg's "least typical poem," one that is his "most highly praised" yet also, for his readers, a source of "embarrassment" for its frank portrayal of Naomi's breakdowns and hospitalizations (213).

45. Ginsberg, "How *Kaddish* Happened," in *Poetics of the New American Poetry*, ed. Donald Allen and Warren Tallman (New York: Grove, 1973), 345.

46. Morris Dickstein, *Gates of Eden: American Culture in the Sixties* (New York: Basic, 1977), 16.

47. Bruce Comens, *Apocalypse and After: Modern Strategy and Postmodern Tactics in Pound, Zukofsky, and Williams* (Tuscaloosa: Univ. of Alabama Press, 1995), 20–21.

48. Maurice Lamm, *The Jewish Way in Death and Mourning* (New York: Jonathan David, 1969), 150.

49. Qtd. in Hyde's "Remarks (from reviews of *Kaddish*)," in *On the Poetry of Allen Ginsberg*, ed. Hyde, 101.

50. Lamm, *The Jewish Way in Death and Mourning*, 172.

51. Alter, *The Art of Biblical Poetry*, 9.

52. See Wittreich, Jr., preface to *Milton and the Line of Vision*.

53. Lamm, *The Jewish Way in Death and Mourning*, 165.

54. M. L. Rosenthal, *The New Poets: American and British Poetry Since World War II* (New York: Oxford Univ. Press, 1967), 112.

55. Ibid., 111–12.

56. *Kaddish*, 213. Ginsberg portrays this interconnection elsewhere, especially in "War Profit Litany" (in *The Fall of America*, 1973), "Who Runs America?" (in *Mind Breaths*, 1978), "On the Conduct of the World Seeking Beauty Against Government" (in *Cosmopolitan Greetings*, 1986), and "Is About" (in *Death and Fame*, 1999).

57. Miles, *Ginsberg: A Biography*, 35.

58. Edelman, "Tearooms and Sympathy," 567.

59. Breslin, "The Origins of *Howl* and *Kaddish*," 423.

60. Ibid.

61. See also Ginsberg's "Plutonian Ode" (1978), in *Collected Poems, 1947–1980*, 702–05.

62. In one of his earliest public readings of *Kaddish*, a 1964 performance at Brandeis University included among the recordings in *Holy Soul Jelly Roll*, Ginsberg revises this line, yet still emphasizes the spatial and the nominative: "caw caw my eye be buried in the same Ground where I stand as Angel."

63. "Allen Ginsberg," Lannan Literary Videos, 1989.

64. Ginsberg, *Collected Poems, 1947–1980*, 791.

65. Ginsberg, *Howl: Original Draft Facsimile*, 143.

CHAPTER 5

1. Foucault, *The Order of Things*, 44.

2. Ibid., 36.

3. Derrida, "The Ends of Man," 123.

4. See Foucault, *The Order of Things*, 386.

5. Francisco J. Varela, Evan Thompson, and Eleanor Rosch, *The Embodied Mind:*

Cognitive Science and Human Experience (Cambridge: MIT Press, 1991).

6. Ihab Hassan, "The New Gnosticism: Speculations on an Aspect of the Postmodern Mind," in *Early Postmodernism: Foundational Essays*, ed. Paul A. Bové (Durham, N. C.: Duke Univ. Press, 1995), 96–97.

Bibliography

Allen Ginsberg. Lannan Literary Videos. Directed by Lewis MacAdams and John Dorr. 1989.

"Allen Ginsberg with R. D. Laing." *Writers in Conversation*. London: ICA Video, 1984; The Anthony Roland Collection of Films on Art, 1989.

Alter, Robert. *The Art of Biblical Poetry*. New York: Basic, 1985.

Bell, G. K. A. "The Church's Function in War-Time." In *The Church and Humanity, 1939–1946*. London: Longmans, 1946.

Bentley, G. E., Jr. *Blake Records*. Oxford: Clarendon, 1969.

Blake, William. *The Complete Poetry and Prose of William Blake*, edited by David V. Erdman. New York: Doubleday, 1988.

―――. *The Marriage of Heaven and Hell*. Commentary by Geoffrey Keynes. Oxford: Oxford Univ. Press, 1975.

Bloom, Harold. *The Anxiety of Influence: A Theory of Poetry*. New York: Oxford Univ. Press, 1973.

―――. "On Ginsberg's *Kaddish*." In *The Ringers in the Tower: Studies in Romantic Tradition*. Chicago: Univ. of Chicago Press, 1971.

―――. *The Visionary Company: A Reading of English Romantic Poetry*. Ithaca: Cornell Univ. Press, 1971.

Bogardus, Emory S. *The Making of Public Opinion*. New York: Association, 1951.

Bracher, Mark. *Being Form'd: Thinking Through Blake's "Milton"*. Barrytown, N.Y.: Station Hill, 1985.

Braidotti, Rosi. "The Politics of Ontological Difference." In *Between Feminism and Psychoanalysis*, edited by Teresa Brennan. New York: Routledge, 1989.

Breslin, James. "The Origins of *Howl* and *Kaddish*." In *On the Poetry of Allen Ginsberg*, edited by Lewis Hyde. Ann Arbor: Univ. of Michigan Press, 1984.

Brown, Lyndon O. *Marketing and Distribution Research*. 3rd ed. New York: Ronald, 1955.

Buck, Claire. *H.D. and Freud: Bisexuality and a Feminine Discourse*. New York: St. Martin's, 1991.

Budge, E.A. Wallis. *The Gods of the Egyptians*. 2 vols. Chicago: Open Court; London: Metheun, 1904.

Comens, Bruce. *Apocalypse and After: Modern Strategy and Postmodern Tactics in Pound, Zukofsky, and Williams.* Tuscaloosa: Univ. of Alabama Press, 1995.

Cooper, Andrew M. *Doubt and Identity in Romantic Poetry.* New Haven: Yale Univ. Press, 1988.

Crisp, Peter. "Pound as Gnostic? Creative Mythology and the Goddess." *Paideuma* 23 (1994): 173–93.

Curtis, F.B. "Blake and the 'Moment of Time': An Eighteenth-Century Controversy in Mathematics." *Philological Quarterly* 51 (1972): 460–70.

Deleuze, Gilles, and Félix Guattari. *Anti-Oedipus: Capitalism and Schizophrenia*, translated by Robert Hurley et al. Minneapolis: Univ. of Minnesota Press, 1983.

Dellamora, Richard. *Apocalyptic Overtures: Sexual Politics and the Sense of an Ending.* New Brunswick, N. J.: Rutgers Univ. Press, 1994.

Derrida, Jacques. "The Ends of Man." In *Margins of Philosophy*, translated by Alan Bass. Chicago: Univ. of Chicago Press, 1982.

Dickstein, Morris. *Gates of Eden: American Culture in the Sixties.* New York: Basic Books, 1977.

Doolittle, Hilda. See H. D.

DuPlessis, Rachel Blau. *H. D.: The Career of That Struggle.* Bloomington: Indiana Univ. Press, 1986.

Edelman, Lee. "Tearooms and Sympathy, or, The Epistemology of the Water Closet." In *The Lesbian and Gay Studies Reader*, edited by Henry Abelove et al. New York: Routledge, 1993.

Edmunds, Susan. *Out of Line: History, Psychoanalysis, and Montage in H. D.'s Long Poems.* Stanford, Calif.: Stanford Univ. Press, 1994.

Erdman, David V. "*America:* New Expanses." In *Blake's Visionary Forms Dramatic*, edited by Erdman and John E. Grant. Princeton: Princeton Univ. Press, 1970.

———. *The Illuminated Blake.* New York: Dover, 1974.

Faas, Ekbert. "Confronting the Horrific." In *On the Poetry of Allen Ginsberg*, edited by Lewis Hyde. Ann Arbor: Univ. of Michigan Press, 1984.

Fish, Stanley. "Inaction and Silence: The Reader in *Paradise Regained.*" In *Calm of Mind: Tercentenary Essays on "Paradise Regained" and "Samson Agonistes,"* edited by Joseph Anthony Wittreich, Jr. Cleveland, Ohio: Case Western Reserve Univ. Press, 1971.

———. *Surprised by Sin: The Reader in "Paradise Lost".* New York: St. Martin's, 1967.

Foucault, Michel. *Discipline and Punish: The Birth of the Prison*, translated by Alan Sheridan. New York: Vintage, 1979.

———. *Madness and Civilization: A History of Insanity in the Age of Reason*, translated by Richard Howard. New York: Pantheon, 1965.

———. *The Order of Things: An Archaeology of the Human Sciences.* New York: Random House, 1970.

Freud, Sigmund. "The Antithetical Meaning of Primal Words." In *The Standard Edition of the Complete Psychological Works of Sigmund Freud*, translated by James Strachey. Vol. 11. London: Hogarth, 1957.

———. *The Interpretation of Dreams*, translated by James Strachey. London: Hogarth, 1953; New York: Avon, 1965.

————. "Negation." In *The Standard Edition of the Complete Psychological Works of Sigmund Freud*, translated by James Strachey. Vol. 19. London: Hogarth, 1961.

————. *Three Essays on the Theory of Sexuality*, translated by James Strachey. New York: Basic, 1962.

Friedman, Susan Stanford. "Against Discipleship: Collaboration and Intimacy in the Relationship of H. D. and Freud." *Literature and Psychology* 33 (1987): 89–108.

————. *Psyche Reborn: The Emergence of H. D.* Bloomington: Indiana Univ. Press, 1981.

————. "The Writing Cure: Transference and Resistance in a Dialogic Analysis." *H. D. Newsletter* 2 (Winter 1988): 25–35.

Frye, Northrop. *Fearful Symmetry: A Study of William Blake*. Princeton: Princeton Univ. Press, 1947.

Gelpi, Albert. "Re-Membering the Mother: A Reading of H.D.'s *Trilogy*." *Poesis* 6.3–4 (1985): 40–55.

George, Diana Hume. *Blake and Freud*. Ithaca: Cornell Univ. Press, 1980.

Ginsberg, Allen. *Collected Poems, 1947–1980*. New York: Harper & Row, 1984.

————. *Holy Soul Jelly Roll: Poems and Songs (1949–1993)*. New York: Rhino Records, 1994.

————. "How *Kaddish* Happened." In *Poetics of the New American Poetry*, edited by Donald Allen and Warren Tallman. New York: Grove, 1973.

————. *Howl: Original Draft Facsimile*, edited by Barry Miles. New York: HarperCollins, 1986.

————. *Indian Journals: March 1962–May 1963*. San Francisco: Dave Haselwood and City Lights, 1970.

————. Interview by Thomas Clark. In *Poets at Work: "The Paris Review" Interviews*, edited by George Plimpton. New York: Viking, 1989 [reprint of 1966 interview].

————. *Journals: Mid-Fifties, 1954–1958*, edited by Gordon Ball. New York: HarperCollins, 1995.

————. *Your Reason & Blake's System*. New York: Hanumen, 1988.

Goddard, Dwight, ed. *A Buddhist Bible*. Thetford, Vt.: E. P. Dutton, 1938; Boston: Beacon, 1994.

Goffman, Erving. "The Moral Career of the Mental Patient." In *Asylums: Essays on the Social Situation of Mental Patients and Other Inmates*. New York: Anchor, 1961.

————. "On the Characteristics of Total Institutions." In *Asylums: Essays on the Social Situation of Mental Patients and Other Inmates*. New York: Anchor, 1961.

Goldsmith, Steven. "The Muting of Satan: Language and Redemption in *Paradise Regained*." *Studies in English Literature, 1500–1900* 27 (1987): 125–40.

Gollin, Gillian Lindt. *Moravians in Two Worlds: A Study of Changing Communities*. New York: Columbia Univ. Press, 1967.

Goux, Jean-Joseph. *Symbolic Economies After Marx and Freud*, translated by Jennifer Curtiss Gage. Ithaca: Cornell Univ. Press, 1990.

Hassan, Ihab. "The New Gnosticism: Speculations on an Aspect of the Postmodern Mind." In *Early Postmodernism: Foundational Essays*, edited by Paul A. Bové. Durham, N.C.: Duke Univ. Press, 1995.

————. *Paracriticisms: Seven Speculations of Our Time*. Urbana: Univ. of Illinois Press, 1975.

————. *The Postmodern Turn*. Columbus: Ohio State Univ. Press, 1987.

H. D. *Bid Me to Live: A Madrigal*. New York: Grove, 1960.

————. *The Gift*. New York: New Directions, 1982.

————. *Notes on Thought and Vision, and the Wise Sappho*. San Francisco: City Lights, 1982.

————. *Tribute to Freud*. New York: New Directions, 1974.

————. *Trilogy*. New York: New Directions, 1973.

Hill, Christopher. *Milton and the English Revolution*. New York: Viking, 1978.

Hilton, Nelson. *Literal Imagination: Blake's Vision of Words*. Berkeley: Univ. of California Press, 1983.

Hollenberg, Donna Krolik. *H.D.: The Poetics of Childbirth and Creativity*. Boston: Northeastern Univ. Press, 1991.

————. "'New Puritans' in a Civil War: Letters Between H.D. and Norman Holmes Pearson (1941–46)." *Sagetrieb* 14.1 and 2 (1995): 27–81.

Homans, Margaret. *Bearing the Word: Language and Female Experience in Nineteenth-Century Women's Writing*. Chicago: Univ. of Chicago Press, 1986.

"Homosexuality in America." *Life*, 26 June 1964: 66–80.

Hunt, Garry, ed. *Uranus and the Outer Planets*. Cambridge: Cambridge Univ. Press, 1982.

Irigaray, Luce. "Sorcerer Love: A Reading of Plato's Symposium, Diotima's Speech." In *Revaluing French Feminism: Critical Essays on Difference, Agency, and Culture*, edited by Nancy Fraser and Sandra Lee Bartky. Bloomington: Indiana Univ. Press, 1992.

Kearney, Richard. *Poetics of Imagining: From Husserl to Lyotard*. London: Routledge, 1991.

Kermode, Frank. *The Sense of an Ending: Studies in the Theory of Fiction*. New York: Oxford Univ. Press, 1967.

Keynes, Geoffrey. "Notes on Blake's Illustrations to Milton's Poems." In *Milton's Miscellaneous Poems*, illustrated by William Blake. London: Nonesuch, 1926. Grosse Point, Mich.: Scholarly Press, [1968].

Kloepfer, Deborah Kelly. *The Unspeakable Mother: Forbidden Discourse in Jean Rhys and H.D.* Ithaca: Cornell Univ. Press, 1989.

Laing, R. D. and Aaron Esterson. *Sanity, Madness, and the Family*. London: Tavistock, 1964; New York: Penguin, 1970.

Lamm, Maurice. *The Jewish Way in Death and Mourning*. New York: Jonathan David, 1969.

Le Comte, Edward. *Milton Re-Viewed: Ten Essays*. New York: Garland, 1991.

Lerner, Robert E. "Medieval Prophecy as Religious Dissent." *Past and Present* 72 (1976): 3–24.

Lieb, Michael. *The Visionary Mode: Biblical Prophecy, Hermeneutics, and Cultural Change*. Ithaca: Cornell Univ. Press, 1991.

Littman, Mark. *Planets Beyond: Discovering the Outer Solar System*. New York: John Wiley & Sons, 1990.

Lowth, Robert. *Lectures on the Sacred Poetry of the Hebrews*, translated by G. Gregory. 1753. Reprinted Boston: Crocker & Brewster; New York: J. Leavitt, 1829.

Marcuse, Herbert. *One-Dimensional Man: Studies in the Ideology of Advanced Industrial Society*. Boston: Beacon, 1964.

Martin, Ronald E. *American Literature and the Destruction of Knowledge: Innovative Writing in the Age of Epistemology*. Durham, N.C.: Duke Univ. Press, 1991.

Mead, G. R. S. *Fragments of a Faith Forgotten*. New Hyde Park, N.Y.: University Books, 1960.

Miles, Barry. *Ginsberg: A Biography*. New York: HarperCollins, 1989.

Morris, Adalaide. "The Concept of Projection: H. D.'s Visionary Powers." In *Signets: Reading H. D.*, edited by Susan Stanford Friedman and Rachel Blau DuPlessis. Madison: Univ. of Wisconsin Press, 1990.

———. "Science and the Mythopoeic Mind: The Case of H. D." In *Chaos and Order: Complex Dynamics in Literature and Science*, edited by N. Katherine Hayles. Chicago: Univ. of Chicago Press, 1991.

Morton, A. L. *The World of the Ranters: Religious Radicalism in the English Revolution*. London: Lawrence & Wishart, 1970.

Mustazza, Leonard. "Language as Weapon in Milton's *Paradise Regained*." *Milton Studies* 18 (1983): 195–216.

Newton, Isaac. *Mathematical Principles of Natural Philosophy*. Tr. Andrew Motte. Rev. Florian Cajori. Berkeley and Los Angeles: Univ. of California Press, 1966.

Ostriker, Alicia. "Blake, Ginsberg, Madness, and the Prophet as Shaman." In *William Blake and the Moderns*, edited by Robert J. Bertholf and Annette S. Levitt. Albany: State Univ. of New York Press, 1982.

———. "'Howl' Revisited: The Poet as Jew," *American Poetry Review* 26 (1997): 28–31.

———. *Writing Like A Woman*. Ann Arbor: Univ. of Michigan Press, 1983.

Pagels, Elaine. *The Gnostic Gospels*. New York: Random House, 1979.

Pearson, Norman Holmes. Introduction to *Trilogy*, by H. D. New York: New Directions, 1973.

Perloff, Marjorie. "A Lion in Our Living Room: Reading Allen Ginsberg in the Eighties." In *Poetic License: Essays on Modernist and Postmodernist Lyric*. Evanston, Ill.: Northwestern Univ. Press, 1990.

Peterfreund, Stuart. "Blake and the Ideology of the Natural." *Eighteenth-Century Life* 18 (1994): 91–119.

Plato. *Cratylus*. Translated by Benjamin Jowett. In *The Collected Dialogues of Plato*, edited by Edith Hamilton and Huntington Cairns. Princeton: Princeton Univ. Press, 1982.

———. *Symposium*. Translated by Michael Joyce. In *The Collected Dialogues of Plato*, edited by Edith Hamilton and Huntington Cairns. Princeton: Princeton Univ. Press, 1982.

Podhoretz, Norman. "A Howl of Protest in San Francisco." *New Republic*, 16 September 1957, 20.

Portugés, Paul. "Allen Ginsberg's Paul Cézanne and the Pater Omnipotens Aeterna Deus." *Contemporary Literature* 21 (1980): 435–49.

———. *The Visionary Poetics of Allen Ginsberg*. Santa Barbara, Calif.: Ross-Erikson, 1978.

Pritchard, James B., ed. *Ancient Near Eastern Texts Relating to the Old Testament*. Princeton: Princeton Univ. Press, 1969.

Raine, Kathleen. *Blake and Tradition*. Princeton: Princeton Univ. Press, 1968.

Rhu, Lawrence F. "After the Middle Ages: Prophetic Authority and Human Fallibility in Renaissance Epic." In *Poetry and Prophecy: The Beginnings of a Literary Tradition*, edited by James L. Kugel. Ithaca: Cornell Univ. Press, 1990.

Robinson, Janice. *H. D.: The Life and Work of an American Poet*. Boston: Houghton, 1982.

Rosenthal, M. L. *The New Poets: American and British Poetry Since World War II.* New York: Oxford Univ. Press, 1967.

Rumaker, Michael. "Allen Ginsberg's 'Howl.'" In *On the Poetry of Allen Ginsberg*, edited by Lewis Hyde. Ann Arbor: Univ. of Michigan Press, 1984. First published in *Black Mountain Review*, Fall 1957.

Scholem, Gershom. *The Messianic Idea in Judaism.* New York: Schocken, 1971.

Schumacher, Michael. *Dharma Lion: A Critical Biography of Allen Ginsberg.* New York: St. Martin's, 1992.

Schweik, Susan. *A Gulf So Deeply Cut: American Women Poets and the Second World War.* Madison: Univ. of Wisconsin Press, 1991.

Sessler, Jacob John. *Communal Pietism Among Early American Moravians.* New York: Henry Holt, 1933. Reprinted, New York: AMS, 1971.

Silverstein, Louis. "Planting the Seeds: Selections from the *H. D. Chronology.*" *H. D. Newsletter* 2.2 (1988): 4–14.

Smith, Paul. "H. D.'s Identity." *Women's Studies* 10 (1984): 321–37.

Stempel, Daniel. "Blake, Foucault, and the Classical Episteme." *PMLA* 96 (1981): 388–407.

Sword, Helen. *Engendering Inspiration: Visionary Strategies in Rilke, Lawrence, and H. D.* Ann Arbor: Univ. of Michigan Press, 1995.

Tannenbaum, Leslie. *Biblical Tradition in Blake's Early Prophecies: The Great Code of Art.* Princeton: Princeton Univ. Press, 1982.

Thompson, E. P. *Witness Against the Beast: William Blake and the Moral Law.* New York: Norton, 1993.

Trungpa, Chögyam. *Crazy Wisdom.* Boston: Shambhala, 1991.

Tylee, Claire M. *The Great War and Women's Conciousness: Images of Militarism and Womanhood in Women's Writings, 1914–64.* Iowa City: Univ. of Iowa Press, 1990.

Tytell, John. *Naked Angels: The Lives and Literature of the Beat Generation.* New York: McGraw-Hill, 1976.

Varela, Francisco J., Evan Thompson, and Eleanor Rosch. *The Embodied Mind: Cognitive Science and Human Experience.* Cambridge: MIT Press, 1991.

Vendler, Helen. "American X-Rays: Forty Years of Allen Ginsberg's Poetry." *New Yorker* 4 November 1996: 98–102.

Warburton, William. *The Divine Legation of Moses Demonstrated.* 6 vol. London: Fletcher Giles, 1738–1765. Reprinted, New York: Garland, 1970.

Weber, Burton Jasper. *Wedges and Wings: The Patterning of "Paradise Regained."* Carbondale: Southern Illinois Univ. Press, 1975.

Wittreich, Joseph Anthony, Jr. Preface to *Milton and the Line of Vision.* edited by Wittreich. Madison: Univ. of Wisconsin Press, 1975.

———. "William Blake: Illustrator-Interpreter of *Paradise Regained.*" In *Calm of Mind: Tercentenary Essays on "Paradise Regained" and "Samson Agonistes,"* edited by Wittreich. Cleveland, Ohio: Case Western Reserve Univ. Press, 1971.

Wojcik, Jan and Raymond-Jean Frontain. "Introduction: The Prophet in the Poem." In *Poetic Prophecy in Western Literature*, edited by Wojcik and Frontain. London: Associated University Presses, 1984.

Youngquist, Paul. "Criticism and the Experience of Blake's *Milton*." *Studies in English Literature, 1500–1900* 30 (1990): 555–72.

———. *Madness and Blake's Myth*. University Park: The Pennsylvania State Univ. Press, 1989.

Index